Modernizing Bavaria

Monographs in German History

Volume 1
Osthandel and Ostpolitik: German Foreign Trade Policies in Eastern Europe from Bismarck to Adenauer
Mark Spaulding

Volume 2
A Question of Priorities: Democratic Reform and Economic Recovery in Postwar Germany
Rebecca Boehling

Volume 3
From Recovery to Catastrophe: Municipal Stabilization and Political Crisis in Weimar Germany
Ben Lieberman

Volume 4
Nazism in Central Germany: The Brownshirts in 'Red' Saxony
Christian W. Szejnmann

Volume 5
Citizens and Aliens: Foreigners and the Law in Britain and the German States 1789–1870
Andreas Fahrmeir

Volume 6
Poems in Steel: National Socialism and the Politics of Inventing from Weimar to Bonn
Kees Gispen

Volume 7
"Aryanisation" in Hamburg
Frank Bajohr

Volume 8
The Politics of Education: Teachers and School Reform in Weimar Germany
Marjorie Lamberti

Volume 9
The Ambivalent Alliance: Konrad Adenauer, the CDU/CSU, and the West, 1949–1966
Ronald J. Granieri

Volume 11
Recasting West German Elites: Higher Civil Servants, Business Leaders, and Physicians in Hesse between Nazism and Democracy, 1945–1955
Michael R. Hayse

Volume 12
The Creation of the Modern German Army: General Walther Reinhardt and the Weimar Republic, 1914–1930
William Mulligan

Volume 13
The Crisis of the German Left: The PDS, Stalinism and the Global Economy
Peter Thompson

Volume 14
"Conservative Revolutionaries": Protestant and Catholic Churches in Germany After Radical Political Change in the 1990s
Barbara Thériault

MODERNIZING BAVARIA

The Politics of Franz Josef Strauß and the CSU, 1949–1969

Mark S. Milosch

Berghahn Books
New York • Oxford

First published in 2006 by

Berghahn Books

www.berghahnbooks.com

Library of Congress Cataloging-in-Publication Data

Milosch, Mark S., 1964-

Modernizing Bavaria: the politics of Franz Josef Strauss and the CSU, 1949-1969/ Mark S. Milosch.

p. cm.—(Monographs in German history; v. 15)

Includes bibliographical references and index.

ISBN 1-84545-123-6 (alk. paper)

1. Bavaria (Germany)—Politics and government—1945-. 2. Strauss, Franz Josef, 1915-. 3. Christlich-Soziale Union—History—Germany—Bavaria. 4. Political parties—Germany—Bavaria—History. I. Title. II. Series.

DD801.B423M55 2005

320.943'309045—dc22 2005057027

British Library Cataloguing in Publication Data

A catalogue record for this book is available from the British Library

Printed in the United States on acid-free paper

ISBN 1-84545-123-6 hardback

Meina liabn Frau!

TABLE OF CONTENTS

PREFACE

In 1949 Bavaria was the most industrially backward of the states of what was then being founded as the Federal Republic of Germany (West Germany). In the next twenty years Bavaria became a natural home, perhaps *the* natural home of German high-technology and growth industries, so that by 1970 it had become one of the most industrially modern states in Germany. Similar if less dramatic changes were taking place in other regions of Europe and, in a general sense, throughout western Europe. In the past thirty years much has been written about industrial modernization. Various approaches have been taken: political history, economic history, new cultural history, social history, business history, sociology of science and technology, Marxist history, cultural criticism, et cetera. I have taken yet another approach, one that is quite unusual. I have tried to write the *political* history of an *economic* transformation; I have tried to answer the question, "What were the politics (politics, more than policies) by which the Christian Social Union (CSU) led Bavaria's industrial modernization?" This question is rarely asked, since, for one thing, it is usually thought that party politics has little effect on industrial modernization. Whether or not this is generally so, I do not think it was in Bavaria. Bavaria was unique in important ways. For one thing, in Bavaria the CSU established a political dominance unequalled by any other party in any other country of postwar western Europe; and in Bavaria the transformation was greater and quicker than perhaps anywhere else in Europe and involved industries dependent on politics. In Bavaria, if anywhere, the question deserves an answer. For another thing, the effects of the CSU's politics are very difficult to measure. Certainly they cannot be measured by econometric techniques, since they were largely psychological—the CSU changed Bavaria's image, establishing it as an appropriate location for high-technology industries—and since almost everything a political party does has some economic effects and can thus be connected to industrial modernization.

I have dealt with these difficulties by concentrating on the CSU's core leadership group, especially its chairman, Franz Josef Strauß, who was one of the most important, controversial, talented, and colorful German politicians of the postwar period and who by the 1960s utterly dominated the CSU. The CSU's core leadership group changed little after 1954, when most of the threads of interest-group politics led to Strauß's hands. I have also concentrated on four spearheads of Bavaria's industrial modernization: the aerospace and defense industries, "big research," atomic sciences, and energy. These were not only the industries in which politics intervened, but in the 1950s and 1960s they seemed the very horizon of the future.

Considerable respect and interest are due the CSU's accomplishment, but this book was not inspired by party spirit or admiration for Franz Josef Strauß. There has always been a duality to the work of the CSU. On one hand, the industrial modernization that the CSU helped to effect brought growth, stability, wealth, and employment to Bavaria; on the other hand, it altered the Bavarian character and tradition—and the alterations were a result not only of industrial modernization itself but also of the way the CSU effected this modernization and used it to promote itself. Much of the old, "pre-postwar" Bavaria was bad (a bigoted and xenophobic clinging to outdated forms of thought and life) and much of the new postwar Bavaria good (increased prosperity and openness to modern life); yet old Bavaria was also marked by a humane tempo and scale of life, and by an honest conservatism and love of *patria,* while the new Bavaria is often marked by a dishonest conservatism and a superficial love of tradition used to bolster a collective egoism. The case becomes even more complicated when one considers the argument, often made by the CSU, that it is only through modernization that tradition can survive. There is some truth to this, and also to the counterargument that no one can so effectively destroy a tradition as its own representatives, when they instrumentalize and thereby kitschify it. It is not my point to takes sides in this argument, but to point out that thirty years have passed and neither Bavarians nor Germans have come to terms with the losses and gains involved in the postwar creation of a new Bavaria. This too indicates that the process of Bavaria's industrial modernization was bound up with politics. Perhaps this book, one of the few histories of a politics of industrial modernization, will make it easier for them to do so.

ACKNOWLEDGEMENTS

I am grateful to the Fulbright Commission, the German Academic Exchange Service (DAAD), the Hanns-Seidel-Stiftung, and the University of Iowa for grants that made it possible for me to spend two and a half years conducting research for this book in Germany.

I am deeply indebted to my dissertation advisor, David Schoenbaum, whose suggestion of this topic grew out of his own encounter with Franz Josef Strauß, whom he interviewed thirty-five years ago for his own book on the Spiegel Affair. It also grew, I think, out of gracious consideration for my wife's declared wish that if she and I must move to Germany, then only to Munich. Professor Schoenbaum's support was unwavering and his advice excellent.

In many cases I was able to speak with people who were involved in the events I investigated. For their cooperation I would like to thank Otto Barbarino, Manfred Baumgärtel, Alfred Bayer, Mathilde Berghofer-Weichner, Karl Böck, Hermann Bößenecker, Werner Disko, Rudolf Forster, Oskar Hatz, Sepp Hort, Emilio Humouda, Werner Kalb, Franz Sackmann, Ludwig Voelkl, and Julia Weichselgartner. I would also like to thank many scholars for their advice and assistance, including Oliver Braun, Werner Bührer, Stephan Deutinger, Paul Erker, Maximilian Lanzinner, Stefanie Lerch, Jürgen Seidl, Helmuth Trischler, and Petra Weber. I would also like to thank the members of my dissertation committee at the University of Iowa, Elizabeth Heineman, Gerhard Loewenberg, Colin Gordon, and Stephen Vlastos. Ronald Granieri of the University of Pennsylvania gave excellent advice on restructuring the final manuscript. Others who were of assistance, in writing letters of recommendation or in similar capacity, include Erik von Kuehnelt-Leddihn and John A.A. ter Haar (both deceased and sorely missed), John Lukacs, and Hans Woller. I would like to thank Monika Hohlmeier, the daughter of Franz Josef Strauß and currently minister in the Bavarian state government, for the rare grant of permission to see her father's papers. Many librarians and archivists gave me assistance in researching this book, and thanks are especially due to Andrea Schwarz at the Bayerisches Hauptstaatsarchiv; Renate Höpfinger, Claus Brügmann, Fritz Hopfenmüller, and Andreas Bitterhof at the Archiv für Christlich-Soziale Politik der Hanns-Seidel-Stiftung; Eva Moser and

Richard Winkler at the Bayerisches Wirtschaftsarchiv; also to the archivists of the Bundesarchiv in Coblenz, the Militärisches Archiv in Freiburg im Breisgau, the Deutsches Museum in Munich, the Munich Stadtarchiv, the Bayerische Landesamt für Statistik und Datenverarbeitung, the Bayerische Staatsbibliothek, and the libraries of the University of Iowa.

On a more personal level, I would like to thank Karl-Ulrich Gelberg, Wissenschaftliche Mitarbeiter at the Historische Kommission der Bayerischen Akademie der Wissenschaften, and Thomas Schlemmer, Wissenschaftliche Mitarbeiter at the Institut für Zeitgeschichte in Munich. Both are fellow historians of Bavaria and were generous not only with their advice and time but with their friendship. Other friends who made this project easier include Fabrizio Amore, Matthias and Dana Lindl, Chris and Bonnie Moon, Christoph Randak, Lorenzo Rossi, and Dr. Carl-Werner and Brigitte Curtius.

Finally, I am deeply grateful to my mother and father for their support, and to my wife, Jane, who, little knowing where it would lead, introduced me to Bavaria in December of 1987, who steered me toward this topic in 1995, who accompanied me to Bavaria in 1998, and who has made enormous sacrifices for this book, always in a spirit of love.

ABBREVIATIONS

BDA	Bundesvereinigung der Deutschen Arbeitgeberverbände; Federal Association of German Employer Federations
BDI	Bundesverband der Deutschen Industrie; Federation of German Industry
BDLI	Bundesverband der Deutschen Luftfahrtindustrie; Federation of the German Aircraft Industry
BHE	Bund der Heimatlosen und Entrechteten; Alliance of the Homelandless and Wronged
BP	Bayernpartei; Bavaria Party
BWB	Bundesamt für Wehrtechnik und Beschaffung; Federal Office for Defense Technology and Procurement
CDU	Christlich-Demokratische Union; Christian Democratic Union
CSU	Christlich-Soziale Union; Christian Social Union
DFG	Deutsche Forschungsgemeinschaft; German Research Society
DFS	Deutsche Forschungsanstalt für Segelflug; German Research Institute for Glider Flight
DGB	Deutsche Gewerkschaftsbund; German Trade Union Federation
DIHT	Deutscher Industrie- und Handelstag; German Assembly of Industry and Commerce
DKfW	Deutsche Kommission für Weltraumforschung; German Commission for Space Research
DP	Deutsche Partei; German Party
DVL	Deutsche Versuchsanstalt für Luftfahrt; German Aviation Research Institute
ECSC	European Coal and Steel Community
EDC	European Defense Community
EEC	European Economic Community
EURATOM	European Atomic Community
FDP	Freie Demokratische Partei; Free Democratic Party

FFO	Flug-Funk-Forschungsinstitut Oberpfaffenhofen; Aerospace Communications Research Institute in Oberpfaffenhofen
FhG	Fraunhofer Gesellschaft; Fraunhofer Foundation
IPP	Institut für Plasmaphysik; Institute for Plasma Physics
LBI	Landesverband der Bayerischen Industrie; Federation of Bavarian Industry
MPG	Max-Planck-Gesellschaft; Max Planck Foundation
NATO	North Atlantic Treaty Organization
SPD	Sozialdemokratische Partei Deutschlands; Social-Democratic Party of Germany
VBCI	Verein der bayerischen Chemischen Industrie; Association of the Bavarian Chemical Industry
VCI	Verband der Chemischen Industrie; Federation of the Chemical Industry
VwG	Volkswirtschaftliche Gesellschaft (Bayern); Economic Society of Bavaria
WAV	Wirtschaftliche Aufbau-Vereinigung; Economic Reconstruction Party
WbdU	Wirtschaftsbeirat der Union; Economic Advisory Board

INTRODUCTION
BAVARIA, 1949

The Question

An economic miracle, a *Wirtschaftswunder,* took place in Bavaria after World War II, one that built on the postwar German economic miracle. It transformed Bavaria, for centuries one of the most backward regions of Germany, into the natural and favored home of many of Germany's most technologically advanced industries. How did this happen? More precisely, since Bavaria has since 1946 been the near monopoly of one political party, the Christian Social Union (CSU), and since the aerospace, defense, research, and energy industries that found a home in Bavaria depended on government largess and connections, what was the CSU's role in this modernization? What were the politics by which the CSU promoted the industrial modernization of Bavaria?

The answer is not obvious. If we look elsewhere, the politics of industrial modernization in the postwar era has been quite varied. In many countries after World War II a large part of the story was of publicistic efforts to promote industry and modernity. In Scandinavia the big story was how powerful political parties dominated the economy. The popular historiography of France tells how the state took over key sectors of the economy in the name of national prestige. An important role in the *aggiornamento* of postwar Italy was played by politicians allowing themselves to be bought and dominated by wealthy industrialists. In many oil-rich countries the story was of how the state exploited its natural resource; and in some Asian countries of how a free-enterprise regime unchained Adam Smith's invisible hand.

But none of these things happened in Bavaria. The CSU preferred to associate itself with rural-agricultural life and tradition, and only after the process of industrial modernization was well advanced did Franz Josef Strauß, the party's longtime and controversial chairman, begin to promote its accomplishments in that field—and even then only in a minor key. Nor could the CSU dominate the

Notes for this section begin on page 16.

economy—it was merely a regional party and economic policy was the prerogative of the national government. Nor did it stand for the nationalization of key industries—quite the opposite, it defended private property with all the fervor of a dyed-in-the-wool antisocialist party appealing to western Europe's most conservative, not to say reactionary, voters. Nor did industrialists dominate the CSU: though Franz Josef Strauß worked closely with them (Marxist intellectuals scored him as a capitalist lackey), few people close to the situation doubted that Strauß dominated the relationship. Nor was Bavaria rich in natural resources; and of all Germany's nonsocialist parties the CSU was the least likely to object to the state's visible hand.

The CSU created a politics sui generis of industrial modernization. We contend that between 1949 and 1969 Franz Josef Strauß and a few other CSU politicians, such as Hanns Seidel and Otto Schedl, created a politics of industrial modernization that took advantage of the particular circumstances of the CSU and Bavaria in ways that benefited a remarkable list of entities, not excluding themselves, the CSU, Bavarian industry, and Bavarian voters. Often the circumstances they took advantage of included the freedom from responsibility the CSU enjoyed as the junior partner in the coalition that governed Germany, and the freedom of movement it enjoyed as the result of its overwhelming domination of Bavaria. Often too the circumstances were events that enabled the CSU's tacticians to take advantage of broader trends that were remaking postwar Europe: Americanization and, later, the reaction against Americanization, the gradual reawakening of regional consciousness and constitutional federalism across Europe, the oil glut of the late 1950s and early 1960s, the development of the new industries of atomic power and aerospace, and the growing recognition of research capacity as a factor in the national economy. At first the CSU leaders discovered these circumstances and the tactics by which the CSU and Bavaria could profit from them almost accidentally. Later they understood what they had done and honed their politics.

Hence industrial modernization in postwar Germany was about more than Ludwig Erhard, liberal political economy, and the integration of markets. For Bavaria it was about enjoying the benefits of the wider liberal environment while at the same time enjoying the benefits of some unliberal political interventions in the economy. This was possible because economies are basically local things, and national economies are to a considerable degree "potpourris" of local economies. As Jane Jacobs demonstrated, notwithstanding the nationally uniform character of central governmental economic policies, "most nations are composed of collections or grab bags of very different economies, rich regions and poor ones within the very same nation."[1]

Scholars have written little about the politics of industrial modernization in Bavaria. This is largely because they take Bavaria's postwar growth to be merely a peculiar instance of a German and European development driven by broad political, market, and sociological forces. Yet the real story in Bavaria was not that Bavaria *grew*, which was only to be expected, but that it *caught up* to the rest of

Germany. This was not an inevitable but a contingent development, dependent on individual actions, events, institutions, and the precise way and time in which they came together. In this sense it is less suited to a political-scientific than to a historical treatment.

This makes it all the more important to understand the historical context, which we will introduce in a series of contracting frames. The first will look at the over one thousand-year history of Bavaria and Germany. The second will describe the postwar climate of opinion, the third the CSU's relations with the Christian Democratic Union (CDU), and the fourth the political-industrial situation in Bavaria and Germany in 1949, our baseline year.

Bavaria and Germany

Industrial modernization meant something different in Bavaria because, put shortly, Bavaria was different from the rest of Germany. For centuries Bavaria had grown increasingly backward within Germany, and Bavarians had been the object of condescension and the butt of jokes. As a result, Bavarians experienced Bavaria's rapid postwar industrial modernization and the success of the CSU as something like a sweet revenge, or at least a sweet reversal of a historical long wave that had battered them for centuries.

Unlike other Germans, Bavarians have a state tradition embedded in their character. While almost all of the other states of postwar Germany were first created in 1945, Bavaria has been a state-like entity for over one thousand years. The Bavarians, originally a Germanic tribe like the Saxons, Franconians, Swabians, and Alemanni, began their state history as a duchy of the Holy Roman Empire of the German Nation. This empire allowed its member states to govern themselves in most of their internal affairs, and, especially after the Reformation, even to pursue their own foreign policies toward states outside the empire. Bavaria was generally one of the most content states within the empire and the Bavarian dukes and their subjects were outstandingly loyal to the emperor; but also outstandingly determined to govern themselves in their internal affairs. From the sixteenth through the nineteenth centuries, these traits deepened and became more self-conscious. The Holy Roman Empire dissolved in 1806, but the Napoleonic Wars left Bavaria aggrandized by parts of Franconia and Swabia and promoted to the rank of kingdom within the Germanic Confederation, where Bavaria maintained its tradition of loyalty to Germany and determined independence within it. When in 1871, Prussia coerced Bavaria into its German Empire, Bavarian antipathy to Prussia's centralizing propensities was so strong that Bismarck permitted the Bavarians to keep their own king, army, postal service, and diplomatic representation abroad. While Saxons, Swabians, Alemanni, and Franconians were more or less content to submerge their local and historical identities into the German Empire, Bavarians remained more ambivalent, not only about the German national movement because of their particularist loyalties, but even more about the Protestant Prussians, who condescended to the Bavarians, their Catholic faith, and their peasant baroque culture. Later Prussian attempts to erode the Bavarian prerogatives and centralize power in Berlin only made Bavarians more self conscious and defensive, often fiercely so. Bavarian voters even maintained, within the German Empire, a Bavarian political party whose raison d'être was to defend the Bavarian state from the encroachments of the central government in Berlin. By the twentieth century this insistence on membership yet distinction within Germany, this loyal independence, pride in being German, and determination to live in a Bavarian state had become as much a part of the Bavarian character as republican democracy is of the American. As a Bavarian maxim had it, "We want to be German and stay Bavarian."

Bavarians' satisfaction in catching up to the general German level of industrial development was magnified by other differences between Bavaria and the rest of Germany. The most important difference can be expressed in the dichotomy: backward Bavaria—modern Germany. Some hint of this can be found as long ago as the Middle Ages, when Bavarians had the reputation of a red-blooded, mule-headed people, pious and dogmatic, unsubtle and unreflective, somewhat extravagant, vulgar and coarse and rowdy, indolent and more inclined to drink than their northern neighbors, loving earthy jokes and belly laughs. After Protestantism triumphed in much of the rest of Germany, the Protestants cultivated a *leyenda negra* according to which the Bavarians were ridiculous hayseeds, undisciplined and ignorant. This hurt all the more for having an element of truth to it. But backwardness became the dominant element in Bavaria's image only during the nineteenth and twentieth centuries, when a stagnant Bavaria became the poorest state in Germany east of the Oder and Neisse rivers and a dynamic Germany one of the richest countries in the world. While Germany became the industrial heart of Europe, Bavaria became the agricultural heart of western Germany, relatively unindustrialized well into the twentieth century. While Germany became the preeminently modern country, with modern industry, politics, social structure, class struggle, art, literature, and music, Bavaria continued, through the Weimar Republic and beyond, to be marked by "feudal mentalities." Bavaria remained the center, within Germany, of an antimodern reaction that gloried in its attachment to its patria, its traditions, its monarchy, and its Catholic baroque culture, and remained unmoved by calls to arms in the names of nation or class. Not that Bavaria was entirely a rural backwater: Bavarians enjoyed a competent administration (modelled on that of Napoleonic France) and Munich, their capital, had some advanced industries and an excellent academic, artistic, and musical life. Nonetheless large areas of Bavaria were backward—economically, politically, socially, and culturally.

Other differences between Bavaria and the rest of Germany came from Bavaria's historical experiences. The Reformation and Counter-Reformation, for example, left Bavaria in an anomalous position: Bavaria was not the only predominantly Catholic region in what in 1871 became the German Empire; but it was the only one that had been shaped by the baroque religion-culture of Austria,

Hungary, and Bohemia, so that even today Bavarian Catholics have a faith that is more sacramental, more dogmatic, more "popular," less intellectual, less progressive, and less moralistic than Rhineland Catholics. The growth of the bourgeoisie, so important to the development of neighboring Swabia and Franconia, as well as the Rhineland, Prussia, and Saxony, happened slowly in "old Bavaria" (Bavaria excluding the Franconian and Swabian acquisitions of the Napoleonic era), being largely restricted to Munich. The Industrial Revolution affected Bavaria less than the rest of Germany, and came to seem much more alien to Bavarians than to other Germans; this was partly due to the anti-industrial romantic movement, whose idealization of the medieval and the rural sank deep roots in the Bavarian mind. Well before 1871 the Bavarians had developed a defensive sense of inferiority, aware that the centers of German wealth, industry, power, culture, and learning had, since the seventeenth century, shifted northward. After 1871 this sense was magnified by the political dominance of Protestant Prussians, by the industrialization of the Rhineland, and by the intellectual leadership northern Germany exercised in Europe, in which Catholic Bavarians hardly participated. Even liberalism was different in Bavaria.[ii] After 1871 liberalism and democracy came into tension with each other everywhere in Germany, but the tension was sharpened by religion in Bavaria, where the liberals (mostly Franconian Protestants and urban bourgeois) were self-consciously antidemocratic (since conservative rural Catholics were the majority) and the democrats (the agricultural and village *demos*) were decidedly antiliberal (and anti-urban, anti-Protestant, and anti-free-market, preferring guilds and restraints on trade). We have already pointed out how many Bavarians felt ambivalent about the German Empire. Not a few of them despised it. The feeling of Bavarian representatives present at the Prussian ceremonies proclaiming the empire, "everything so cold, so proud, so glossy, so pompous and boastful and heartless and empty," remained with Bavarians during the empire's fifty-year life.[iii]

Even recent history had taught Bavarians different lessons. While the collapse of the German Empire in 1918 was followed by socialist insurrections throughout Germany, only in Munich did the socialists create a Soviet Republic. The Bavarian reaction soon marched in and smashed it, but a period of Red terror left conservative Bavarians furiously antisocialist. Although during the Weimar Republic Germany's two Catholic political parties, the Center Party and the Bavarian People's Party, had a greater voice in the central government than they had ever had before, the republic was disliked in Bavaria as nowhere else in Germany—chiefly for its centralizing constitution. The conservative state government in Munich allowed Bavaria to become a sort of "Wild West" where all sorts of Rightists—reactionaries and revolutionaries, Bavarian particularists and National Socialists—agitated for the republic's overthrow. Though the National Socialist movement got its start in Bavaria, by the elections of 1932 Bavaria had become its electoral weak point (excepting some Protestant cities in Franconia, which were the most highly Nazified places in Germany). Adolf Hitler obviously had no interest in federalism, and soon after he took power reduced Bavaria to an administrative district within a centralized Reich. This was one reason why, if there was no more resistance to National Socialist rule in Bavaria than in the rest of Germany, there may have been less enthusiasm for it. The catastrophic military defeat of 1945, the revelations about the death camps, and the recriminations that followed were also experienced differently in Bavaria. Germans in general had no one but themselves to blame for all of this, and if a few northern Germans blamed Bavaria for giving birth to the Nazi movement, that was nothing compared to the way many Bavarians blamed northern Germany for voting for Hitler, supporting him, and providing him with his generals. Incredible as it seems to us, more than a few Bavarians saw the crimes of the Third Reich as the logical result of the liberal tradition of centralism and anticlericalism.

If the long view of the Bavarian-German relationship provides little clue of how the CSU might create a politics of industrial modernization in Bavaria, it shows that whoever would do so had indeed much to overcome.

Postwar Climate of Opinion

In the first years after the end of World War II, while Germans dug out from the rubble and struggled to feed themselves and reconstruct their cities and factories, industrial modernization was naturally not a political issue. Yet the question of constitutional centralism versus federalism in the new Germany, which was indeed a major issue, was in a sense the transposition of the question of industrial modernization onto the constitutional plane.

The quarrel between the centralist and federalist traditions—and each was a bona fide German tradition—was about much more than the division of power between the national and state governments. These traditions implied opposed visions of Germany. The centralist tradition, created in the late nineteenth century as part of the struggle to create and aggrandize the German nation-state, was popular with all those who had celebrated that nation-state; with nationalists, liberals, Protestants, and Prussians, and generally with northern Germans. The nationalist and liberal Right saw a strong central government as a necessary means to restore German greatness; business and industrial interests, distrusting state governments as potential bastions of anticapitalist conservatism, looked to the central government as the best means for promoting a coordinated economic policy; socialists and organized labor saw centralism as a precondition of economic planning. The federalist tradition, on the other hand, was upheld by those who looked fondly back to images of a pre-Bismarckian Germany, to the Germany of small, semi-independent states, and by Catholics, who saw it as a shield against Germany's Protestant majority. Federalism implied a conservative Germany where regional and religious traditions would be cultivated, where agrarian interests would be protected and religion would be taught in the state schools. Hence it was strong in Catholic regions of Germany—above all in Bavaria, where it was *the* hot-button issue.

Hence also the transposition. Centralism was the cause of those who held themselves to be modernizing and progressive. It was the cause of those who wanted to create economies of scale, who valued efficiency and expertise in planning, administration, and legislation. Federalism was the cause of conservatives, Catholics, defenders of small scales in politics and business, of parochial and agrarian interests, traditions, guilds, and personal networks, and, often enough, of an antimodern "reactionary" mentality. While the correspondence between federalism, conservatism, and the Catholic faith was not perfect—one could find progressive federalists in the Social-Democratic Party organizations of Bavaria as well as in the proud old city-states of Hamburg and Bremen, Protestant federalists in Saxony's German Party, and Catholic centralists in the Rhineland—the relation was strong.

The federalists prevailed at the constitutional convention of 1949. Though they were a minority, they had the support of the American and French military governors and the Bavarians of the CSU went to the convention prepared to fight, as it were, for the Holy Grail, while the centralists treated their convictions like a bargaining chip. Among European constitutions, only the Swiss gave more authority to regional or state governments than did the one Germany adopted in 1949. The "Basic Law" gave the state governments complete authority over all matters relating to education, religion, and culture, and provided that state governments were to appoint and control members of the federal parliament's upper chamber, the Federal Senate, which had a limited veto over federal legislation.

But Bavarians were divided about the federalist victory. For one thing, not all Bavarians were Bavarian, at least not in the same way. Parts of northern and western Bavaria, added to the Bavarian state in the early nineteenth century, were populated by people who did not consider themselves Bavarian, but Franconian or Swabian, and, though they had developed a certain feeling for the Bavarian state, they spoke a different dialect, had different traditions and a different character, and were less particularist and therefore also less federalist than the "old Bavarians." This was true not only of Protestant Franconians (Upper and Middle Franconia), but even of the Catholic Franconians (Lower Franconia).

For another thing, even the "old Bavarians" were divided. They were overwhelmingly federalist, in that they wanted the Bavarian state government to have influence within the federal government as well as wide latitude for self-government. But, though most of them were content to see Bavaria a member state in a Germany roughly as federal as the United States of America, no small number were "hyper-federalist." The hyper-federalists wanted something more than a federal Germany, but on what they could not agree. Many of them wanted to restore the Bavarian monarchy, but some were republicans; some wanted Germany to be confederal rather than federal, that is, a loose commonwealth of states; a few even wanted Bavaria to secede from Germany and unite with Austria or to form its own country (they could argue that Bavaria was geographically larger than Denmark, Switzerland, the Netherlands, Belgium, Ireland, and Luxembourg, and, with 9.12 million residents, more populous than each of these as well as Sweden, Norway, and Greece, and moreover had enjoyed continuous existence as a significant political entity longer than most of these countries). Yet these latter were always a splinter group and their desire a fantasy. Hyper-federalism was perhaps less a position than an attitude, marked by a paraded animus against Prussia, and a propensity to view Bavarians who viewed the national government warmly as "traitors."

There was never any question but that any party that sought the votes of Bavarian farmers, craftsmen, and the Catholic middle class would have to represent some degree of federalism. But there was an important question as to how far it would have to go. For by 1949 there were two parties competing for the votes of Bavarian federalists: the CSU, a Christian-Democratic party of a peculiar conservative-liberal and Catholic-Protestant sort, and the Bavaria Party, a hyper-federalist party. The result was that while from 1946 to 1948 the CSU had straddled its liberal (Christian-Democratic) and conservative (Bavarian traditionalist) constituencies, in 1949 the newly-licensed Bavaria Party forced the CSU into a bidding war for the support of the latter group, which created the acute danger that the CSU would lose its liberal voters to other parties, or even that it would fall between two stools and losing both. Yet the CSU could not let the challenge of the Bavaria Party go unanswered. This became evident when the CSU responded to the Bavaria Party's campaign against ratification of the insufficiently federalist Basic Law by voting against it in the constitutional convention—that is, the CSU voted against a constitution whose federalist provisions it had brokered. The Basic Law went into effect anyway—Bavaria was the only state to vote against ratification—so that, after 1949, the best either the CSU or Bavaria Party could promise was to defend the Basic Law as it was ratified.

Yet it remained to be seen whether the Basic Law as it was ratified could be defended. After all, the Basic Law was merely a document: the practice of Germany's first governments would create the new republic's working constitution. And formidable forces were determined to interpret the Basic Law in favor of a strong central government: the Social-Democratic Left and the nationalist and liberal Right, organized labor and industry. Even Germany's other Christian-Democratic party, the CDU, became ambivalent about federalism after it won the federal election of 1949.

Nor did anyone have a promising strategy for defending the Basic Law. The conservative wing of the CSU was committed to a rigid "forward defense," the same policy incarnated by the Bavaria Party, one of nay-saying and uncompromising resistance to everything that tended to aggrandize the federal government at the expense of the states. This approach would be appreciated by conservative federalist voters, at least in the short term. Yet it was easy to foresee that uncompromising resistance would lead to political isolation in Bonn and end in failure. The CSU's liberals and moderates had little better to offer. Their defense would presumably be more flexible, and possibly more successful in influencing the CDU and, as a member of the government, occupying ministries of key concern to federalists, but they had little strength of conviction, and the CSU's conservative wing was right to fear that their compromises would only lead to further compromises on terms ever less favorable to the federalist cause. Alternatives to these approaches were not on hand in 1949. No one seems to have thought that industrial modernization might be part of a strategy to defend the constitution or Bavarian identity. After all, federalism and modernization had always been mutually exclusive.

CSU and CDU

Whatever the CSU could achieve for Bavaria, it would have to achieve within the German party system, which took shape after the first federal election in September 1949.

The novel element in the party system created in Germany after World War II was the Christian-Democratic parties, the Christian Democratic Union (CDU) and the Christian Social Union (CSU). These were the first parties in German history to appeal to both Catholics and Protestants ("Union" referred to the union of both confessions in one party) and to commit themselves to a broadly Christian program combining Catholic and Protestant elements (namely Catholic social teaching and the political and economic liberalism favored by Protestants). They sought to be multi-class parties, appealing at the same time to agricultural, lower-middle, middle, and upper-middle class voters, and thereby to dominate the political center and Right. The idea worked surprisingly well. Christian-Democratic governments dominated the German government from 1949 to 1969, and were widely credited with reintegrating Germany into Europe, integrating it into the Western military alliance, reconciling the German Right with liberal democracy, deconfessionalizing political life, and consolidating a liberal economy (called the "social market economy"). Certainly the Christian Democrats have been criticized on these grounds as well, but perhaps no criticism has been so widely accepted as that they operated as a culturally conservative force. The CDU has also been criticized as having been an economically conservative force, doing little to promote new technologies and industries, so that Germany has never recovered its prewar position as a technological leader. Whether or not this is true of the CDU, it has rarely been said of the CSU. The CSU, almost alone among the new Christian Democratic movements of postwar Europe, became an aggressive promoter of modern technology and industry.

The CDU was by far the more important of the two Christian-Democratic parties. It was present throughout West Germany except Bavaria, and the CSU operated only in Bavaria. In 1949 the CDU and CSU together won 31 per cent of the national vote. The CDU's Catholic leaders proved pragmatic and liberal, carefully respecting the sensibilities of their party's Protestant minority, and decided that their party's preferred enemy would be Social Democracy. The CDU leader, Konrad Adenauer, was a bourgeois Catholic from Cologne, adept at managing the conflicts between Catholics and Protestants, between representatives of the mostly Catholic working class and Protestant and bourgeois economic liberals (such as Ludwig Erhard, the popular Economic Minister and incarnation of the liberal social market economy), both for the good of the party and his own good. The CDU managed to win votes from the Catholic working class and financial support from industry.

The other important party of the Right, the Free Democratic Party (FDP), won 12 per cent of the national vote in 1949. The FDP, in most respects to the Right of the CDU, was classically liberal (opposed to state intervention in the economy, and in tune with the interests of the upper middle class) in the German tradition (nationalistic and anti-Catholic). Its support came from the Protestant middle and upper classes. In proportion to the FDP's size, industry funded it more generously than it did the CDU, and the FDP faithfully promoted industry's policies.

The Left was dominated by the Social-Democratic Party of Germany (SPD), which, maintaining its prewar faith in Marxism and democracy, regained its working-class constituency and won 29 per cent of the vote in 1949. Its old rival, the Communist Party, received only 5.7 per cent of the vote in 1949 and played no role in subsequent elections.

Most of the other German parties tended to the Right or even the extreme Right, and had limited appeal. They represented special issues (such as the Alliance of the Homelandless and Wronged, which represented German refugees from lost eastern territories), or confessions (such as the Center Party, which sought to re-create the prewar Catholic confessional party in the teeth of episcopal opposition), or extreme positions (such as the conservative nationalists of the German Party, the German Conservative Party, and the Party of the German Right). Remnants of the prewar world, they soon lost their voters to the Christian Democrats, Social Democrats, and FDP, and disappeared entirely from the federal parliament by 1957. They play little role in our story.

In Bavaria the party system was rather different. The first Bavarian twist was that the Right was dominated not by the CDU but by the CSU, which won 29 per cent of the Bavarian vote in 1949. The similarity and difference in the names of the CSU and the CDU evidences the desire of the Bavarian Christian Democrats to connect themselves to Christian Democrats in the rest of Germany, yet to keep them at some distance. When in 1945 the Bavarian Christian Democrats decided to call their party the Christian Social Union they had not yet resolved whether their party would one day merge into the CDU. Certainly there were those who wanted it to do so—Josef Müller, the party's founder, and many of his liberal followers, who wanted to create a real "union" of Catholics and Protestants, a Christian-Democratic party like those being created in the rest of Europe. But there were also those who were determined that the CSU maintain its status as a separate party, cooperating with the CDU in some loose arrangement. This view was upheld by the party's conservative wing, which was less interested in the new and exotic idea of Christian Democracy than in reviving the tradition of Bavarian Catholic politics, and which wanted a Catholic-Protestant union only in the sense that it wanted to convince Franconian Protestants to vote for a party that would represent the Bavarian Catholic tradition. To get the Protestant vote the CSU's conservative wing was unwilling to taint the party with any but the slightest admixture of liberalism, nationalism, and secularism. From 1946 to 1948 the CSU's conservative and liberal wings fought vociferously about the confessionalization of the Bavarian school system, the place of Bavaria within a yet-to-be-constructed Germany, the restoration of the Bavarian monarchy, and the creation of an office of "State President" (by which the conservatives thought to distinguish Bavaria from the other German states).[iv] Yet the combatants were bound together by their desire to win elections and the need of each other to do so. In 1949 the two sides arranged compromises that prevented a formal rupture in the party, but for the most part the conservatives came out on top and there was never again any question of the CSU merging into the CDU. The CSU would maintain a separate party structure with its own membership roll, finances, and governing officers.[v] As for the other parties in Bavaria, the Social Democrats received only 23 per cent of the Bavarian vote in 1949, its electoral weakness corresponding to the smallness of the industrial working class in rural-agricultural Bavaria. The FDP received only 8.5 per cent of the Bavarian vote that year, most of its support coming from the Protestant regions of Franconia.

The second twist was the Bavaria Party, which won 21 per cent of the Bavarian vote in 1949. This meant that it was no splinter party but would play a major role in Bavarian politics and have a profound effect on the CSU. A hyper-federalist party, licensed by the allies in 1948, its aggressive particularism and populism immediately won village-artisanal and rural-agricultural voters who had previously supported the CSU–some CSU leaders even switched parties.

But what constitutes a party system is the relations between the parties. These were formed after the election, when CDU leader Konrad Adenauer rejected the prospect of a coalition with the Social Democrats in favor of a coalition with the FDP and the German Party, the most respectable of the Rightist parties. Adenauer's strategy was to isolate the Social Democrats and blur the distinction between the CDU and the minor Rightist parties so as to win the latter's voters. Though there was never any question but that the CSU would be part of a CDU-led coalition, Adenauer often treated the CSU not as a sister Christian-Democratic party but as another small Rightist party, seeking to dominate it by playing it off against the others. The CSU could do little about this in 1949, but it did manage to prevent Adenauer from including the Bavaria Party in the governing coalition. For the CSU's strategy vis-à-vis the Bavaria Party was not to suffocate it in a tight embrace, as Adenauer hoped to do to the FDP and the German Party, but to marginalize and delegitimize it. Vis-à-vis the CDU, the CSU's goal was to maintain its independence. The CSU's leaders had little idea in 1949 that they might be able to increase that independence, much less that in important ways the CSU tail could wag the CDU dog. This dynamic, in which the nonsocialist parties of the Right maneuvered against each other for position but stood together against the Social Democrats, became the basic characteristic of the German party system from 1949 through 1966. During this entire period the CDU led center-Right governments in Bonn in which the

CSU was a vital coalition partner, and the coalition parties rarely flirted with the Social Democrats, and even then as a tactic to signal that they had an option on the Left.

Within this system, the politics of industrial modernization got short shrift. Not only were many other issues of the late 1940s and early 1950s more pressing than industrial modernization, but the party system worked against it becoming an issue. The Social Democratic Party, which in the 1940s and early 1950s was still a working-class Marxist party, opposed industrial modernization since it considered modernization (understood to mean rationalization) a threat to union jobs. Likewise the CDU had little reason to push in this direction, for, on one front, it sought to maintain its strength among the Catholic working class against Social Democratic inroads. On its other front, its contest with the FDP and the other small Rightist parties for the votes of the conservative middle class had little to do with industrial policy. Though the FDP was more forward-looking than the CDU in industrial matters, it preferred to prospect for Protestant Christian-Democratic votes by stirring up anticlerical feeling than to associate itself with big industry too publicly. There was little reward for the CDU and the FDP in being more forward-looking on industrial issues than industry itself, and in 1949 industry was much less concerned to get strategic assistance from the poor fledgling republic than to see that it stayed out of the economy, kept taxes low, and permitted industry to organize itself as it saw fit. Industrial modernization would become a political issue only later, when industry raised it in a manner that set the parties scrambling.

Least of all was the CSU interested in industrial modernization in 1949. The CSU's target voters were the supporters of the Bavaria Party, typically populist agrarians, often hostile to the very idea of industrializing Bavaria. From the first, the CSU had a "special competitive relationship" with the Bavaria Party: it was obvious that almost all the Bavaria Party's votes in the 1949 federal election came from people who had voted for the CSU in the 1946 Bavarian state election, and the easiest way for the CSU to increase its vote was to reduce that of the Bavaria Party. This relationship persisted throughout the 1950s; even as the Bavaria Party declined and the CSU grew, the percentage of the Bavarian vote that went to the CSU and the Bavaria Party remained remarkably stable; at issue was only how the CSU and the Bavaria Party would divide it.[vi] This relationship forced the CSU to take up some of the Bavaria Party's themes, as that latter party's agrarian populism and its anti-complex (especially anti-Prussianism and anti-urbanism) had obviously resonated with the CSU's base. The CSU would have to emphasize even further an image of itself as agrarian, traditionally Bavarian, and aggressively federalist, and de-emphasize any connections to the financial and industrial interests–that is, until someone in the party leadership found a way to promote the interests of both agriculture and industry, tradition and modernization.

Industrial Modernization in CSU-Dominated Bavaria

When the new German state was founded in 1949 the economic prospects were better than most people thought, especially for the heavily industrialized Rhineland. The German "economic miracle" had not yet gotten underway and rebuilding would obviously take years, but the outlook was never as bad as it seemed in the chaos, poverty, and unemployment of the late 1940s, and many things boded well. Though factories had been bombed and dismantled, wealth is produced not by factories but people and the German people had the same essential skills and work ethic that they had before the war. The new Germany stood poised to benefit from the new order of global free trade promoted by America and Britain, and from new ideas about managing the business cycle. Above all, a new doctrine of economic liberalism was at hand to unleash their energies—new in that the "neoliberal" promoters of the social market economy, as it was felicitously named, had learned real lessons from the failure of the old European liberalism in the first third of the twentieth century, mostly lessons about not permitting capitalists to push the doctrines of economic liberalism beyond what the social structure and the political system would bear. The victory of the Christian Democrats in the 1949 election, followed by Konrad Adenauer's formation of a coalition with the FDP to carry the banner of the social market economy, was very much part of the bright outlook.

The same could not be said of Bavaria in 1949. Bavarians lived in what was not only the most self-conscious and distinct state in the new Germany, but also a state that had always been relatively poor and unindustrial, with 30.6 per cent of its working population still in agriculture, more than any other of the republic's states, and a per capita GDP that measured only 85 per cent of that of Germany as a whole.[vii] Bavaria was the largest, most thinly populated, and most agricultural of the states, and great swaths of its countryside were devoted to some of Germany's most inefficient agriculture. Its one large city, Munich, had nothing to compare with the manufacturing, commerce, and finance of Berlin, Hamburg, Frankfurt, or Cologne. Bavaria was a center of local commerce possessed of some light consumer industry, a tourist destination renowned for its joie de vivre, Oktoberfest, beer, and onion-domed rococo churches.

Indeed there were plenty of bad signs in 1949, indicating that however the Bavarian economy might grow in absolute terms, Bavaria was on course to become relatively poorer within Germany. German industry seemed less likely than ever to locate in Bavaria. One problem was that the lost war and division of Europe had moved Bavaria from the center to the periphery, making it an eastern march of western Germany, sharing hundreds of miles of frozen border with communist German Democratic Republic and Czechoslovakia. The movement for European integration threatened to make Bavaria even more eccentric, as the Rhine valley and Ruhr industrial area would become the geographical center of an integrating Europe. Another was that, as a result of the division of Europe, two million German refugees from the East, most of them driven out of the neighboring Czech Sudetenland, had settled in Bavaria, which could not provide sufficient employment for them. Again, the energy situation seemed bound to become worse. Demand for electricity, heat, and fuel was obviously going to increase sharply in the 1950s and 1960s, but nearly all of Bavaria's coal had to be transported from the Ruhr and Saar—no other state was as far from the German coalfields as Bavaria, and none paid so much for its coal. Likewise for gasoline and oil, which had to be transported to Bavaria from the northern seaports. Again, agriculture was bound to decline and it seemed obvious that most farmers would have to move on to employment in wealthier, more industrial parts of Germany, along with the refugees. Even the climate of opinion seemed to oppose Bavaria. While the postwar climate of opinion in northern Germany was marked by interest in the possibilities of economic planning, Bavaria became more deeply conservative, seemingly hypnotized by romantic images of its past. While in northern Germany politicians debated nationalization and neoliberalism, in Bavaria they often argued about restoring the monarchy, corporatism, and Christendom.

In 1949 the CSU seemed one of the more ominous of these bad signs. It was the most backward-looking Christian-Democratic party in Europe. We have already indicated how in 1949 it was more than ever dominated by its conservative wing—central European conservatives, that is, reactionaries and clericalists deeply ambivalent to or even hostile to modern industrial society, who had attached themselves to the Christian Democratic movement with substantial reservations, being themselves part of a Bavarian demos that was suspicious of democracy and looked back proudly on its baroque agricultural past and a tradition of Bavarian Catholic politics that was anti-Protestant, antiliberal, suspicious of the German national state, and certainly anti-industrial and antimodern. Even Franz Josef Strauß, who later developed an insatiable appetite for controversy, didn't dare protest when in 1949 the CSU conservatives replaced his patron, Josef Müller, the leader of the party's liberal wing as well as its founder and chairman, with the conservative Hans Ehard. Not to be confused with the Federal Economic Minister Ludwig Erhard, Hans Ehard was a "man of the state," profoundly devoted to conservative federalism, with hardly any interest in industry or modernizing Bavaria's industrial base.

Yet in 1949 the CSU utterly dominated Bavarian politics. In the 1946 Bavarian state election, a four-party contest, it won 52 per cent of the vote; in the 1949 federal election its vote was cut to 29 per cent, but this was still 6 per cent more than the Social Democrats and 8 per cent more than the Bavaria Party had received.

In retrospect we see that the future of Bavaria and the CSU was closely related to the modernization of Bavarian industry. If Bavarian industry did not modernize, then Bavaria would lose yet more ground, which would have consequences for the CSU. Its vote reduced, the CSU would lose ground in Bonn, and be able to do even less for Bavaria.

But in 1949 few politicians were thinking about this. It is no wonder. German politicians had their plates full with the work of inventing a new country, a new constitution, a new political tradition, new parties, with the tasks of securing themselves against the Soviet threat and finding ways to relate to the United States, France, and Britain, with creating a liberal economic order that would be politically salable, reducing unemployment, and providing housing for refugees. Bavarian politicians were busy rebuilding cities and universities, and feeding German refugees. But if the priorities were elsewhere, time was pushing the question of Bavarian industrialization forward. The two million German refugees in Bavaria and the millions of Bavarians who would soon be leaving the farm made this a certainty.

But even if industrial modernization had been a priority, the CSU did not have many options in 1949. We have said that between 1949 and 1969 CSU politicians created a politics that took remarkable advantage of certain circumstances of their party and of Bavaria. Yet in 1949 no one could imagine what those circumstances would be. It was very difficult to see how a regional party could make an impact in reshaping the Bavarian economy. The Bavarian state government did not have the money or even the jurisdictional competences to pursue an economic policy different from that of the German government. The chief task of the Bavarian Economic Ministry was to distribute aid to depressed regions and groups. Support for scientific research came under the competence of the Bavarian Ministry of Education and Culture, but this ministry had to devote its meager resources to rebuilding schools and universities. Nor did the German government yet intervene in the economy to such an extent that it could reshape regional industrial structures. The federal government awarded few large government contracts and, having no armed forces, supported no defense industry. As far as industrial modernization went, the only option before the CSU in 1949 was whether or not it would pursue friendly, cooperative relations with Bavarian industry and support industry's interests in whatever ways it could on a case-by-case basis. With Hans Ehard as minister-president of Bavaria and chairman of the CSU, even this seemed too much to hope for. In 1949 few things drew the attention of CSU politicians to the problems of promoting industrial modernization, and nothing that did pointed them toward any solutions.

Notes

1. Jane Jacobs, *Cities and the Wealth of Nations* (New York, 1984), 32.
2. Throughout this book we will use the words "liberal" and "conservative" in their European meanings. European liberals promoted both moral and economic individualism, and tended to nationalism and anticlericalism. European conservatives promoted order, tradition, and Christian faith but were distrustful of individualism and market forces.
3. Benno Hubensteiner, *Bayerische Geschichte. Staat und Volk, Kunst und Kultur,* thirteenth ed. (Munich, 1992), 431 (Prinz Otto writing to Ludwig II).
4. Thomas Schlemmer, *Aufbruch, Krise und Erneuerung: Die Christlich-Soziale Union* 1945 bis 1955 (Munich, 1998), 111ff.
5. Schlemmer, *Aufbruch,* 24ff, 382ff.
6. Konstanze Wolf, *CSU und Bayernpartei: Ein besonderes Konkurrenzverhältnis 1948–1960* (Cologne, 1982).
7. Paul Erker, "Keine Sehnsucht nach der Ruhr. Grundzüge der Industrialisierung in Bayern 1900–1970," *Geschichte und Gesellschaft. Zeitschrift für Historische Sozialwissenschaft* 17, no. 4 (1991): 485, 489, 491 (figures given are from 1950).

CHAPTER 1

INDUSTRIAL MODERNIZATION JUST BELOW THE HORIZON, 1949–1954

In a Tight Corner

It became possible for the CSU to create a politics of industrial modernization only after it got itself out of the tight corner it occupied in the German party system.

In 1949 the CSU was unable to tack to the Right and Left or to play the other parties off against each other. This was because it was dominated by the CDU. This was most evident in the federal parliament. At the beginning of the first parliamentary term, the CSU deputies in Bonn were treated by the other parties and the major interest groups like representatives of a de facto state party organization of the CDU, as if the CSU were akin to the CDU state party organizations of Hesse or Rhineland-Palatinate, permitted to bear a slightly different name only in order to humor Bavarian sensibilities. This was understandable. A national party organization was not the only attribute of a serious party that the CSU lacked: it "owned" no national issues; its political profile was distinguishable from the CDU's only on issues of import to people many considered Bavarian Catholic bumpkins; it did not have its own candidate for the chancellorship; its leader did not, like the leaders of other parties, bear the title of "party chairman" but of "state chairman"; and it lacked important industrial clients. The CSU's status as a formally independent but practically dependent party put it under serious disadvantages vis-à-vis the various state party organizations of the CDU: the leaders of the CSU were not admitted into the inner leadership circle of the CDU; CSU leaders were not treated by the CDU as eligible for the highest political offices (the chancellorship, the presidency, and the foreign ministry); the

Notes for this section begin on page 44.

CSU could not expect Bavaria to receive the same favored treatment that the CDU-led national government gave to CDU-dominated states. The CSU even depended on the CDU for money: for the 1949 federal election German industry gave money to the CDU and let the CDU finance the CSU—the former naturally took care of its own needs first and tried to use its power over the purse to control the CSU. If the CSU's status as a separate party gave it any advantages over the CDU, in 1949 it was hard to see what they were.

And if in 1949 the CSU was not cornered in Bavaria, its position was growing more constricted. The CSU state deputies awaited the 1950 state election with trepidation. Though the CSU had won 52 percent of the Bavarian vote in the state election of 1946, the conservative victory in the infighting that followed alienated Bavarian Protestants and the urban middle class, while the creation of the Bavaria Party in 1948 threatened the CSU's rural Catholic base. The result had been evident in the 1949 federal election, when the CSU won only 29 percent of the Bavarian vote.

The victory of the CSU's conservative over its liberal wing had also reduced the party's appeal to industry, on which all of the nonsocialist parties depended for money. While the CDU and FDP stood for economic liberalism while quietly supporting selective intervention in the economy in support of industry, the CSU showed little interest in either. Its party program said nothing about industrialization, and with good reason industry considered the CSU deputies in Bonn to be second-string representatives of rural agricultural and village artisanal interests. Something like this had been the tradition of Bavarian Catholic politics since the days of Bismarck, and there was little indication that the CSU meant to break with it. As a CSU internal report admitted: "If one considers the parliamentary work done by the state and federal CSU deputies, it is striking that it is chiefly political or legal, but not economic. If we deal with economic matters, then for the most part we talk about agriculture. Or commerce. Very rarely do we talk about industrial problems."[1]

It is no exaggeration to say the CSU was in a corner. By the mere fact of the creation of the German state in 1949, it seemed that the CSU might well lose its raison d'être, or that a short term might be set to the appeal of particularistic conservatism. Yet, while between 1946 and 1949 the CSU had become too conservative and Catholic for Bavarian Protestants and for industry, and fallen into financial crisis, the results of the 1949 federal election had indicated that the CSU was not conservative enough for its Catholic base.[2] In 1949 there was a real question whether the CSU could survive—probably it would survive in a crippled form, but perhaps it would be absorbed by the CDU. The CSU had to find some way, as an advisor to the CSU deputies in Bona wrote, "to get out of its corner."[3]

That the CSU quickly got out of its corner was largely the achievement of two politicians, Franz Josef Strauß and Hanns Seidel. They could not make the CSU into the equal of the CDU, or remake it into the FDP, but by 1954 they had begun to make clever use of the valuable advantages of being the second party of German Christian Democracy. And, half unawares, they began to create its politics of industrial modernization. Of course there was no question in the years 1949 to 1954 of undertaking the industrial modernization of Bavaria, much less of undoing the similarities between Bavaria and the Italian *Mezzogiorno.*

Strauß and Seidel executed a tour de force of a different sort. Though neither man was in a position to set the CSU's political course, each man was marvellously effective in what appeared to be an inglorious office, from which they effectively maneuvered the CSU out of its corner, and in the process set it on the road toward a politics of industrial modernization.

Sealing the Deal with Industry

In 1949 the CSU leaders had to decide what would be their party's relationship to the CDU. They feared that if the CSU tried to operate in Bonn as an independent Christian-Democratic party, its two dozen deputies would quickly become isolated and ineffective: though in the parliamentary system small "swing" parties can exercise considerable power, the CSU could hardly swing since the CSU's supporters had voted for it believing it would support the CDU on the great issues of the day. So the CSU leaders agreed with the CDU that for the parliamentary term 1949–1953 the two parties would form a joint parliamentary caucus: within the federal parliament and government they would act vis-à-vis other parties as a single entity, the CDU/CSU.4 Yet this created the danger that the CSU deputies would become incapable of acting separately in Bonn, and would then be gradually absorbed into the CDU.5

To defend against this danger, the CSU leaders formed the State Group (Landesgruppe), an association of CSU deputies within the CDU/CSU caucus. The State Group proved much more cohesive and durable than the ephemeral associations occasionally created by parliamentarians from other states. Immediately before the meetings of the CDU/CSU joint parliamentary caucus, the twenty-four CSU deputies would assemble for closed meetings at which they would agree on common positions they would take within the CDU/CSU caucus. These meetings would preserve the deputies' CSU identity and would put them in a position to exercise influence out of proportion to their numbers—particularly since Franz Josef Strauß led the State Group.

In 1949 Strauß was little known outside the CSU. He was only thirty-four years old, but was already the natural leader of the generation of CSU deputies that had no pre-Nazi political experience. Strauß was born the son of a Munich butcher; his parish priest recognized his talents and insisted that his reluctant father give him a classical education, and "Franzi" wrote the best university entrance examination in all Bavaria while winning national bicycle races. A classicist writing a doctoral dissertation on the Roman imperial idea when World War II started, he served from 1939 to 1945 in France and Russia. After the war Strauß naturally claimed that he had been anti-Nazi, and he cited as evidence his father, a rather reactionary Catholic active in the Bavarian People's Party. But it seems doubtful that any reservations the hard-living, hard-loving son may have had about the Nazis stemmed from piety, or that he was much influenced by his father's monarchism. In the last days of the war, Strauß threw off his uniform but was taken prisoner by the Americans, to whom he soon made himself useful. The Americans appointed him assistant county councillor (Landrat) in Upper Bavaria and later county councillor in his own right. He joined the CSU and allied himself to its liberal chairman, Josef Müller, who, recognizing his political talents, made Strauß his protégé. But when in May 1949 the elderly conservatives that dominated the CSU gathered to vote Müller out of his party chairmanship, Strauß refused to share his patron's defeat. He took the podium, and his fellow liberals, expecting a brilliant defense of Müller, sat "as if turned to stone" when Strauß failed to defend his patron.[6]

In the years 1949 to 1953, while the liberal wing of the CSU was in eclipse, Strauß performed astonishing feats as the leader of the State Group. He maneuvered it out of its corner, built up its influence and its finances, and knocked down its opponents. He treated it not as an immovable federalist bloc but a mobile force, directed not so much toward the realization of any ideological program as toward increasing the CSU's influence in Bonn. He proposed positions on which the other CSU deputies could agree, especially federalist positions. While these positions appealed to the other deputies' political passions, Strauß learned to exploit their nuisance-value.[7]

Strauß demanded that his "community of conspirators," as he called the State Group, get paid off for its cooperation. As we will see, he learned to do this rather quickly, though some years passed before he learned to demand payoffs that promoted Bavaria's industrial modernization.

Yet the State Group was a necessary but not sufficient means to getting the payoffs Strauß wanted. The CSU required connections to industrial interests. Strauß formed these when he created a special alliance between the State Group and the leaders of Bavarian industry.

This alliance came as an unpleasant surprise to the other parties. In the first years of the new German republic the nonsocialist parties scuffled anxiously to determine which parties would represent which interest groups, above all industry, the source of money to finance election campaigns. Though the CSU was certainly a nonsocialist party, through 1949 it had not established itself as a representative of any major branch of industry, even Bavarian industry, which, dominated by liberals and Protestants, favored the FDP and cultivated direct connections with the CDU, hoping that the latter would absorb the CSU.[8]

It was by no means a given that Bavarian industry would represent its interests through the CSU. The CSU might well have come to mean no more to Bavarian industry than the CDU state party organization in Hesse came to mean to Hessian industry. In Bonn, Bavarian industry had the option to bypass the CSU and represent its interests through the Federation of German Industry (BDI, Bundesverband der Deutschen Industrie), the CDU, and the FDP. Even in Munich, the FDP was a real alternative to the CSU. Though the CSU received support from individual industrialists, mostly conservative Catholics or those who did business with the Bavarian state, through 1949 Bavarian industry seems to have preferred the FDP to the CSU in Bavarian politics.

It was a specific configuration of institutions, people, and circumstances that drove Bavarian industry toward the CSU. The institutions, on industry's side, were two trade associations, the Federation of Bavarian Industry (LBI, Landesverband der Bayerischen Industrie) and the Association of the Bavarian Chemical Industry (VBCI, Verband der Bayerischen Chemischen Industrie). The LBI, the general trade association for all of Bavarian industry, was founded in 1949 by the leaders of industry-specific trade associations to represent Bavarian industry to the Bavarian government and to collect and distribute money to the nonsocialist parties.[9] The Association of the Bavarian Chemical Industry (VBCI, Verein der Bayerischen Chemischen Industrie) was the most important of the industry-specific trade associations driving the LBI to pursue a hard line.

Both the LBI and VBCI were dominated by pragmatic characters. Otto Seeling founded and served as president of the LBI. He was a Frankish Protestant, a glass manufacturer from Nuremberg. His private rhetoric is revealing: postwar Germany's labor unions had been built up by "Jewish-communistic elements within the occupation governments," and the idea that labor should be represented on corporate boards (codetermination) was "humanitarian drivel." He worked tirelessly to persuade industrialists to coordinate their political donations so that, through the offer or withholding of money by one central donor (the LBI), they could put greater pressure on the nonsocialist parties to represent their policies.[10]

It was similar with Siegfried Balke, chairman of the VBCI and a member of the LBI's presidium. If Balke seems to have been more tractable than Seeling, he was more successful at politics. Balke began his rise to eminence as a front man for the Bavarian chemical industry in 1945 and 1946, becoming VBCI chairman largely because, being half-Jewish and having therefore spent the war years in an inconspicuous position in a minor chemical firm, he was politically clean in an industry that was notoriously unclean.[11] Yet Balke's Weltanschauung was not very different from Seeling's. He was a Protestant and a right-wing national-liberal, and stood out in the late 1940s for his zeal to exonerate the accused in the IG-Farben trials, his private expressions of hostility to the Western allies and their economic policies, and his opposition to Adenauer's policy of binding Germany to the Western powers.[12] Balke's idée fixe was "public relations." He dedicated himself to convincing Bavarian industrialists to coordinate their political contributions so as to increase their leverage over the nonsocialist parties.[13]

Seeling and Balke, the LBI and the VBCI, turned to the State Group to solve specific problems—for Seeling, to secure coal for Bavarian industry. In the winter of 1950 to 1951 a crisis of coal production forced many Bavarian factories to close or work part-time while Ruhr industry had enough coal to keep working at full capacity. This profoundly affected how the leaders of Bavarian industry understood the position of Bavarian industry within Germany. Seeling and other Bavarian industrialists believed with good reason that Ruhr industry had used its superior influence with the CDU, particularly with Adenauer and Erhard, to secure its own supply at Bavaria's expense.[14] (It was no accident that Seeling came from the Bavarian glass industry, which, along with the porcelain industry, suffered more than any other from the coal crisis. In order to secure Bavarian industry's coal supply Seeling met personally with Adenauer and Erhard in the winter of 1950–1951.[15]) In mid-1951, Bavarian industrialists expected the coming winter would bring another coal crisis. In fact, Seeling saw coal as the chief problem of Bavarian industry and Balke, by this time the chairman of the LBI's Energy Committee, expected that while the situation would be somewhat better in the winter of 1951–1952 energy would long remain a fundamental problem for Bavarian industry.[16]

As to the Bavarian chemical industry, Balke and the VBCI feared that, in the general reorganization of the German chemical industry following the Allies' breakup of the I.G.-Farben conglomerate, the Bavarian industry might be reorganized out of existence. In 1951 the leaders of the Federation of the Chemical Industry (VCI, Verband der Chemischen Industrie, the national trade association for the chemical industry) and in particular Karl Winnacker, the president of Hoechst, who had used political contributions to purchase influence with the CDU and the FDP, was urging Adenauer and Erhard to incorporate specific Bavarian chemical firms into Hoechst, claiming, with widespread agreement among the country's industry, banks, and ministerial bureaucracy, that the Bavarian firms would otherwise not be competitive.[17] Winnacker wanted to absorb the most important Bavarian chemical firm, Wacker-Chemie, as well as Lech-Chemie Gersthofen, Kunstseidenfabrik Bobingen, Süeddeutschen Kalkstickstoff-Werken, and Anorgana-Gendorf, while another I.G.-Farben successor, Bayer, sought to absorb the AGFA-Camerawerk.[18]

If in early 1951 Bavarian industry, struggling against the Rhine/Ruhr industrial complex and its allies in the CDU and FDP, had increasing need of a political patron, in early 1951 Strauß was looking for a cause to take up against the CDU. The State Group had felt its oats when it successfully resisted Adenauer's rather unfederalist project to create a national police force-cum-army, and had followed this up with a demand for "equal treatment" within the CDU/CSU joint parliamentary caucus. Adenauer agreed to the demand but then failed to deliver.[19] Strauß led the State Group's debate as to how to respond. He suggested to the CSU deputies that they dissolve the CDU/CSU joint parliamentary caucus; this the deputies were not prepared to do, though Strauß convinced them, "after long and forceful remarks," that should the occasion arise the State Group might at least threaten to do so.[20] Strauß was looking for a pretext to raise the price of the CSU's cooperation, and the pattern of discrimination against Bavarian industry, coinciding with a governmental initiative for investment aid to industry in the Rhine and Ruhr, according to which Bavaria, with 17 percent of the Federal Republic's population, would receive only 10 percent of the investment aid, presented itself as if made to order.[21]

Strauß took the initiative. His idea was that the CSU follow the CDU and the FDP in setting up an association to which tax-deductible and anonymous donations could be made and that would publish an information service retailing political news useful to industry—in effect, selling inside information from ministries that the party held. The CDU and FDP were already doing this, and an advisor to the State Group warned Strauß: "The CSU can still point to no such organization or achievement. Yet so long as its economic base has not been secured it cannot break out of its current cramped position [in the German party system]." But Strauß's ambitions soon extended beyond an information service.[22]

In July 1951 Strauß invited Balke to become an "advisor" on economic affairs to the State Group. If the two men had not known each other well before this time, they got to know each other well enough after Balke accepted and convinced Seeling that the LBI foot the bill for Strauß's information service and an office in Bonn. Thus Strauß overcame German industrialists' notorious reluctance to associate themselves publicly or closely with one political party, and convinced the LBI to bear costs estimated at DM 100,000 annually—at the time a very substantial sum.[23] Strauß and Balke came to an agreement that Strauß would lead the State Group in fighting for a cheaper and more secure coal supply for Bavaria, and in the defense of the Bavarian chemical industry.[24] And Strauß agreed to address a whole list of other concerns, including how many CSU candidates in the next federal election would come "from Bavarian industry," the prospects for future "defense contracts for Bavarian industry," and political assistance to the LBI for the "immediate creation of Christian trade unions" (yellow unions created to undermine the monopoly over the trade-union movement exercised by the Social-Democratic-dominated German Trade Union Federation).[25]

Fortified by his new alliance, Strauß made himself heard in Bonn. In late August 1951 he called the State Group to a strategy session in the Bavarian palace of Kirchheim, and it is plain that the arrangements with Balke had already changed things. According to the minutes of the Kirchheim meeting: "The joint parliamentary caucus with the CDU, which we have worked for and realized for technical reasons of political coalition ... has not always proven itself good for Bavaria's economy and therefore also for the State Group.... Economically speaking, there is within the CDU, in view of the numerical dominance of North Rhine-Westphalia, an effort to treat the economy of North Rhine-Westphalia as the North Star for the economic policy of the entire republic and to neglect ... Bavaria. To more strongly emphasize Bavarian economic interests seems to the CSU a matter of practical survival." Strauß again persuaded the State Group to threaten to dissolve the joint parliamentary caucus, this time if the CDU did not agree that the CSU receive more money for its own offices and employees, separate office space, its own speaking time in the federal parliament, and placement on the same level as other government parties in negotiations for the division of ministries. Almost all of the demands were quickly granted by Heinrich von Brentano, the chairman of the CDU/CSU joint parliamentary caucus, who had recognized in this a "serious political crisis" and announced to his colleagues "the intentions of the State Group to pursue in the future a more independent political line."[26]

For their part, the CDU, FDP, and BDI were alarmed by the new alliance, which they soon saw institutionalized in what was variously called the "Bonn Office," or the "Strauß office," out of which a small staff produced the Nachrichten aus Wirtschaft und Politik Industrial and Political News and in coordination with which Strauß lobbied the Bonn ministries and government on behalf of Bavarian industry.[27]

Strauß and the LBI had created their alliance for the long term, bringing the CSU and the LBI together because the CDU and the BDI had already come together. The former pair understood themselves to be gravely threatened by the axis of the latter, the inevitable effect of which would be to keep the CSU out of the loop in matters of economic policy (and therefore financial contributions), and to give permanent priority to the industrial interests of the CDU-governed states. Of particular concern here was North Rhine-Westphalia, the most populous state in the Federal Republic as well as the home state of Chancellor Adenauer and many of his CDU advisors and ministers, which many Bavarian politicians and officials saw as the new Prussia, the rich, industrialized, and dominant northern German state. They were not entirely wrong. Though North Rhine-Westphalia later learned that it had common interests with Bavaria, it aggravated Bavarian suspicions by using promises of special tax reductions, credits, and state loan guarantees to entice Bavarian industry to relocate.[28]

It was a good thing for the State Group that Seeling and Balke were not valuing their alliance by its short-term yield, for that was varied. As to coal supplies, Strauß advocated the Bavarian cause but was unable to prevent power outages in the winter of 1951–1952. If coal supplies became less of a problem, this was due chiefly to an improvement in the general situation.[29] As to the Bavarian chemical industry, Strauß secured money from Erhard for its buildup and stabilization and met with Adenauer to warn him that in the decisions over the IG-Farben decartelization Bavarian interests must not be trampled on; the LBI reported internally that, "in sharp words a full consideration of all of the Bavarian requests was demanded. If this was not granted Strauß threatened to take the CSU out of the government coalition"; as the negotiations for the reorganization of the IG-firms continued Balke was satisfied that the Bavarian chemical industry suddenly got a more reasonable response from the powers in Bonn.[30] On more minor issues, the results were thinner.[31] If the LBI found out that the CSU continued to refuse some of its demands, this did not matter too much.[32] No party could afford to give industry all that it demanded, yet through the alliance with the State Groups, the voice of Bavarian industry was heard in Bonn. The range of action that Strauß undertook on behalf of Bavarian industry in the fall of 1951—arm-twisting, complaining, threatening, soliciting, and lobbying—was remarkable. And Balke reported to the LBI that it had created "an entirely new atmosphere."[33]

For the State Group the alliance with the LBI cost practically nothing and yielded a rich harvest. Its efforts on behalf of Bavarian industry did not alienate the CSU from any of its core constituencies, and, since it corresponded to

Bavaria's interests, was in the CSU's own long-term interest. In return for its efforts the State Group got the full support of Bavarian industry: not only increased financial contributions, but the fundamental decision of industry to favor the CSU over the other parties, especially the Bavaria Party. In 1949, the year the Bavaria Party had cut the CSU's vote nearly in half, the LBI had financially supported the Bavaria Party. But in September 1951, immediately after Strauß and Balke came to their agreement, Balke, who together with Seeling dominated the "Committee of Six" that decided how to apportion industry's contributions to the nonsocialist parties, wrote a note to himself that, "It is absolutely necessary that the Bavaria Party be financially wiped out."[34]

There is little doubt what the alliance with the LBI did for Franz Josef Strauß. Beyond increasing his influence with the CDU, it consolidated his dominance of the State Group and his position within the CSU. Hans Limmer, the State Group's go-between in its relations with Bavarian industry, reported to Strauß that the LBI was tired of being approached for money by swarms of "collectors and political panhandlers." "The LBI would like to coordinate the political efforts of industry so that from now on there should only be one donor [the LBI itself] and one person designated to receive money for each party.... If you move now, you should be able to pull the rug out from under your esteemed colleagues Ochsensepp [Josef Müller's nickname], Hundhammer, Ehard, Seidel, Elsen and all the rest of them." And this seems to be what happened; for at the same time Limmer reported to Strauß, Balke instructed the LBI: "Str. will open an account with the Bavarian Credit Bank. Our payments will be made only to this account. Str. will be the only person with the right to withdraw money from the account and he will be responsible to us in all financial matters."[35] There are indications that the Bonn Office was not only, as Strauß wrote to Ehard, an institution "out of whose proceeds not inconsiderable sums flowed to the party or rather to the political aims of the CSU," but that after 1951 the LBI's financial contributions to the CSU passed chiefly and perhaps even exclusively through Strauß's hands.[36]

Both Strauß and the LBI appear to have been well satisfied with their alliance. Balke reported to Seeling: "It's already clear that the operation in Bonn is going to bring us usable material ... and that above all the increased activity of the CSU (which is made possible by us) in support of Bavarian industry in Bonn has created an entirely new atmosphere ... On balance our expenditure has been worth it, for when we force the people in Bonn to realize that they can no longer use politics to drive us economically against the wall, then that will gradually make a difference."[37] And Strauß crowed at the official opening of the Bonn Office that from now on all efforts to promote Bavarian economic interests in Bonn would be made "in the closest cooperation" with the State Group.[38]

Strauß Pushes Forward

When in the early 1950s Germany began to plan its rearmament as a member of the Western alliance, Bavarians did not dare to dream that its new defense industry might be concentrated in their state. Since the late nineteenth century, the German defense industry had been concentrated in northwestern Germany, near the Rhine and Ruhr steel mills.

But Strauß and the State Group did eventually achieve a concentration of the German defense industry in Bavaria, and the story of that achievement begins in the early 1950s, when Strauß began to stake his claim to the not-yet-existing Defense Ministry. Strauß did not want to be Germany's first postwar Defense Minister out of any calculation that he could use this ministry to bestow a high-technology defense industry on Bavaria, but for personal reasons. He was extremely ambitious and powerfully attracted to defense issues, especially as they related to foreign policy and Germany's position in the world. In this sense the postwar Bavarian defense industry originated in Strauß's own personality. Strauß's almost obsessive interest in defense matters marked his entire political career—from 1950 until his death in 1987 he was either working to become Defense Minister, or was Defense Minister, or was acting as a kind of self-appointed shadow Defense Minister, and his defense concerns extended beyond the military defense of Germany's eastern borders to the recovery of Germany's position in the world, its national pride, its military power, and the reestablishment of its defense industry: four things he understood to be profoundly connected. In his *Memoirs* Strauß wrote that he became the CDU/CSU speaker on defense issues "not as the result of long-term planning, but rather through a series of accidents, through Providence."[39] We will see that if Strauß's leadership on defense issues came through a series of accidents, then only because he worked to make himself accident-prone.

Strauß's drive to become Defense Minister went through two phases. In the first, which went from 1950 through the federal election of 1953, Strauß tried to use party-political levers to remove obstacles to his ambition. In the second he learned to work industrial-political levers.

It was in working the party-political levers that Strauß and the State Group got their education in the advantages that came with being the second party of German Christian Democracy. In the early 1950s defense politics were about the proposed European Defense Community (EDC, a pan-western-European army in which the German role was the subject of controversy). Adenauer maintained personal control over the negotiations, appointing Theodor Blank, a tractable and self-effacing Catholic trade-union leader from North Rhine-Westphalia who would not be able to maintain his position without Adenauer's support, to oversee defense matters through the so-called Blank Office. Later, when treaties permitted, he would transform the Blank Office into the Defense Ministry. Adenauer planned to handle the EDC negotiations personally, as a confidential diplomatic matter, and to stonewall the federal parliament until he was ready to present it with a completed treaty for ratification. Any Christian-Democratic deputies who did not like this were to be disciplined with all the means Adenauer had at his disposal.

But it didn't work out that way. Adenauer found that his means did not suffice to control the CSU State Group, and especially not Strauß, who had already been making a name for himself on defense issues. On 13 July 1950, less than three weeks after North Korea launched its drive down the Korean peninsula, John McCloy, the American High Commissioner in Germany, privately sounded out some German parliamentarians on the idea of German rearmament; Strauß was among those invited to dinner and he was already egregious for his eagerness to rearm, his interest in rebuilding German power in the world, his demand for equal rights for a German army, and the anti-American undertones to his language. Hardly had a month gone by before Strauß began to raise the issue before voters and the federal parliament.[40] He was soon doing so more often and more insistently than any other German parliamentarian and became, at a time when the German public was overwhelmingly opposed to rearmament, the leading parliamentary advocate of rearmament, speaking to the CDU/CSU joint parliamentary caucus with great energy of the need to organize an effective defense with "modern weapons."[41]

When the EDC negotiations got under way, Strauß used the State Group to coordinate resistance to Adenauer. Strauß created a division of labor according to which he spoke to themes involving German national feeling, stirring it up on such issues as allied restrictions on German defense manufacturing and French proposals for subordinating and controlling German forces. He threatened that, since the CSU deputies were not being kept informed about the treaty Adenauer was negotiating, they would be free to reject it.[42] Other CSU leaders acquired their own profile on defense issues: Richard Jaeger, who came from the CSU's conservative wing, spoke to the constitutional changes required by the proposed army, parliamentary oversight of the army, and the Defense Committee; and Hans Ehard, as Bavarian Minister-President, demanded federalism within the new army—that Bavarian soldiers be drafted into Bavarian units that would serve their term of duty within Bavaria, and led the successful fight against Adenauer's project for a paramilitary national police force.[43] All of this intensely annoyed Adenauer but, since the CSU deputies were free to say things the CDU deputies could not, many of the latter were happy to accept the CSU's leadership on rearmament issues. When Strauß launched "thundering philippics" against Adenauer's stonewalling of the parliament, they rewarded him with "showering applause."[44]

The issue between Adenauer and Strauß was less policy than power. On defense policy the two men were more often in agreement than Adenauer could afford to let on. Power was something else entirely. Adenauer understood defense issues to be part of foreign policy, which he was determined to keep within his personal control, either directly or indirectly through the appointment of weak ministers dependent on him. And given Strauß's personality and domination of the CSU State Group, it was clear that he would never be a weak minister.

Yet nothing stood behind Strauß's push but the State Group; and it did not suffice to force Adenauer to give the future Defense Ministry to a man like Strauß. Strauß and the State Group were increasingly bold about Strauß's ambitions for the Defense Ministry. At first the CSU claimed that it wanted only a "place" in the new ministry. In January 1951 Strauß told the State Group that the CSU would have to have "decisive influence" in the Blank Office and began beating the drums to the effect that Blank "seems to be losing his grip on the situation."[45] In January 1952 Strauß founded the CDU/CSU Defense-Political Working Group to prepare the parliamentary debate on the EDC and to constitute an expert body "which the Chancellor couldn't ignore."[46] In February 1952, in the federal parliamentary debate on German rearmament within the EDC, Strauß clinched his role as the Christian Democrats' most prominent defense politician and the hope of all those who wanted a more aggressively "national" foreign and defense policy.[47] Strauß gave the nation a taste of his oratorical brilliance—the debate was broadcast, and in city centers crowds gathered to listen to them. Strauß spoke after Adenauer and gave what many believe to have been his greatest speech ever.[48] In June 1952 Strauß proposed creation of the European Defense Community Committee, of which he was made first chairman on July 10—Adenauer having been forced to give up his plan to present the parliament with a fait accompli—a position from which Strauß could exercise considerable influence on the legal and constitutional framework of the new defense forces. By mid 1952 the State Group was calling openly for Strauß to be made Defense Minister. In August 1952 Strauß and Heinrich von Brentano, the chairman of the CDU/CSU joint parliamentary caucus, intrigued to force Adenauer to accept a Cabinet reshuffle which would give the Foreign Ministry to Brentano and promise the Defense Ministry to Strauß.[49] But Adenauer fought them off; and after this Strauß became more careful. Strauß tried to put pressure on Adenauer by spreading rumors that the CSU might form a coalition with the Social Democrats—incredible as such a thing might be, the rumors signalled Strauß's resolve—and met secretly with people who acted as his eyes and ears within the Blank Office.[50]

Insufficient as Strauß's engines were, it was in working them that Strauß and the State Group discovered the political dynamics that drove the CSU's relation to Germany's military-industrial complex for the next forty years. One of them was to make use of the CSU's relative freedom from foreign policy responsibility to outflank the CDU on the right. As the senior party of German Christian Democracy, the CDU conducted and got the credit for the success of Germany's foreign relations, but it was constrained by its responsibility: dependent on good relations with the Western allies, it could not openly represent national feeling, certainly not the resentments that many Germans felt toward the Western allies. The FDP often did this, and Strauß was never reticent, neither by nature, nor when he saw a chance to connect himself to Germany's potential defense industry, which was itself nationalistic in its political heart of hearts and rightly feared the Western allies' plans to shape Germany's rearmament to the advantage of their own domestic industries.

Another dynamic was that hawkishness on defense issues tended to integrate the CSU. In the rearmament debates of 1952 and early 1953 Strauß positioned himself as the most vehement advocate of rearmament. Though the great majority of Germans opposed rearmament, for almost all CSU politicians and party members, rearmament was a matter of course and gave rise to no serious inner-party quarrels.[51] It appealed to the CSU's conservatives through their Catholic anticommunism (and their eagerness to defend Christendom against Bolshevism), and to its liberals' national feeling (national liberals in Bavaria, mostly Protestants from Franconia, were probably more national and less liberal than elsewhere in Germany). To insist more sharply than Adenauer that the new German army receive "equal rights" and that Germany be given back its "sovereignty" connected Strauß to both groups, and not only in the CSU. It also won him a following among the right-wing nationalists of the CDU and appealed to the often nationalistic and resentful supporters of the FDP and the Bavaria Party.

Yet other dynamics worked against the CSU. While Strauß's rhetoric won him support in many circles, it turned Adenauer strongly against him. Bluster was exactly what the French and British did not want in a German Defense Minister, so that as far as Adenauer was concerned, the more Strauß raised the temperature of his rhetoric, the more necessary it became to deny his claim to the Defense Ministry. Moreover, as Chancellor and CDU chairman, Adenauer had no use for Bavarian particularism and the CSU's insistence on its autonomous structure. In fact, he was considering "disciplinary attempts" and "plans to break the CSU political machine."[52] This could not make Adenauer eager to increase Strauß's influence by appointing him Defense Minister. Even beyond these considerations, Strauß incarnated stereotypically Bavarian traits that Adenauer despised. Adenauer was the type of a late nineteenth-century patrician, a stiffly bourgeois Rhinelander repelled by Strauß's Bavarian vulgarity, his bluster, boastfulness, unpredictability, impudence, imprudence, drunkenness, and lechery—if Adenauer could have stepped out of Buddenbrooks, Strauß had all too much in common with father Karamazov.

The negative dynamics weighed heavily. Before Strauß would be able to wrest the Defense Ministry from Adenauer, he would have to strengthen the positive dynamics. And to do that Strauß needed support beyond the State Group: he would need the support of German industry, the group most interested in German rearmament. But German industry had no reason to support Strauß unless it somehow became clear that he would serve its interests better than Adenauer and Blank. How could he convince them of this?

Strauß's basic problem was that as late as 1953 he had little relationship with German industry outside of Bavaria. After all, his relationship with Bavarian industry had been founded on his willingness to work with it against industry in the rest of Germany. Bavarian industry was, moreover, neither influential on all-German issues nor particularly ambitious for defense contracts.[53] Strauß and Balke had agreed that one aspect of the cooperation between the State Group and the LBI would be that the CSU use its influence to secure defense contracts for

Bavarian firms, but the LBI's ambitions were quite modest: it wanted Bavarian industry to get its fair share and the State Group had taken up this cause in March 1952. At that time the CSU deputies called for a "general distribution to the states" to prevent the lion's share of the contracts from going to firms in North Rhine-Westphalia, and they pressed the Economic Ministry on the matter.[54] Beyond this Bavarian industry did not go, mostly because everyone expected that the kinds of armaments Germany would produce—to the extent it produced any, for each of the western allies wanted Germany to buy its future arms from its own defense-industrial complex—would be the typical weapons of the "Age of Steel" that would naturally be produced in the Ruhr.

And in Adenauer, Blank, and Erhard, Strauß had rivals for the favors of extra-Bavarian industry. Adenauer was close to the BDI, the representative of the potential defense industry, which counted on him to make sure that Germany's arms would have a "German character," as the euphemism went. Adenauer understood very well that the Defense Ministry, when formed, would be a gold mine exploitable for political contributions and kickback-income for whichever party held it. Though Adenauer could not hold it personally, he did the next best thing in setting up Blank as presumptive minister. Already in 1953 Blank permitted the BDI's Working Group for Questions of Rearmament to participate in the deliberations of his proto-Defense Ministry.[55] As to Ludwig Erhard, industry was counting on him to oppose industrial cartels and special interests—not German ones, of course, but French. Erhard's role was to oppose French efforts to impose a dirigisme that would give the French defense industry the upper hand over the German.[56] In sum, German industry had no reason to look to Strauß to represent it so long as it had Adenauer, Blank, and Erhard. This team would have to falter before Strauß could gain a hearing from the industry.

Yet the second phase of Strauß's drive, in which he actively sought to build up his extra-Bavarian industrial clientele, began with the 1953 federal election and the formation of a new CDU-led government. The election dramatically improved the CSU's position in Bonn. The Bavaria Party was literally "wiped out," as Strauß and Balke had wished, none of its seventeen deputies returning to the federal parliament, while the State Group grew from twenty-four to fifty-two deputies.

Strauß forced Adenauer to give ground before his push for the Defense Ministry. Strauß demanded three ministries, as many as the FDP, which had forty-eight deputies. Fritz Schäffer's position at the Finance Ministry was secure, but Wilhelm Niklas was not returning to the government so that, since the Defense Ministry did not yet exist, there were the questions of what ministry Strauß would get and of whether Hans Schuberth would keep the Postal Ministry. Adenauer tried to force Strauß to accept the Ministry for the Family, which Strauß saw as an insult to his ambitions as well as an attempt to make him, a bachelor playboy, look ridiculous. Strauß refused and, after some violent quarreling, Adenauer agreed to make Strauß Federal Minister for Special Tasks (that is, Strauß became a minister, enjoying Cabinet-level rank, without a ministry, being responsible for special tasks to be agreed upon as the occasion arose). As to the future, the CSU did not dare demand that Adenauer promise to make Strauß Defense Minister—that seemed beyond the just ambition of a 38-year-old—but did extract from Adenauer a written promise to entrust one of its representatives "with a decisive role in the defense area."[57]

Adenauer counterattacked on the Postal Ministry. He announced that he would not have Schuberth back and drove a wedge by arguing plausibly that it would not do for all of the CSU's ministers to be Catholic. The real issue was not Schuberth (a political nonentity who had been given the ministry due to his professional background in the postal service), but Adenauer's attempt to rule the CSU from without. At first the CSU insisted on Schuberth; then it relented; then Adenauer, without consulting the CSU, offered the Post Ministry to Karl Sigmund Mayr, a Protestant CSU deputy from Franconia; without consulting the CSU leadership, Mayr accepted. This caused an uproar within the CSU. Strauß and Schäffer threatened to expel Mayr, a notorious Adenauer "agent" within the CSU, and forced him to retract and apologize in a humiliating manner.[58] Strauß and Adenauer then agreed on a compromise: the CSU would name another Protestant for the Post Ministry.

Strauß pulled a fast one and proposed Siegfried Balke, who was not only not a deputy, but was not even a member of the CSU. The State Group bridled, but Strauß persuaded a majority to approve his choice.[59] Thanks to Strauß, precisely those Bavarian industrialists over whom Strauß and Adenauer had battled two years earlier now saw their man sitting alongside Strauß at federal cabinet meetings—indeed a new way, as Balke put it in his euphemistic style, "in which the increasing discrepancy between the political-economic desires of industry and the possibilities of practical politics can be bridged."[60]

As Federal Minister for Special Tasks Strauß acted, wags said, as if he were Federal Minister for Self-Assigned Tasks, assigning himself tasks that prepared him for the Defense Ministry and put him in the position to work for the first time with extra-Bavarian industrialists. He involved himself in the Franco-German negotiations to resolve the question of the Saarland, in the EDC negotiations, and in atomic matters. The latter proved important for his future, leading into his promotion to Minister of Atomic Affairs in 1955. It is reported, perhaps not too reliably, that Adenauer had suggested to Strauß only "in passing" that he "look after atomic questions," but however it came about Strauß was eager to take up the responsibility. He seems to have been genuinely fascinated by atomic energy, and atomic research and energy had obvious potential military applications.

All of these fields allowed Strauß to make up his "deficit in extra-Bavarian connections." They gave Strauß a chance to step onto the foreign-political stage and make contacts in America, France, and Britain.[61] Strauß's ministerial status, the responsibilities he had taken over, and his susceptibility to influence by money made him interesting to people involved in these industries. Although it is impossible to say whether this was one of his purposes in seeking these tasks, his involvement with the Saar question involved him with Saar industry and industrialists like the Roechling family. Involvement with the EDC negotiations allowed him to appeal, for example, in *Industriekurier,* to industrialists who feared that the arrangements Adenauer and Blank were making would allow French industry to shut out German. As for atomic energy and research, in 1954 his charge to deal with atomic things got Strauß onto the Planning Committee for the future Atomic Affairs Commission, where he met Karl Winnacker, the President of Hoechst, and a number of Germany's leading industrialists.[62] Strauß also expanded his network at meetings of Fritz Schäffer's Economic and Socio-Political Club, where chemical and oil interests dominated.[63]

Still, at the end of 1954 none of this was a matter of the politics of modernization, but of industrial interest politics in the service of the political ambition of the State Group, and to a considerable degree of Strauß's own ambition for higher office. But we will see how the industrial interests to which Strauß connected himself were set to become modernizing interests.

Turning the Economic Ministry to Account

Hanns Seidel, the Bavarian Economic Minister from 1947 to 1954, came to a solution to the problems facing the CSU in Munich strikingly similar to that which Strauß promoted in Bonn. Yet the CSU was in a very different situation in Munich. If in Bonn Strauß tried to play David against the CDU, in Munich Seidel had to ensure that the CSU didn't play Goliath to the FDP and the Bavaria Party.

Seidel did so by winning the support of Bavarian industry. Seidel came from the CSU's liberal wing, but his achievement in doing this cannot be understood if we assume, as it would be so natural to do, that there was a natural harmony between liberal ministers and industry. One of Seidel's predecessors as Bavarian Economic Minister was Ludwig Erhard, but though Erhard incarnated German liberalism, as Bavarian Economic Minister from 1945 to 1946 he failed miserably to win the confidence of Bavarian industry, as did Seidel's successor, Otto Bezold of the FDP.[64] In truth industry was not genuinely liberal; it opposed state intervention in the economy only when the state intervened in favor of interests other than its own. As a leading economic historian wrote, although German industry "tirelessly emphasized its 'fundamental agreement' with Ludwig Erhard's policies," it was still determined to organize the market and restrict competition, and demanded state intervention in the market in its favor. "Despite repeated professions of faith in the American ideology of 'free enterprise,' the willingness to accept 'foreign' political-economic systems and ideas was very slight indeed."[65]

What mattered to industry was less whether a minister was liberal than what kind of liberal a minister was. Ludwig Erhard had failed in Bavaria partly because he was first and foremost an economic liberal, a doctrinaire who considered that his mission was to unyieldingly defend the purity of the free market against the intrusions of politics. Seidel, on the other hand, was at heart a political liberal, interested in the working of liberal democracy, who thought that while politics should not be sordid, neither should it try to be too pure. He did not scorn interest groups as something that polluted politics but saw the competition for their support as part of a healthy liberal democracy.[66] Seidel was comfortable with the primacy of politics over economics and did not hesitate to subordinate his economic liberalism to the political situation and the need of his party to secure the support of interest groups and win elections. Though Seidel's economic ideas were similar to Erhard's, he rejected Erhard's dogmatism and tendency to think in exclusive categories ("planned economy" versus "market economy") and accepted the necessity of a mixed economy while working to move the CSU and Bavaria gradually in the liberal direction.[67] Not surprisingly, industry preferred to work with someone like Seidel.

All this positioned Seidel wonderfully well to serve Bavarian industry—how well came as something of a surprise to many Bavarian industrialists, many of whom scorned the CSU and looked to the CDU and the FDP. But while the CDU was eager to answer industry's call, it also tried to represent Catholic labor voters and had a progressive Catholic wing, so that it was constrained, on the one side, by Social-Democratic-leaning elements in its voting base, and, on the other, by Ludwig Erhard, the standard-bearer of neoliberalism, and his many supporters among the CDU's parliamentary deputies. For its part the FDP was even more eager to represent the interests of industry, but at the same time its voting base was in the professions and among owners and managers of family- and medium-sized businesses, who took the liberal ideals of free markets and government nonintervention in the economy more seriously than did industry. Seidel, on the other hand, found that on many issues a CSU Economic Minister was less constrained than many realized. This was so because the CSU was not committed to liberal principles, was not seriously threatened by the Social Democrats in Bavaria, had no outstanding "social Catholics" among its state and federal deputies, and, most interestingly, precisely because its voting base was in some interesting ways more antisocialist and antiliberal than industry itself.

This latter point requires some explaining. Bavarian Catholics were notably more traditional than Rhenish Catholics and even in the 1950s the Bavarian faithful bore in their hearts a strong "subsidiarist-corporatist" rejection of welfare-state centralism as well as an appreciation for regulated markets. Again, the CSU's willingness, born of its conservative Catholic Weltanschauung, to brand Social Democracy as Bolshevism and to defend private property rights unflinchingly could be turned against Social Democracy in general and against the progressive wing of the CDU. Again, the relative weakness of the liberal political-economic ideology and of labor unions in Bavaria meant that it was politically possible for the CSU to support an aggressively proindustrial politics in a way that was more difficult for the FDP or the CDU. All this meant that—just as Strauß discovered in Bonn—there were a number of issues on which the CSU could out-industry industry's parties without fear of offending its voting base. Seidel began to explore them in the late 1940s and early 1950s.

The principal issue was the prohibition of industrial cartels. Industry vigorously opposed the prohibition, treating it as a defining issue throughout the 1950s. This put the CDU in a difficult position. It pitched itself to voters for its excellent relations with the Western allies and on the success of the social market economy. The allies were pressing for the abolition of cartels and Ludwig Erhard was ready to lead the charge against cartels. At the same time the anticartel Social Democrats, Catholic trade unionists, and progressive Rhineland Catholics pressed the CDU hard in several of Germany's western states. Accordingly, the CDU pursued a middle position, watering down Erhard's proposals for a complete ban on cartels in favor of a ban on their abuse. The FDP opposed the prohibition of cartels, but felt itself squeezed between its financial supporters in industry and its voting base in the professions and family- and medium-sized firms, which, as liberal true believers, supported the prohibition. And so the CSU, free of all these constraints, turned its Catholic conservative dislike of economic liberalism to account for industry. We have already seen Strauß's support of industrial interests, but it was Seidel who made the CSU the hard core of public political support for cartels. Though cartels were an issue of federal law, in 1954 Seidel spoke to the issue in the Federal Council (the upper chamber in the German parliament, to which the states appointed delegates), letting no one take a stronger procartel position than the CSU, calling cartels indispensable to the German economy in times of recession and their prohibition unnecessary and legally dubious. Erhard contradicted Seidel angrily—which no doubt proved helpful in teaching industry which of the two Christian Democratic parties it could count on.[68]

Codetermination was another issue industry used to identify its real friends. In the early 1950s industry passionately resisted the drive of German unions for legislation giving employees equal representation in corporate boardrooms—many industrialists saw codetermination as the opening wedge of Bolshevik revolution. The unions were supported by the Social Democrats (of course), but also by the CDU's Catholic trade-union/progressive wing. Once again the CDU steered a middle course, negotiating in 1951 a very mild form of codetermination, which applied only to the iron and steel industries and in which the unions were represented in the boardroom at just below parity. Once again the CSU, not under pressure from the socialist Left or Catholic trade unionists, made itself the hard core of resistance to codetermination.

Yet Seidel was quite different from Strauß. Lacking Strauß's oratorical brilliance, his role was less to stake out public positions than to work patiently behind the scenes, with industrialists, within the Bavarian State Cabinet, and with Minister-President Ehard.[69] For example, one of Ehard's few efforts on behalf of the Bavarian economy was a campaign to persuade large national banks to establish themselves in Munich. But this he undertook at the urging of Seidel, who had been coached on the issue by Seeling, Bavarian firms having had trouble acquiring sufficient capital from Frankfurt banks.[70] Another example of Seidel's work as an "honest broker" was his effort on behalf of the Bavarian chemical industry—here again, Seidel's efforts linked up with Strauß's. More determined than his colleagues in the Bavarian cabinet to promote the Bavarian interest before Adenauer and Erhard, Seidel persuaded the cabinet to authorize him to negotiate on behalf of Bavarian firms with the IG-Farben Control Group. He argued for, variously, ownership and management of Bavarian chemical plants to be given to the Bavarian state, to a financial group to be put together by Bavarian banks, or to the industrialist Friedrich Flick. Though Seidel was frequently forced to give way, the Bavarian chemical industrialists believed that he was their best friend in Bavarian politics, that he had achieved as much as anyone could have, and that, while doing so, he had preserved good working relations with the northern German chemical industry. Thus Seidel stole a march on the FDP, which had spared no effort to make itself the political patron of the German chemical industry.[71]

Like Strauß with his LBI-subsidized "Strauß Office" in Bonn, Seidel institutionalized his relationship with industry. In June 1948, less than a year after he became Economic Minister, he founded the Economic Advisory Board (Wirtschaftsbeirat der Union), a group of industrialists and businesspeople who were invited to advise the CSU on economic questions—though many were not even CSU party members. From the CSU's point of view, the purpose of the Economic Advisory Board was to put CSU leaders into contact with leading circles of Bavarian industry, acquainting these disproportionately liberal and Protestant circles with the CSU's liberal wing and giving them a stake in the party's success. Naturally this led to financial contributions, which strengthened Seidel's hand within the party. By the early 1950s the Economic Advisory Board exercised direct influence over the CSU's party program. Although Seidel was not the sole founder of the Economic Advisory Board, as Bavarian Economic Minister he was the most highly placed friend of industry and commerce within the Bavarian state government and became the politician industry looked to in Munich—just as in Bonn it looked to Strauß.[72]

Adenauer's high estimation of Seidel provides one index of Seidel's success in winning the support of Bavarian industry. In 1950 Adenauer, who understood the primacy of politics over economics as much as any politician in Germany, repeatedly and insistently requested Seidel to give up the Bavarian Economic Ministry for the federal Cabinet-level position of State Secretary in the Office of the Federal Chancellor, where his task would have been to coordinate the policies of the three ministers most involved in the economy, Wilhelm Niklas (Agriculture Minister, CSU), and Franz Blücher (Vice-Chancellor and Minister for the Marshall Plan, FDP), and of course Ludwig Erhard. In effect, his assignment would have been to force them to respect "the primacy of politics" and to stand between Erhard and the major economic interest groups. Seidel politely but adamantly refused—not that, in 1950, he had reason to be confident of a glorious future in a CSU still dominated by its conservative Catholic wing, but it seems because he could find no one suitable to take over his ministry.[73]

Balke provides another index. In 1961 he wrote to Seidel, when the latter was on his deathbed: "When I got to know you in 1947, when you became the Bavarian Economic Minister, it seemed to me that in the general chaos of the times the only possible political-economic policy with which we could salvage something from Germany's catastrophe was that of the former liberals, who then reconstituted themselves as the FDP.... In the next few years I was able to see that the only new political idea since 1945 was the Christian-Democratic. I drew the appropriate conclusions and for several years worked to convince influential circles that the only party that could be the party of industry in Bavaria was not the FDP but the CSU. This was made possible above all by your activity, dear Herr Seidel, which for me was decisive from the beginning.... I would like to expressly emphasize that the changed attitude of Bavarian industry toward the CSU was by no means due to the Minister-President [Hans Ehard] and the general politics of the CSU, but was based exclusively on the work you were doing..."[74]

Seeing Industry in Science

The issue of industrial modernization first presented itself in the reconstruction of Germany's scientific research institutes. Hanns Seidel took up the struggle against the scientific establishment and other German states, so that Bavaria could reconstruct as many of the institutes as possible within its borders.

Defeat, occupation, and the construction of the new republic offered the scientific have-not states a chance to reshuffle some cards, and Bavaria was the biggest have-not of all. Since the founding of the German Empire in 1871 the country's scientific power had been concentrated in Prussia, a great deal of it along the lower Rhine and near Berlin, where the neighborhood of Dahlem had been established as a great state-supported research colony, a German answer to Oxford. Under the German Empire, Bavaria had contributed very little money to furthering the sciences and had received few institutes. Several factors made a reshuffling of the cards possible. One was the destruction wreaked by World War II together with the postwar poverty, chaos, and allied prohibitions on many kinds of research, all of which had scattered scientists and loosened institutes from their geographical moorings. During the last years of World War II some institutes had been moved out of range of allied bombing, and they were often moved to Bavaria, but they were by no means anchored to their new sites.[75] Another factor was the Basic Law, which gave the states jurisdiction over "culture," meaning religious affairs, education, and scientific research. This meant that research institutes had to look to the states for money, and that many of them would be more or less up for auction to the highest bidder—at least this is how it seemed in the first years of the West German republic, before the federal government managed to undermine the states' exclusive jurisdiction. Most of the states coveted research institutes, expensive though they were, for their prestige and out of the expectation that, if a state could create a concentration of research institutes, a concentration of related industries would follow.

In this competition for institutes Bavaria suffered from a grave handicap: lack of money. The Bavarian state government was comparatively poor and unwilling to devote its scarce resources to its Culture Ministry, which was for its part unwilling to devote its resources to scientific research. The first part of the problem needs little explanation: Bavaria was a relatively agricultural and tax-poor state and in the first postwar years the reconstruction of cities, schools, universities, and infrastructure and the housing of German refugees (of which Bavaria had a disproportionate share) took priority over scientific research. The second part of the problem takes us into the peculiar politics of the Bavarian Culture Ministry, a traditional bastion of federalism and clericalism.

The inflexible resistance of the Bavarian Culture Ministry to any federal role in matters of education, culture, and research soured Bavaria's relations with the scientific community. The latter was overwhelmingly oriented to the tradition of German liberalism and centralism, believing that if the responsibility for funding science belonged to the central government, preferably to a single federal ministry, it would be more generously, securely, and wisely funded. And the federalist-minded CSU was the major political obstacle to such centralization.[76]

Seidel worked to overcome Bavaria's problems, its lack of money and alienation from the scientific community, in different ways with different institutes.

Relations proved most difficult with the Max Planck Foundation. The question after World War II was whether the Max Planck Foundation, the dominant research organization, would continue to favor northern Germany. Its predecessor had always been an overwhelmingly Prussian institution, with very few institutes in Bavaria, and its reorganization had been a northern German project. Its governing board, which had broad powers in apportioning its moneys and locating institutes, was dominated by scientists who took a dim view of Bavarian federalism. From 1948 to 1950 there was a tremendous migration of institutes from the Soviet occupation zone to the west, but only two of them ended up in Bavaria.[77] Bavaria had to lobby very hard to secure the Institute for Silicate Research in Würzburg. But then it sought to delay and even escape its obligation to contribute to the institute's support, which confirmed the prejudices of the foundation's leaders.[78]

It says a lot that even the Fraunhofer Foundation, organized and dominated by Bavarians, proved a hard sell in Bavaria. Fraunhofer was founded in Munich in 1949 under Hanns Seidel's patronage and with a membership that was almost exclusively Bavarian, dominated by mining interests.[79] Fraunhofer aspired, however, to become a foundation of national importance, to do for applied research what the Max Planck Foundation did for pure science. Yet the responsibility for supporting applied research belonged to the Culture Ministry, controlled by the conservative Catholics Hundhammer and Schwalber, who in 1950 gave Fraunhofer the paltry subvention of DM 1,000—as Fraunhofer called it, "a sort of recognition duty."[80] Fraunhofer spun into crisis. Although its leaders declared their desire that the foundation serve all of Germany, it received practically no support from other states, which saw it as a stalking horse for Bavarian interests, or from the scientific community, which considered it an unhealthy division in the organization of state-supported research and worked actively to destroy it. But in 1951 Ludwig Erhard's Federal Economic Ministry rescued Fraunhofer, providing it with Marshall-Plan money and gradually, with the willingness of Baden-Württemberg to contribute to the support of institutes located within its borders, the Fraunhofer Foundation oriented itself away from Bavaria. But the reorientation took some years, and from 1949 to 1952 Bavaria received the lion's share of funding: DM 1,037,000 of Marshall Plan funds; second-place Baden-Württemberg received only DM 177,000, Lower Saxony DM 108,000 and North Rhine-Westphalia DM 35,000.[81]

Adolf Butenandt, Germany's leading biochemist, provides a case study of his own. Here it was a matter of a far sighted administrator in the Bavarian Culture Ministry pushing to "acquire" Butenandt. When representatives of the Bavarian Culture Ministry tried to interest Butenandt in moving from the University of Tübingen in Baden-Württemberg (his Max Planck Institute for Biochemistry would come with him), Butenandt named his price. In addition to his salary, he demanded that a new building be constructed for his institute and that he be provided with a "private house with a garden." The Baden-Württembergers were furious but refused to match Bavaria's offer. Hans Meinzolt, the State Secretary in the Culture Ministry and a Protestant CSU liberal (according to CSU tradition at that time, the Culture Minister must be Catholic and the State Secretary Protestant), took the decision to give Meinzolt whatever it took. The conservative civil servants thought Butenandt's demands outrageous, but Meinzolt nullified their objections with the overly optimistic argument that it might be possible to cover the cost with private donations from Bavarian industry. Meinzolt prevailed by presenting the "acquisition" of Butenandt as a step toward acquiring other Max Planck Institutes and, if Butenandt should succeed Otto Hahn as the President of the Max Planck Foundation, conceivably toward making Munich the foundation's headquarters. Meinzolt was looking even further ahead than this: he foresaw that if Munich had Werner Heisenberg and Adolf Butenandt, perhaps the two greatest figures in German science, this could create the synergy to transform Munich into a mecca of German science.[82] As we will see, all of these things happened in the 1960s.

Werner Heisenberg provides another case study. Seidel encouraged the great theoretical physicist, a leader in making science policy for the new republic, to move to Bavaria. Two factors gave special urgency to Seidel's efforts. The first was the Bavarian energy crisis, which made the prospect of atomic power very attractive to Bavaria.[83] Energy was both lacking and expensive in Bavaria. Bavarian consumers and industrial users paid the highest energy prices in Germany, and the problems that this caused were becoming more serious as energy consumption was increasing. Industries where energy costs were a substantial proportion of total costs could not afford to come to Bavaria, and it seemed some that were already there would have to leave; and the chemical industry was one such—it alone was responsible for 40 percent of Bavaria's total industrial power consumption.[84] The second was the decision of the Allies, in 1952 and 1953, to loosen their grip on German science—after the war they had utterly banned all aspects of atomic research and energy, particularly reactors and particle accelerators. On 8 December 1953 Eisenhower announced the American "Atoms for Peace" program, an offer to sell reactors and support atomic research programs in friendly countries, very much including Germany.[85]

And so Seidel responded vigorously when Heisenberg sought his assistance in moving his Max Planck Institute for Physics to Munich, where he wanted to construct Germany's first atomic reactor. Heisenberg, a Protestant Franconian who had studied in Munich, was eager to return to Munich, and Seidel convinced the Bavarian Cabinet to resolve "to raise no objections to the construction of the Federal Reactor Station near Munich" and in December 1953 he launched a publicity campaign. Seidel declared to the press that the atomic research would do much for Bavaria and implied that it was pretty much decided that Heisenberg's institute would be moved to Bavaria. But Adenauer had reserved the final decision to himself and scolded Seidel for damaging Germany's foreign policy interests by publicly raising the subject of atomic reactors before the allies had formally lifted their prohibition.[86] The Bavarian Culture Minister also tried to rein in Seidel, claiming that he "has gotten involved in areas beyond his sphere of responsibility" and that since the Max Planck Foundation fell within its jurisdiction, the Culture Ministry should be "duly" involved in any planning and negotiation involving the MPI for Physics. But Heisenberg and Seidel knew what they had in each other. To Heisenberg and the physicists Seidel was "*the* minister for our cause."[87]

Aerospace research institutes were a more complicated case, and one with a short-term payoff. Their attraction was that, given the postwar prohibition on aircraft production and the resultant backwardness of the German aircraft industry, the location of research institutes could go some way toward determining where Germany's aircraft industry would be reconstructed—if it were to be reconstructed at all.[88]

North Rhine-Westphalia was Bavaria's chief opponent in the struggle for the aircraft industry and aerospace research. In the early 1950s North Rhine-Westphalia tried to entice the firms of Dornier, Siebel, and Messerschmitt to leave Bavaria for the Ruhr, and succeeded in persuading Messerschmitt to cover its bets by founding Messerschmitt GmbH Rheinland in Essen, after which it provided Messerschmitt's subsidiary with financial support for research and development, and even production, which it hoped would lead to the construction of trainers and sport planes in Essen. This unsettled the connection of Dornier, Siebel, and Messerschmitt to Bavaria, all the more so as it took place in June 1953, while Walter Scheel (then a rising FDP deputy in North Rhine-Westphalia, later Federal President) was putting himself forward as the advocate of the aircraft industry, and shortly after North Rhine-Westphalia used financial contributions to persuade the Federation of the German Aircraft Industry (BDLI, Bundesverband der Deutschen Luftfahrtindustrie) to move its headquarters from Berlin to Düsseldorf in North Rhine-Westphalia, and the DVL (Deutsche Versuchsanstalt für Luftfahrt, or German Aerospace Research Institute) to move its headquarters to Essen in North Rhine-Westphalia.[89] And so it became crucial for Bavaria to show some commitment to its aircraft industry by fighting to keep DVL institutes within Bavaria. North Rhine-Westphalia coveted the DVL more than any other aerospace research institute. Like the Max Planck Foundation and Fraunhofer Foundation, the DVL supported a number of affiliated research institutes, some of them in Bavaria. Though the institutes had been plundered and shut down by the allies after World War II, they continued to exist as shells around which the field might one day reorganize itself. In 1949 and 1950 North Rhine-Westphalia began awarding aerospace scientists professorial chairs and giving substantial support to rebuild the shells of those DVL institutes located within its borders. In return many of the DVL's leaders were willing to support North Rhine-Westphalia's drive for hegemony over their field. In 1951 one of those who refused to play this role warned Minister-President Ehard and Hanns Seidel of what would happen if North Rhine-Westphalia purchased effective control of the DVL: "Impoverished Germany will hardly be able to afford the luxury of several such institutions [foundations supporting aerospace research]. One may assume that in the long run the DVL, the oldest German aerospace research foundation, will become the only one." While North Rhine-Westphalia's contributions to the DVL ran into the millions of marks, Bavaria's were insignificant and those of other states small and diminishing. As we have seen, after 1951 Bavaria's policy was paralyzed by the poverty and federalism of its Culture Ministry and the struggle for responsibility over the field between the Bavarian Culture and Economic Ministries, so that by 1954, when the Bavarian Economic Ministry finally won jurisdiction over the field from the Culture Ministry, a Bavarian civil servant summed up the situation, "North Rhine-Westphalia is well on the way to making the DVL the sole aerospace research institute in Germany and to erecting its institutes in North Rhine-Westphalia."[90]

The Bavarian Economic Ministry steered a course for conflict. The showdown came at the DVL's annual meeting in June 1954, and the Bavarian civil servants had planned their moves. The Bavarian state was not a member of the DVL but Seidel's ministry arranged to have one of its sympathizers within the DVL invite Bavaria to the meeting and the ministry organized the Bavarian aircraft manufacturers to support Bavarian interests by electing Bavarians to the DVL's board and putting pressure on Federal Transport Minister Hans-Christoph Seebohm to assist Bavaria "in eliminating the danger of being permanently outnumbered and outvoted." They warned Seebohm that "the understandable striving of the federal government to reanimate an aerospace research institute which can work with the ministries must not lead to centralization and geographical concentration nor to personal hegemony in this field. Rather must there must be a healthy dispersion within West Germany..." Within the DVL there was tremendous tension between the backers of North Rhine-Westphalia (Friedrich Seewald, the chairman of the supervisory committee, who had drawn seven former members of the DVL to the Aachen Polytechnic) and Bavaria (Otto Fuchs). The Bavarians, determined "to pull no punches," arranged a pre-meeting conference where they secured agreement that both Bavaria and North Rhine-Westphalia would become members of the DVL supervisory committee, as would the Bavarian aircraft manufacturer Claudius Dornier.[91] Yet North Rhine-Westphalia's supporters were determined to run the DVL their own way, forcing Fuchs to admit that in 1952 North Rhine-Westphalia had given the DVL DM 300,000, while only in 1953 did Bavaria begin contributing to the DVL: a paltry DM 25,000. And as the Bavarian civil servants had expected, Fuchs was not reelected to the supervisory committee and the DVL closed its Munich office.[92]

This tested the CSU's willingness to gamble on the future. In the expectation that the Western allies would soon lift the ban on German aircraft production and aerospace research, the German aircraft industry began lobbying the federal government for large subventions.[93] Bavaria was the home of Messerschmitt, Dornier, and BMW, three firms likely to be resuscitated; Messerschmitt and Dornier were struggling to stay afloat manufacturing other products (prefabricated homes, cars, refrigerators, and sewing machines) and building small planes in Spain, while BMW returned to automobile production but was waiting for defense contracts to finance the reconstruction of its aircraft engine-manufacturing subsidiary BMW Triebwerkbau GmbH, considered its "pearl," a sure profit-maker.[94] The CSU came under pressure to actively support them, for it would not have required much for the firms to move to states that would support them—most of these firms were little more than shells owning wrecked sites and maintaining contact with scattered engineering teams.

The CSU was willing—or rather the spirit was willing but the flesh was weak. The first move came in late 1951, when in response to the allied lifting of the ban on sport gliders and the expectation that all other bans would soon be lifted, a movement developed in Seidel's Economic Ministry and in the Bavarian state parliament to support the Bavarian institutes of the DVL and, since Bavaria could not give the DVL anything like the financial support it received from North Rhine-Westphalia, to offer it the site, physical plant, and airfield of the former Aerospace Communications Research Institute in Oberpfaffenhofen (FFO, Flug-Funk-Forschungsinstitut Oberpfaffenhofen), title to which was held by the federal government but which could be transferred to Bavaria. The Bavarian state parliament unanimously passed a motion to this effect.[95]

Whether Bavaria could really afford to support aerospace research was a different question. The DVL understood its value to the states and tried to play them off against each other to increase their donations. North Rhine-Westphalia gave inordinate amounts of money to the DVL, so much that no other state could compete, least of all Bavaria, which tried to work together with Baden-Württemberg against North Rhine-Westphalia.[96] Already in 1952 it was apparent that this strategy had failed, as Baden-Württemberg bowed out of the competition; but by then the Bavarian Economic Ministry felt that "the housing of the DVL on the former site and in the facilities of the FFO seems to be a sure thing." The Bavarian civil servants took up the strategy of working to get the FFO site made available to the DVL and beyond that to put up no more than "a certain initial capital" in exchange for representation in the DVL's supervisory organs.[97]

But time was working against Bavaria. It proved to be no easy thing to have the FFO site, which was being used by the United States Air Force as a military airfield, transferred to Bavaria. To keep North Rhine-Westphalia from monopolizing aerospace research the Bavarian government had to spend more and more money—or find other substitutes for money. The Bavarian government applied to the Federal Transport Ministry to have Munich made Lufthansa's headquarters, but Minister Seebohm, who was from the German Party, a northern-German Protestant party which had few voters in Bavaria and more than a few prejudices toward it, awarded Lufthansa to Hamburg. As a consolation prize Seebohm promised to send the German Research Institute for Glider Flight (DFS, Deutsche Forschungsanstalt für Segelflug) to Munich—if the State Government would cover the "running accommodation costs." The State Government doubted it was worth the money and only on the assurance that the Bavarian contribution would not be subject to annual increases did the Bavarian Finance Ministry agree to contribute DM 80,000.[98] In another instance, in mid 1954 the Bavarian Economic Ministry, "after protracted negotiations," got Seebohm's agreement to provide money to reestablish the FFO (which related to the Bavarian electronic industry) at the Munich-Riem airport. North Rhine-Westphalia resisted this strongly but Bavaria pushed it through, promising one day to make the FFO part of the DVL. These successes were counterbalanced by problems getting the FFO going—the federal government expected Bavaria to contribute money, but Bavaria dithered and pled poverty. This reinforced its well-established reputation: when Bavaria staked its claims to the Central Collection of Aviation Documentation (Zentralstelle für Luftfahrtdokumentation), the reaction in the Federal Transport Ministry was to sneer, "that it is precisely Bavaria that in all likelihood will make many claims, but then when it comes down to putting up some money for the building up of aerospace research centers or for similar purposes, in contrast to other states will be unwilling to make any actual expenditures."[99]

Between Interest-Group Politics and Industrial Modernization

During the "rosy-fingered dawn" of the issue of industrial modernization—for even by 1954 we cannot say that it had risen above the political horizon—Strauß and Seidel showed themselves oriented to the future. They believed that the CSU was going to be the dominant party in Bavaria for some time and that therefore the CSU had to make Bavaria's future in the new liberal environment. The politics by which they sought to do so were something more than the sort of pork-barrel politics made by all political parties, yet something less than a politics of industrial modernization. Certainly there is no reason to think that at this time either Strauß or Seidel had a plan for the modernization of Bavarian industry, much less a grand strategy or a theory.

Though Strauß and Seidel shared an orientation to the future, this had a different character in each man. Seidel was convinced of the importance of reconciling Bavarian industry with the CSU, and of the economic importance of research, especially applied research, and beyond this the whole character of his politics and the policies of his ministry sought to secure the CSU's and Bavaria's future—already in 1953 he was lobbying to bring the Winter Olympics to Munich.[100] Strauß's politics were different, being strongly colored by his personal ambition. He used the State Group as the instrument of his advancement, and cultivated whichever interest groups could assist him to move up the routes natural to his personality, which was fascinated by modern technology, above all military technology.

In 1954 the economic situation in Bavaria was not good, and it was open to question whether the liberal economy was the problem. Though in the state election campaign that year the CSU could present its voters with impressive figures of absolute economic growth, economic health is a matter of not only absolute but also relative growth. By this measure Christian Democracy had not yet proven itself able to master Bavarian history. Bavaria had not completely pulled itself out of stagnant southern Europe or participated fully in the Rhenish postwar "economic miracle." Seidel discussed this openly with the Economic Advisory Board: "The Bavarian share of the national income is too small," he admitted. "While in 1936 per capita income in Bavaria was 8 percent lower than in the area that today constitutes the Federal Republic [of West Germany], in 1950 and 1951 it was about 14 percent lower. To put it another way: while in 1951 per capita income in the Federal Republic was already 5 percent more than it was in 1936, in Bavaria it was 2 percent less than it was in 1936. This is something worth thinking about… in absolute terms, we in Bavaria have indeed kept pace with economic developments, yet in relative terms we have remained backward…."[101] Relative to other states, in the early 1950s Bavaria was losing tax strength and had higher unemployment, and its workers were paid less.[102]

Industrial modernization is different from economic growth, but here too the indications were not good. As of 1954 the visible fruits of the politics and policies we have described were minimal. Strauß was far from realizing his ministerial ambitions; he played an important role in party politics but did not loom large in policy. Seidel's policies were bearing fruit in some Max Planck Institutes, much Fraunhofer money was being spent in Bavaria, and Bavaria was creating conditions under which it might succeed in keeping some of its aerospace research institutes. But taken together these institutes employed only a few hundred researchers and were still quite disconnected from industry. There was as of yet no "synergy" between them: Heisenberg and Butenandt were not yet even resident in Bavaria; no significant atomic research was being conducted anywhere in Germany; nor were any airplanes being built.

But in 1954 it did not matter that Strauß and Seidel had few conspicuous results to show for Bavarian industry, nor that none of the chief events that were to promote industrial modernization in Bavaria had occurred. After all, the issue of which states would attract "big science" and high-technology and growth industries remained open. Not even North Rhine-Westphalia, the only state that would pursue a conscious politics of industrial modernization earlier and more earnestly than Bavaria, had been able to resolve it in its favor. Neither did it matter that in the early 1950s industrial modernization was barely an issue in the CSU, nor that it did not have a plan of modernization or political concern with the issue.

At that time it was more important that broad developments were moving forward, developments conducive to a modernizing politics: Strauß and Seidel had gotten the CSU out of its tight corner; they had made themselves and their party useful to Bavarian industry; Strauß had shown he knew how to increase the CSU's influence in Bonn; and Seidel had taken the first steps to ensure that Bavaria would not remain a scientfic and technological backwater.

Yet something was missing. Before these developments could really change things in Bavaria, before high-technology industry could be directed to Bavaria, the CSU would have to acquire significantly more power in Bonn. But before that happened, everything changed in Munich. In December 1954 the Social Democrats, the FDP, the Bavaria Party, and the Alliance of the Homelandless and Wronged joined together in a "carnival coalition" that relegated the CSU to the political opposition.

Notes

1. ACDP, NL Balke, 44/4, Denkschrift, 7.8.51 (correcting an error in the original).
2. Schlemmer, *Aufbruch,* 339–363.
3. ACSP, NL Strauß, BMVg, 900, "Notwendigkeit der Gründung eines Vereins."
4. Wolfgang Dexheimer, "Die CSU-Landesgruppe. Ihre organisatorische Stellung in der CDU/CSU Fraktion," *Zeitschrift für Parlamentarische Fragen* 3, no. 3 (1972): 307–313.
5. Schlemmer, *Aufbruch,* 382.
6. Schlemmer, *Aufbruch,* 328.
7. Franz Josef Strauß, *Die Erinnerungen* (Berlin, 1989), 139f, 145.
8. Gerard Braunthal, *The Federation of German Industry in Politics* (Ithaca, N.Y., 1965), 112; Frank Boesch, *Die Adenauer-CDU. Gründung, Aufstieg und Krise einer Erfolgspartei 1945–1969* (Stuttgart; Munich, 2001), 199.
9. Hanns Egon Freund, "Die Gründung des Landesverbandes der Bayerischen Industrie im Jahre 1949," in, *40 Jahre Landesverband der Bayerischen Industrie e. V.* (n.p., n.d.). BWA, LBI, Balke to VBCI, 22.6.51.
10. BWA, LBI, Aktennotiz, 13.4.50; Niederschrift, 22.10.51; Seeling to Balke, 1.6.50. Werner Bührer, "Geschichte des Bundesverbands der Deutschen Industrie" (forthcoming). Adolf Schwammberger, "Otto Seeling" in vol. 4 of *Fränkische Lebensbilder,* Gerhard Pfeiffer, ed. (Würzburg, 1971), 243–256.
11. BWA, LBI, Balke to Seidel, 23.5.51; Balke to Weyhenmeyer, 23.5.51. Siegfried Balke, "Ein Vierteljahrhundert Organisationen der Chemiewirtschaft in Bayern" (n.p., 1971). Ludwig Voelkl interviewed by author, 26.7.00 in Munich.
12. ACDP, NL Balke, 044/4, Aktennotiz, 10.7.51.

13. BWA, LBI, Ordner, 1949–3.1950. There are indications that in the 1940s, Balke was literally industry's bagman in its financial relations with the political parties, including disreputable right-wing parties. ACDP, NL Balke, 44/4, Aktennotiz Balke, 10.7.51. Petra Weber, "Föderalismus und Lobbyismus. Die CSU-Landesgruppe zwischen Bundes- und Landespolitik 1949 bis 1969," in Thomas Schlemmer and Hans Woller, *Bayern im Bund* vol. 3 (Munich, 2004).
14. BWA, LBI, Niederschrift, 12.1.51, p. 3f; Hauptausschußsitzung, 30.3.51; Seeling to Adenauer, 16.7.51. BWA, Best. V13-7, LBI, Rundschreiben 3/51, 23.1.51. ACSP, NL Seeling, 5.1.3, Ansprache, 25.6.51. Werner Abelshauser, "Korea, die Ruhr und Erhards Marktwirtschaft: Die Energiekrise von 1950/51," *Rheinische Vierteljahresblätter* 45 (1981): 287–316.
15. BWA, LBI, Seeling to Kloepfer, 2.1.51; Seeling to Enzmann, 2.1.51.
16. ACSP, NL Seeling, 5.1.3, Ansprache, 25.6.51. BWA, LBI, Seeling to Adenauer, 16.7.51.
17. Hans-Dieter Kreikamp, "Die Entflechtung der I.G. Farbenindustrie A.G. und die Gründung der Nachfolgegesellschaften," *Vierteljahrshefte für Zeitgeschichte* 25, no. 2 (1977): 229ff. Raymond G. Stokes, *Divide and Prosper: The Heirs of I.G. Farben under Allied Authority, 1945–1951* (Berkeley, 1988), 175ff.
18. BHA, StK, 114293, Seidel to Ehard, 6.2.51; Ehard to Adenauer, 14.2.51. Balke, "Chemiewirtschaft in Bayern," 17. Stokes, *Divide and Prosper,* 179f.
19. Schlemmer, *Aufbruch,* 389.
20. Schlemmer, *Aufbruch,* 391.
21. ACSP, NL Seeling, 5.1.3, Ansprache Seeling am 25.6.51. Petra Weber, "Föderalismus und Lobbyismus. Die CSU-Landesgruppe zwischen Bundes- und Landespolitik 1949 bis 1969," in Thomas Schlemmer and Hans Woller, *Bayern im Bund* vol. 3 (Munich, 2004).
22. ACSP, NL Strauß, BMVg, 900, "Notwendigkeit der Gründung eines Vereins." ACDP, NL Balke, 44/4, Strauß to Balke, 5.7.51; Bayer to Balke, 24.8.51. BWA, Best. V13, V13-52, Balke to Kolke, 12.8.51.
23. ACDP, NL Balke, 044/4, Strauß to Balke, 5.7.51; Balke to Bayer, 29.8.51. Schlemmer, *Aufbruch,* 472. NL Strauß, BMVg, 900, Protokoll vom 18.4.51. BWA, Best. V13-52, Balke to Thom, 20.11.51; Balke to Kolke, Heisel, Gammert, 5.4.50, 2.4.51, 21.9.51. BWA, LBI, Niederschrift, 28.8.51; Besprechung am 22.10.51. BWA, Best. V13-7. Ludwig Voelkl interviewed by author, 26.7.00, in Munich.
24. BWA, Best. V13-52, Niederschrift 31.7.51; Balke to Kolke, 12.8.51. ACDP, NL Balke, 44/4, Seeling to Strauß, 11.9.51; Balke to Seeling, 24.9.51; Aktennotiz Balke, 6.10.51; Seeling to Bender, 7.10.51; Limmer to Balke, 4.11.51.
25. Schlemmer, *Aufbruch,* 473. ACDP, NL Balke, 044/4, Balke to Bender, 14.9.51; Balke to Seeling, 24.9.51; Seeling to Balke, 26.9.51; Bayer to Balke, 24.8.51; Aktennotiz, 24.8.51; Balke to Bayer, 29.8.51, 5.9.51.
26. ACSP, LG, 31.8.51/1.9.51. Helge Heidemeyer, ed., *CDU/CSU-Fraktion im Deutschen Bundestag. Sitzungsprotokolle 1949–1953* (Düsseldorf, 1998), il, lxi, 435ff.
27. Friedrich Voss, *Den Kanzler im Visier: zwanzig Jahre mit Franz Josef Strauß* (Mainz, 1999), 325. Heidemeyer, *CDU/CSU-Fraktion,* lv, 758. *40 Jahre Schäffer-Club e. V. 1952–1992* (n.p., n.d.), 15–25, 36. On Bonn Office, see ACDP, NL Balke, 044/4, Limmer to Strauß, 29.12.51. ACSP, NL Strauß, BMVg, 900, Limmer to Strauß, 14.7.51; "Aufgabengebiet des Büros Bonn," Protokoll 30.11.51; 8.12.51; Limmer to Strauß, 27.11.52; Sackmann to Limmer, 27.11.52, Limmer to Strauß, 30.11.52. BWA, LBI, Bayer to Balke, 15.9.51; Ordner 10.51-12.52; Besprechung mit Strauß, 1.2.53 (Strauß and Limmer made Balke nervous with plans to turn the Bonner Büro into a limited partnership—"Kommanditgesellschaft"—organized so as to allow Strauß to exercise secret influence).
28. ACDP, NL Balke, 044/4, 7.8.51; Seeling to Balke, 26.9.51. BHA, StK, 130518, Planung; Benachteiligung Bayerns. BWA, LBI, Sottong to LBI, 1.4.50. Schlemmer, *Aufbruch,* 391. ACSP, NL Seidel, 29, Seidel to Zietsch, 20.11.51. BHA, MWi, 13160, 13181.
29. BWA, LBI, LBI Rundschreiben, 18.10.51; Balke to Strauß, 11.10.51. Werner Bührer, "Der BDI und die Außenpolitik der Bundesrepublik in den fünfziger Jahren," *Vierteljahrshefte für Zeitgeschichte* 40, no. 2 (1992): 250. Abelshauser, "Korea, die Ruhr": 287–316.

30. "Ausbau der bayerischen Chemie," SZ, 29/30.9.51. "CSU-Politiker bei Adenauer," SZ, 6.11.51.
31. ACDP, NL Balke, 044/4, Aktennotiz, 6.10.51; Balke to Bender, 7.10.51. BWA, Best. V13-52, Jahresbericht, 14.5.52. "Zersplitterung unerwünscht," *FAZ*, 7.9.51. Bührer, "Der BDI und die Außenpolitik": 251. Schlemmer, *Aufbruch*, 352.
32. BWA, LBI, Seeling to Landesausschuß, 7.1.51. ACSP, NL Seeling, 5.1.3, Ansprache am 25.6.51.
33. ACDP, NL Balke, 44/4, Aktennotiz, 6.10.51; Balke to Bender, 7.10.51.
34. ACDP, NL Balke, 044/4, Aktennotiz, 25.9.51. Henning Köhler, *Adenauer: eine politische Biographie* (Frankfurt a.M/Berlin, 1994), 800ff.
35. ACDP, NL Balke, 044/4, Limmer to Strauß, 29.12.51.
36. BHA, NL Ehard 1206, Strauß to Ehard, 5.1.54. BWA, LBI, Seeling to Bender, 17.10.52. When Karl Mayr (MdB) was authorized by CSU chairman Ehard to approach Seeling for money for a special election in his area, he was informed that the matter was between Strauß and Balke and that Strauß should be getting in touch with him soon. BWA, LBI, Karl Mayr to Seeling, 12.9.51; Seeling to LBI Geschäftsstelle, 26.9.51; LBI Geschäftsstelle to Mayr, 29.9.51. LBI made direct financial transfers to Strauß. BWA, LBI, Bericht, 31.12.52. It appears that every month the LBI transferred DM 5000 to Strauß, which more than covered the costs of the Bonn Office. NL Strauß, BMVg, 900, Einnahmen- und Ausgabenabrechnung. "Das Geld, die Macht und FJS," *Der Spiegel* 50, no. 30 (22.7.96): 52–57.
37. ACDP, NL Balke, 044/4, Balke to Bender, 7.10.51.
38. ACDP, NL Balke, 044/4, Limmer to Balke, 4.11.51 (erroneously dated).
39. Strauß, *Erinnerungen*, 157.
40. Strauß, *Erinnerungen*, 244ff. Otto Eckhardt, *Geschichte der CSU-Landesgruppe in Bonn* vol. 1 (n.p., n.d.), 61. Jürgen Ammann, "Die Haltung der CSU in Bayern zur Frage der Wiederbewaffnung und Aufstellung der Bundeswehr 1950–1956" (Master's thesis, Augsburg, 1994), 34.
41. Heidemeyer, *CDU/CSU-Fraktion*, 283.
42. Eckhardt, *CSU-Landesgruppe*, 83f (vol. 1), 2, 25–27, 113 (vol. 2). Ammann, "Haltung der CSU," 58.
43. Ammann, "Haltung der CSU," 78ff.
44. Heidemeyer, *CDU/CSU-Fraktion*, 613f.
45. ACSP, Protokolle der Landesgruppe, 9.1.52. Ammann, "Haltung der CSU," 63.
46. Heidemeyer, *CDU/CSU-Fraktion*, 497, 501. Eckhardt, *CSU-Landesgruppe*, vol. 2 (n.p.), 124f. Ammann, "Haltung der CSU," 58.
47. Strauß, *Erinnerungen*, 163. Hans-Peter Schwarz, *Adenauer*, vol. 2, *Der Staatsmann, 1952–1967* (Munich, 1994), 30. Mark Milosch, "Die Rolle von Franz Josef Strauß bei der Ansiedlung der Luftfahrtindustrie in Bayern," in, *Franz Josef Strauß—Ludwig Bölkow—Sepp Hort*, vol. 2 of *Bayerische Lebensbilder: Biografien, Erinnerungen, Zeugnisse*, ed. Renate Höpfinger (Munich, 2004), 15–18.
48. *Verhandlungen des Deutschen Bundestages*, 1. Wahlperiode, 190. Sitzung, 7.2.52, pp. 8118–8128. Strauß, *Erinnerungen*, 159–164.
49. ACSP, Protokolle der Landesgruppe, 19.6.52. Strauß, *Erinnerungen*, 201–203. Hans-Volkmann, "Die innenpolitische Dimension Adenauerscher Sicherheitspolitik in der EVG-Phase," in *Anfänge westdeutscher Sicherheitspolitik* 1945–1946, vol. 2, ed. Militärgeschichtlichen Forschungsamt (Munich, 1990), 332. Wolfgang Krieger, *Franz Josef Strauß: der barocke Demokrat aus Bayern* (Göttingen & Zurich, 1995), 29f. Schwarz, Adenauer, vol. 2, 28ff. Ammann, "Haltung der CSU," 47.
50. ACSP, NL Elsen, 4.1.2; NL Seidel, 31; NL Mayr, Seidel to Mayr, 7.4.53; NL Strauß, BMVg, 900, Limmer to Strauß, 19.5.53. Eckhardt, *CSU-Landesgruppe*, 194.
51. Alf Mintzel, *Geschichte der CSU. Ein Überblick* (Opladen, 1977), 284ff.
52. Köhler, *Adenauer*, 797ff.
53. BWA, LBI, LBI Rundschreiben 9/54, 21.10.54. "An der Schwelle der Wiederaufrüstung," *MM*, 16/17.10.54.
54. ACSP, Protokolle der Landesgruppe, 13.3.52.
55. Werner Abelshauser, "Wirtschaft und Rüstung in den fünfziger Jahren," in *Anfänge westdeutscher Sicherheitspolitik* 1945–1956, vol. 4, 139ff.

56. Abelshauser in *Anfänge westdeutscher Sicherheitspolitik* 1945–1956, vol. 4, 131.
57. BA, B136, 2163, Adenauer to Strauß, 13.7.1955. Heinrich Krone, *Tagebücher,* vol. 1, *1945–1961,* ed. Hans-Otto Kleinmann (Düsseldorf, 1995), 126. Ammann, "Haltung der CSU," 60. Thomas Dalberg, *Franz Josef Strauß, Porträt eines Politikers* (Gütersloh, 1968), 85. Schwarz, *Adenauer,* vol. 2, 110–113.
58. ACSP, Protokollen der Landesgruppe, 13.9.53. ACSP, NL Mayr, 3.2, Adenauer to Mayr, 28.12.49; Mayr to Adenauer, 1.5.50; Mayr to Adenauer, 31.3.50; Adenauer to Mayr, 2.1.51. "Schuberths Auftreten löst Heiterkeit aus," *MM,* 4.12.53. Karl-Ulrich Gelberg, *Hans Ehard: Die föderalistische Politik des bayerischen Ministerpräsidenten, 1946–1954* (Düsseldorf, 1992), 198f, 269. Schlemmer, *Aufbruch,* 321, 364, 383.
59. "Den Balke im Auge," *Der Spiegel* 7, no. 48 (25.11.53).
60. BA, NL Höcherl, 170, Vortrag, 16.12.60.
61. ACSP, NL Strauß, BMVg, 900, Limmer to Strauß, 21.1.53. Interview with Richard Stücklen in *Geschichte einer Volkspartei. 50 Jahre CSU* (Grünwald, 1995). Dalberg, *Strauß: Porträt,* 73–77, 80. Krieger, *Strauß: barocke Demokrat,* 30. Michael Eckert, "Die Anfänge der Atompolitik in der Bundesrepublik Deutschland," *Vierteljahreshefte für Zeitgeschichte* 37, no. 2 (1989): 138.
62. ACSP, NL Strauß, BMVg, 900, Hammerle to Strauß, 27.1.53. Protokolle des CDU-Bundesvorstandes 1953–1957, 30.9.55, pp. 621, 631. Strauß, *Erinnerungen,* 219f. Köhler, *Adenauer,* 798.
63. ACSP, NL Strauß, BMVg, 900, Liste der Mitglieder.
64. Hermann Bößenecker, *Bayern, Bosse und Bilanzen: Hinter den Kulissen der weiß-blauen Wirtschaft* (Munich: Kurt Desch, 1972), 23.
65. Werner Bührer, "Zum Wandel der wirtschafts- und sozialpolitischen Zukunftsvorstellungen in der deutschen Industrie zwischen Weltwirtschaftskrise und Wirtschaftswunder," in *Politische Zäsuren und Gesellschaftlicher Wandel im 20. Jahrhundert: regionale und vergleichende Perspektiven,* eds. Matthias Frese and Michael Prinz (Paderborn, 1996), 102.
66. Hanns Seidel, *Vom Mythos der öffentlichen Meinung* (Aschaffenburg, 1961).
67. Hans Ferdinand Groß, *Hanns Seidel 1901–1961: Eine politische Biographie* (Munich, 1992), 70–71, 83. Gerhard Kleinhenz, "Wirtschafts- und Sozialpolitik—die Verwirklichung einer Sozialen Marktwirtschaft durch die Landespolitik der CSU," in *Geschichte einer Volkspartei,* 267.
68. Groß, *Hanns Seidel,* 62f, 71, 89. Kleinhenz, "Wirtschafts- und Sozialpolitik," 268. Maximilian Lanzinner, *Zwischen Sternenbanner und Bundesadler: Bayern im Wiederaufbau 1945–1958* (Regensburg, 1996), 205. P. Hüttenberger, "Wirtschaftsordnung und Interessenpolitik in der Kartellgesetzgebung der Bundesrepublik 1949–1957," *Vierteljahreshefte für Zeitgeschichte* 24, no. 3 (1976): 287. Eckhardt, *CSU-Landesgruppe,* 175.
69. ACSP, NL Strauß, BMVG, 900, Limmer to Strauß; 16.4.53, Notiz, 29.12.52; Limmer to Strauß, 31.12.52. IFZ, NL Hoegner, Protokoll des Ministerrats vom 11.12.51, 28.12.51, 22.1.52, 26.2.52, 13.5.52, 2.7.52, 8.7.52, 21.10.52, 2.6.53, 31.8.54. Karl Winnacker, *Nie den Mut verlieren: Erinnerungen an Schicksalsjahre der deutschen Chemie* (Düsseldorf, 1971), 195, 200ff.
70. BWA, LBI, Seeling to Verbindungsstelle, 28.7.50.
71 Winnacker, *Nie den Mut verlieren,* 298. Theodor Heuss, *Theodor Heuss, Politiker und Publizist: Aufsätze und Reden* (Tübingen, 1984), 389ff.
72. ACSP, LVor, 28.6.49. BWA, LBI, Seeling to Seidel, 13.5.50. Alf Mintzel, "Die CSU in Bayern: Phasen ihrer organisationspolitischen Entwicklung," *Politische Vierteljahresschrift* 12, no. 2 (1972): 220. Schlemmer, *Aufbruch,* 434. Groß, *Hanns Seidel,* 105f.
73. Konrad Adenauer, *Briefe 1949–1951,* ed. Hans Peter Mensing (Berlin, 1985), 201f, 503. Groß, *Hanns Seidel,* 112ff.
74. ACDP, NL Balke, 042/2, Balke to Seidel, 22.6.61. ACSP, NL Seeling, 5.1.3, Rundfunkansprache, 12.10.51.
75. Stephan Deutinger, *High-Tech-Staat: zur Geschichte des Forschungsstandorts Bayern 1945–1980* (Munich, 2001), 44ff.
76. Deutinger, *High-Tech-Staat,* 46f.

77. Rudolf Vierhaus and Bernhard vom Brocke, eds., *Forschung im Spannungsfeld von Politik und Gesellschaft. Geschichte und Struktur der Kaiser-Wilhelm-Gesellschaft* (Stuttgart, 1990), 461.
78. Deutinger, *High-Tech-Staat,* 82–83.
79. Rainer Rilling, *Kriegsforschung und Vernichtungswissenschaft in der BRD* (Cologne, 1970), 77. Helmuth Trischler and Rüdiger vom Bruch, *Forschung für den Markt. Geschichte der Fraunhofer-Gesellschaft* (Munich, 1999), 31ff. Deutinger, *High-Tech-Staat,* 185ff. BHA, MK, Repertorien Band, Vorläufiges, VI/1106, Fraunhofer Ges., 1949–1970.
80. BHA, MK, Repertorien Band, Vorläufiges, VI/1106, Fraunhofer, 1949–1970.
81. Trischler and vom Bruch, *Forschung für den Markt,* 39f., 50, 56. Deutinger, *High-Tech-Staat,* 188.
82. BHA, MA 114004, Rucker to Hoegner, 31.3.55. Deutinger, *High-Tech-Staat,* 118ff.
83. Eckert, "Anfänge," 120f. Vierhaus und vom Brocke, *Forschung im Spannungsfeld,* 908. Florian Staudt, "Anfänge Bayerischer Atompolitik in den 50er Jahren" (Master's thesis, University of Munich, 1997), 27.
84. BWA, LBI, Ordner 7.50–12.52. ACSP, NL Seidel, 29, 30, 31. "Chemische Industrie in Bayern," *Chemie-Ingenieur-Technik* 23, no. 11 (1951): 281. Klaus Schreyer, *Bayern—ein Industriestaat. Die importierte Industrialisierung. Das wirtschaftliche Wachstum nach 1945 als Ordnungs- und Strukturproblem* (Munich, 1969), 175.
85. See Wolfgang D. Müller, *Geschichte der Kernenergie in der BRD. Anfänge und Weichenstellungen* (Stuttgart, 1990), 245, 423ff. Eckert, "Anfänge," 137f.
86. ACSP, NL Seidel, 32, Seidel to Adenauer, 18.1.54. NL Heisenberg, Korrespondenzen, Heisenberg to Seidel, 5.11.53. NL Heisenberg, Reactor, Heisenberg to Seidel, 25.9.53. Müller, *Geschichte der Kernenergie,* 109. Deutinger, *High-Tech-Staat,* 131ff.
87. Staudt, "Anfänge Bayerischer Atompolitik," 18. Deutinger, *High-Tech-Staat,* 133.
88. Christopher Magnus Andres, *Die Luft- und Raumfahrtindustrie 1945–1970. Ein Industriebereich im Spannungsfeld von Politik, Wirtschaft und Militär* (Frankfurt a.M., 1996), 91ff.
89. Andres, *Luft- und Raumfahrtindustrie,* 157ff. "Schuß auf Seebohm's Luftpolitik," *Die Zeit,* 18.6.53.
90. BHA, MWi, 12869, Betreff, 24.7.51, Besprechung 20.7.51; Fuchs to Ehard, 10.9.51; Fuchs to Ehard, 10.9.51; MWi, 12877, Vermerk, 11.6.54. Helmuth Trischler, *Luft- und Raumfahrtforschung in Deutschland, 1900–1970. Politische Geschichte einer Wissenschaft* (Frankfurt a.M, 1992), 306.
91. BHA, MWi, 12877, Betreff, 21.5.54; Vermerk, 11.6.54; Seidel to Seebohm, undated; Seewald to Fuchs, 10.6.54; Vermerk, 11.6.54, 28.6.54. BA, B136, 9973, Bericht, 14/15.6.54. Rilling, *Kriegsforschung,* 9.
92. BHA, MWi, 12877, 28.6.54, 11.6.54.
93. Andres, *Luft- und Raumfahrtindustrie,* 87, 113–120.
94. Bößenecker, *Bayern, Bosse und Bilanzen,* 180.
95. BHA, MF, 71812, Brief, 24.9.51; Besprechung, 9.10.51; Antrag, 11.10.51. Deutinger, *High-Tech-Staat,* 169.
96. BHA, MWi, 12869, Stuemmer to Kuchtner, 23.5.52; Niederschrift, 26.5.52; Brief, 27.8.52. MWi, 12706, Brief, 16.4.53.
97. BHA, MWi, 12706, 16.5.52; 12922, Satzung des FFO; MWi, 12869, Niederschrift, 8.1.52.
98. Trischler, *Luft- und Raumfahrtforschung in Deutschland,* 321. BHA, MF, 71812, Betreff, 1.3.54; Heilmann to MF, 27.1.54; Guthsmuths to Bundesverkehrsministerium, 16.2.54; MWi, 12706, Bericht, 29.1.54; 12847, Vormerkung, 26.2.54.
99. BHA, MWi, 12706, Huber an MK, 4.11.53; 12707, 5.1.55; 12918, Protokoll über Mitgliederversammlung, 17.1.56. "Forschungsanstalt statt Luftwerft," SZ, 16.2.54.
100. ACSP, NL Seidel, 2b, Etatrede vor dem Landtag, 7/8.2.50; 5a, Ansprache, 14.11.52; 31, Seidel to Schäffer, 6.53.
101. ACSP, NL Seidel, 5, Rede, 18.10.52.
102. Lanzinner, *Zwischen Sternenbanner und Bundesadler,* 249ff.

CHAPTER 2

INVENTING A POLITICS OF MODERNIZATION, 1954–1957

Liberalizing the CSU

"Physician, heal thyself!" The CSU could not lead the modernization of Bavarian industry until it had modernized itself, but it was incapable of modernizing, that is reforming, itself until something had awoken it to the need to do so. That something came in November 1954, when the CSU found itself in opposition in Bavaria. It was a sudden and astonishing development, as the CSU had triumphed in the election, receiving 38 percent of the vote, an increase of 11 percent over its 1950 state election performance, while none of the other four parties in the Bavarian parliament had increased its vote at all. Yet while the CSU deputies argued about their negotiating position, the Social Democrats, the FDP, the Bavaria Party, and the Alliance of the Homelandless and Wronged, galvanized by loose talk within the CSU about Catholicizing education by creating separate teacher training colleges for Protestants and Catholics, formed a "Coalition of Four" under the Minister-Presidency of the conservative Social Democrat Wilhelm Hoegner.[1] It struck the stunned CSU as an outrage and a catastrophe, and created the fear in CSU ranks that the "long wave" of German history that had beaten against Bavaria for centuries was rising again. Yet in retrospect we can see that the CSU learned the lessons of its defeat so well that it has never since been out of the government in Bavaria.

The Coalition of Four presented obvious dangers and a less obvious opportunity to the CSU. The CSU deputies feared that the Coalition of Four, throwing the CSU out of power, would thereby destroy its status as the party of the Bavarian

Notes for this section begin on page 77.

state (Staatspartei), so important, in the Bavarian political tradition, to its prestige.[2] Worse, the Coalition of Four had brought the Bavaria Party into government, reversing its drift toward the political fringe, and given Joseph Baumgartner, its leader, the Bavarian Agriculture Ministry, which he would use as a platform to consolidate his party's support among farmers.

If these dark clouds had a silver lining for the CSU, it was the FDP's membership in the Coalition of Four. The FDP had galled industry by joining the Coalition of Four and thereby putting the Social Democrats in power—effectively sacrificing its industrial financial supporters to its anticlerical voting base.[3] It was true that the FDP received the Bavarian Economic Ministry, but that was poor compensation since the new FDP minister, Otto Bezold, made a poor successor to Hanns Seidel. Bezold was less a bourgeois liberal and friend of industry than an anticlerical old democrat. Several months before Bezold took over the ministry he had argued that it should be dissolved and after taking it over he admitted, "I don't understand anything about the economy." The LBI soon concluded that Bezold neglected his ministry "to such a degree that 'the machine could barely struggle forward against the ocean.'"[4]

To the CSU's liberal wing, the lesson was clear: the time had arrived to set the clock forward on the relationship between religion and politics. The CSU liberals, who had shown no taste for interparty strife since they lost the battles of 1947–1949, cried in public that democracy had been undone by a "Carnival Coalition," while they internally blamed the disaster on Hans Ehard. Strauß, Seidel, and other liberals fed the sense of outrage within the party, and in December 1954 Ehard resigned as party chairman.

The test of the movement to liberalize the CSU was the contest for the party chairmanship. Even before the delegates voted in January 1955, it was clear that the movement had passed the test. The CSU moderates had thrown in their lot with the liberals and no conservative even entered the contest, which came down to Strauß versus Seidel. It seems likely that the favor these two enjoyed with industry worked against potential conservative candidates, since at this time 80 percent of the CSU's funds came from industry.[5] Seidel won handily over Strauß, 380 votes to 239, the party choosing to respond to the Coalition of Four by emphasizing state over national politics.

In 1955 Seidel installed the new liberal team that was to become the Munich face of the CSU for over a decade: Alfons Goppel was entrusted with cultural and legal matters; Otto Schedl became shadow Economic Minister; and the Protestant Rudolf Eberhard became the shadow Finance Minister. On Strauß's recommendation Seidel appointed Friedrich Zimmermann to be the CSU's General Secretary and in July 1955 the CSU Managing Committee (Landesvorstand) completed the revolution by electing seven new members to the party's Governing Committee (Geschäftsführende Landesvorstand), replacing old conservatives and representatives of agricultural interests with young liberals and allies of Strauß and Seidel.[6] Yet the CSU did not in 1955 become a liberal party. Though it was clear that the liberals had grabbed the steering wheel, the conservatives remained strong within the Bavarian parliament, regional party organizations, and the party membership for another fifteen years and even beyond.

Strauß's position in Bonn was made easier by the CSU's new liberalism. The liberal revolution within the CSU in late 1954 and early 1955 did not begin a new era in the history of the State Group, for its politics had been moving gradually in the direction of liberalism ever since the CSU deputies had arrived in Bonn, where the political climate was more liberal to begin with and where the religious elements of Christian Democracy found much less resonance. But the liberal revolution did make for closer coordination between the CSU in Munich and Bonn. Strauß and Seidel had similar priorities, strategies, and ideas and had good personal relations, and this made it easier for the CSU's state and federal deputies to work together and to pursue bolder strategies. And it changed the CSU's image and made it easier for the party to win industrial support. But the choice of Seidel over Strauß did imply a decision to emphasize Bavarian over German politics, and the idea was held by many in Munich that the CSU would live or die on Bavarian rather than national issues. Strauß continued until his death to insist that the opposite was true, that the CSU must justify its existence in Bonn or not at all, and that to do so it required an identity and program distinguishable from that of the CDU, and on certain points in opposition to that of the CDU.

Yet to many observers the CSU still seemed a laggard. Most of the political pros in the other parties and in journalism thought that Seidel and Strauß had made a good start but had not yet caught their party up to the larger trends of postwar German and European history, above all the accelerating secularization of other Christian-Democratic parties, the decline of local political traditions, and the recovery of national feeling. They were mistaken. In fact, Strauß and Seidel had brought the CSU as up to date as it had to be for the moment, positioned the party very well for the future, and begun to create a new tradition of Bavarian politics. The liberalism Seidel, Strauß and the new leadership team stood for was a Bavarian variant, quite different from the liberalism of the other parties and other regions of Germany—and of greater potential use to Bavarian industry. Their liberalism crossed the Bavarian Catholic political tradition with the German liberal tradition. From the former it took its display of its Bavarian patriotism, its naturally democratic tone, its populist elitism (that is, its tendency to entrust matters of import to elites, who for their part relate easily to popular feeling), while rejecting an excessively close identification with Catholic politics, Bavarian provinciality, or xenophobia.[7] From the German liberal tradition, it took its feeling for the German nation-state (whereas the Bavarian Catholic political tradition as well as the old liberal tradition tended to pit Bavaria and Germany against each other, CSU-style liberalism held that each needed the other), its comfortable relationship with modernity, the exercise of power, and not least, its eagerness to represent bourgeois and industrial interests. Strauß, Seidel, and their lieutenants superimposed this marriage of Bavarian traditionalism and the German national-liberal tradition over the Christian-Democratic marriage of

Catholic social thought with Protestant economic and political liberalism, and the result was a Christian-Democratic party of a unique sort, one that was even more naturally a party of governance than the CDU, and complex but flexible enough to integrate Bavaria to a remarkable degree.[8]

The CSU liberals were also skilled at using issues rather than being used by them. Their liberalism was not one of conviction so much as it was driven by the quest for political advantage. The true character of CSU-style liberalism can be seen in the liberals' treatment of religion. For Seidel by no means meant to secularize the CSU. In fact, from 1954 to 1957 the CSU appealed more loudly to religion. As part of the CSU's campaign against the Bavaria Party—the well of votes into which it could most easily dip its bucket—the CSU made endless play of its charge that the Bavaria Party had "betrayed the Christian voter" by joining a coalition that put the godless Social Democrats in power; the CSU state parliamentary caucus retained Father Georg Meixner, a reactionary Catholic priest, as its chairman, though it reduced his power by making Seidel "speaker of the opposition," that is, de facto chairman; and it moralized endlessly against the Coalition of Four's move to legalize gambling casinos in Bavarian resorts.[9] The difference between the clericalists and liberals was that, whereas clericalists like Hundhammer saw politics as a means by which to pursue essentially religious ends (for Hundhammer the reconstruction of the medieval *Bavaria Sancta* !), and thereby led the CSU into costly political battles for marginal religious gains, liberals like Seidel instrumentalized religion for political ends. This way of approaching issues had implications for Bavarian industry.

Challenge: The Social Democrats Make Science and Technology a Political Issue

In his celebrated theory of challenge and response, Arnold Toynbee held that, "the impulse or motive which makes a perfect Yin-state pass over into new Yang-activity comes from an intrusion of the Devil into the universe of God."[10] So it had been with the reform and modernization of the CSU, and so it was also with the CSU's politics of industrial modernization. Though Strauß, as Minister for Special Tasks, had been asked by Adenauer to look into atomic matters, yet little indicates that in late 1954 and early 1955 Strauß, Seidel, or anyone else in the CSU concerned himself with industrial modernization.[11] Though amenable to the influence of Bavarian industry, yet Strauß, Seidel, and their lieutenants did not anticipate its needs. The Coalition of Four intruded into their universe by challenging them on the issue of scientific modernization; and for Strauß and Seidel the path to scientific modernization led through industry.

The Coalition of Four breathed deeply of the euphoria for atomic energy and science that was building in the early 1950s. As the United States, Britain, and France invested themselves in research on the peaceful uses of atomic energy, public interest and even fascination in its possibilities began to grow throughout western Europe, in Germany as much as anywhere. The American "Atoms for Peace" program to support atomic research programs in friendly countries kicked off an "atomic fever" in late 1953, and it became more intense in 1954 and 1955, when the United States staged a conference-exposition in Geneva, highlighting the glorious future atomic energy offered the world and emphasizing the technical advances that were being made in the USA. This, coming at the same time as the opening of negotiations for a European Atomic Community, had an enormous effect in Germany.[12] German industry was particularly interested in the atomic power and the atomic sciences, since, unable to foresee the great oil discoveries of the mid and late 1950s, it feared that Germany's coal production would be unable to keep up with the demand for power, which would become more expensive and make German products uncompetitive on world markets. And Bavarian industry hoped that it would reduce the difference between energy prices in Bavaria and in northern and western Germany.[13]

In truth, the Coalition of Four thought to reap where Seidel had already sown, or at least to continue sowing the same field. The Coalition of Four reaffirmed Seidel's policy in its first Cabinet meeting and Minister-President Hoegner, in his inaugural address, presented the construction of an atomic power plant as the first step toward a sure solution of Bavaria's energy problems.[14]

But the Coalition of Four conducted its atomic politics with a vigor, media flair and ideological fervor that the CSU had not. Atomic energy and, later, scientific modernization, symbolized in the mid 1950s by atomic reactors, became a banner issue for the "Carnival Coalition," the four parties' professed faith in atomic energy providing them with one of the few things Social Democrats and liberals, Bavarian xenophobes and exiles from the East, could agree on, and a steady flow of favorable press coverage. Naturally, each party approached atomic energy from its own point of view, but it was the Social Democrats, many of whom in the 1950s preserved a nineteenth-century belief in material progress, who invented and drove the program. Waldemar von Knoeringen, the Social Democrat's state party chairman, had as much to do with this as Hoegner. Knoeringen saw it as the issue by which the party could identify itself with progress, dissipating the bourgeois fear of the Social Democrats as irresponsible incompetents, and defusing the opposition of capitalistic interests, allowing the party to create a sharp contrast between its futuristic vision and the Christian Democrat's old-fashioned cultural conservatism.[15]

The Coalition of Four came up with a test for itself: it would prove to the voters what it could do for Bavaria by influencing the federal government to construct the new Max Planck Institute for Physics and its Atomic Reactor Station near Munich in Bavaria instead of near Karlsruhe in Baden-Württemberg. These institutes, nearly everyone thought at the time, would become the center of the atomic energy and atomic research in Germany. But the leaders of the Coalition of Four seriously misjudged their ability to influence the decision. They could do almost nothing to influence Adenauer, who had reserved the decision to himself; probably they thought that Heisenberg must in the end have his way. But in early

1955 it became known that Adenauer leaned toward Karlsruhe. It is hardly surprising that Adenauer must have preferred the Christian-Democratic government of Baden-Württemberg to the Coalition of Four. We can be sure Adenauer knew very well that, as Heisenberg warned the Bavarians, "there [were] very powerful forces, especially ... in industrial circles that want the reactor to go to Karlsruhe." Against the weight of German industry and the concentrated influence of the chemical industry, it meant little to Adenauer that the LBI announced in March 1955 that it wanted an atomic reactor in Munich and urged the Coalition of Four to get Heisenberg and his institute to Bavaria and to do all it could to make Bavaria a center for atomic sciences.[16] In March 1955 the Max Planck Foundation, which also leaned toward Karlsruhe, began preparing Hoegner for a compromise in which Bavaria would get the short end of the stick: the Max Planck Institute, with perhaps a small research reactor, might be sent to Munich but the reactor station constructed in Karlsruhe. Yet Hoegner and the Coalition of Four persisted in seeking publicity from the issue and sending ministers to lobby the authorities in Bonn. When Baden-Württemberg offered to pay some of the costs of the reactor station, the Coalition of Four announced its willingness to pay millions of marks toward the construction of both the reactor station and the MPI. Hoegner struggled with his Cabinet for approval of the moneys and, after much back-and-forth and a bidding war with Baden-Württemberg, on 28 June the Bavarian government made a final offer of DM 9,000,000—at the time an extraordinary, almost irresponsible offer.[17]

But the Coalition of Four failed its own test. On 29 June 1955 Adenauer ruled in favor of Karlsruhe, notwithstanding Strauß had joined the Social Democrats to plead Bavaria's cause. Adenauer justified his decision with the idea that Munich was too close to the Iron Curtain for a reactor research station—most observers thought this was absurd. Karl Winnacker, the president of Hoechst and the most important industrialist interested in atomic energy and research, wrote later that he had been willing to accept Munich, was amused at Adenauer's justification for his decision, and had gone to Karlsruhe "very happily."[18]

The Coalition of Four had made the mistake of pressing an issue on which a state government had little real power—and one that could easily be picked up and turned to greater account by the CSU. For most voters atomic energy was hardly even a peripheral issue, while in 1954 and 1955 German industry was developing an enormous interest in all things atomic. The most interested branches of industry included the most politically conservative, machinery and metals, electronics (Siemens and AEG), and, above all, the chemical industry, which was a major energy user and expected to receive, in any national atomic program, lucrative contracts in atomic chemistry. In November 1954 Winnacker and W.A. Menne led sixteen industrial firms in the formation of the Physics Study Society, the purpose of which was to promote the creation of a German atomic industry, and which naturally abhorred the Social Democrat's vision of a nationalized atomic energy and research industry, preferring that the state support their private efforts.[19] It was largely in response to industry that on 15 October 1955 Adenauer appointed Strauß Minister of Atomic Affairs.

Strauß's ministry preempted the field of atomic power and marginalized the role of the Bavarian state government, yet it did not eliminate it. Knoeringen and Hoegner thought that the more sharply Social Democracy drew the contrast between its own scientific ideology and backward-looking Christian Democracy, the sooner it would prevail. Since, in the mid 1950s, the atom was the symbol and horizon of the future, they shrugged off their setback and went full speed ahead "on atomic course."

The leaders of the Coalition of Four responded to Strauß's effective takeover of the atomic field by transferring their emphasis to scientific education to prepare young Germans for the more technologically based economy that was being created by the "second industrial revolution." The Coalition of Four's new take on the issue originated, as did its earlier one, with Waldemar von Knoeringen and the Munich Social Democrats, who, after the failure of the Coalition of Four's Teacher Training Law, launched initiatives to increase technical education, focusing no longer on big science but on "technical training of youth," the expansion of science departments and engineering schools. Knoeringen and his allies imposed this new approach to the issue on the Bavarian party organization, which passed it up to the Social Democratic Party in Düsseldorf where it was worked into the party's national party program.[20]

The publicistic peak of the Social Democrat's new emphasis on science, technology, and education came in July 1956. Culture Minister Rucker gave a major speech informing the Bavarian parliament that he was working on a plan to spend much more money on scientific education and research in Bavaria. Several weeks later the Social Democrats held their national party convention in Munich, taking as their theme the "second industrial revolution." Accompanied by the music of Beethoven's Ninth Symphony, the delegates sang hymns to "atomic energy, beautiful divine sparks" ("Kernenergie, schöner Götterfunken"), and listened to extravagant addresses on the rosy future created by technology. The press was enthusiastic: "In the Social Democratic Party the call to greater achievement receives special pathos, some speak rapturously of their vision of a 'second industrial revolution', with automatization and the use of atomic energy opening up a new age for which society has to prepare itself spiritually and organizationally."[21]

The policy peak was the Rucker Plan itself, which Rucker presented to the State parliament on 8 November 1956 and which proposed spending DM 1,8 billion—a staggering sum for Bavaria—over ten years to promote education, science, technology, and research. More concretely, the money would be used to improve schools, scholarships, dormitories, and scholarships for gifted students, and increase the number of people studying at technical schools.[22]

Strauß and Seidel saw the Rucker Plan enthusiastically received by all the right people—by all the people they had tried to make into their own constituents, by industrialists certainly, but also by journalists for the prestige and liberal newspapers, national-liberal types, scientists, and technical people. Industry heard its calls for programs to train technicians, engineers, and scientists answered. Journalists found plans to spend more on education and technology attractive in principle: then as now, they polish the reputations of the politicians who put the plans forward. As for the national-liberal types, their party was the FDP, whose progressive-liberal wing liked the idea of greater support for education and research, while the national-liberal wing was attracted by the promise of "catching up" with the other Western countries. The FDP deputy Hildegard Hamm-Brücher's speech in support of the Rucker Plan spoke to the hearts of liberal voters when she regretted the expense but declared that the Rucker Plan "nonetheless has both feet firmly planted in this world" and that it could even go farther in support for gifted students, and implying that in any case for years Bavaria had spent too much money educating priests and farmers.[23] The scientists were delighted to be heard after years of crying in the wilderness; particularly the Max Planck Foundation and the German Research Society (the German analogue to America's National Science Foundation and Social Science Research Council) had disliked Bavaria's "strict construction" of the Basic Law, by which the state government, under the CSU, had worked to prevent the federal government from supporting science.[24]

If the Social Democrats' politics of science and technology pleased these people, the very people to whom Strauß and Seidel looked for support in building up and reforming the CSU, the question almost asked itself: couldn't Strauß and Seidel do more for them than the Social Democrats?

Response: Strauß Gains the Upper Hand

The CSU's effective response to the Coalition of Four came on the federal level, when Strauß became Minister of Atomic Affairs. Yet he sought this ministry less in response to the Social Democrats' bid for the Atomic Reactor Station than as a means to advance his claim to the Defense Ministry. As was so often the case in these years, Adenauer began by resisting Strauß's ambition. In the spring of 1955, Strauß was still only Special Minister, responsible, among other things, for Germany's few "atomic affairs," and a member of the Planning Committee for the German Atomic Energy Commission. Still pressing Adenauer to fulfill his promise of 1953, he demanded that Adenauer make him chairman of a Federal Defense Council, which would prepare Cabinet discussion of all defense-related matters, including defense contracting, and threatened to pull the CSU out of the government if Adenauer refused. On 20 May 1955, Strauß and several leaders of the State Group met with Adenauer and demanded that he create a "post for home defense (air-raid precautions, ground-air defense, civil defense, etc.), organized nationally and a post with the status of State Secretary in a Federal Defense Council that coordinates the defense of the entire country." Adenauer refused Strauß a secretaryship in the new ministry but agreed to consider a Federal Defense Council.[25] On 7 June 1955 Adenauer named Theodor Blank Germany's first postwar Defense Minister. Strauß tried to solidify his claim to be

Blank's eventual successor. He demanded that Adenauer create for him a Home Defense Ministry (meaning civil and air defense). On 5 July 1955, the CSU's Managing Committee issued a Five Point Program on federalism and civilian control of the army, and on 9 July 1955 Strauß again pressed Adenauer for a new assignment—among other things he sought to control the Gehlen Office, Germany's foreign intelligence agency.[26] Adenauer was quite unlikely to grant this, but it was reported that before Adenauer made his diplomatic visit to Moscow he promised to give Strauß "certain urgent tasks." The CSU continued to hammer away at Blank; Strauß and Seidel formulated a parliamentary question for Blank and criticized the overwhelmingly "Prussian" character of the Defense Ministry, the complaint being that southern Germans and Catholics were not sufficiently represented in the new ministry. Immediately after Adenauer returned from Moscow in late September 1955, he offered Strauß responsibility for civil defense, though on what terms remains unclear.[27]

Strauß rejected the offer of the position he had long sought, demanding that both a Ministry of Atomic Affairs and a Federal Defense Council be created for him. Adenauer gave in.[28] As to the Ministry of Atomic Affairs, it must have been clear to Adenauer that Strauß saw his Ministry of Atomic Affairs as a sort of secondary Defense Ministry *in potentia*—if or when Germany attained the right to carry, control, co-produce, or produce nuclear weapons, Strauß would fight to ensure that the Ministry of Atomic Affairs took charge. As to the Federal Defense Council, Strauß had to settle for one of two vice-chairmanships.[29] He openly expressed his intention to use it to keep his foot in the door on civil and air defense and the defense economy: a large foot, as he wanted to make the Federal Defense Council into a group with decision-making authority. But on this point Adenauer once again frustated Strauß's ambition.[30]

Strauß seems to have had some of the interested industry on his side, for in September 1955 the Physics Study Society, through which Strauß had gotten to know many German industrialists, joined their voice to Strauß's in demanding a Ministry of Atomic Affairs. Industry was at this moment, after the opening of the Euratom negotiations at the Messina Conference in July, and immediately after the Geneva Conference in August, agitated about the issue of atomic energy, its potential, and the potential of Euratom for putting German industry under French controls. At the Geneva Conference, German industrialists had learned how far behind Germany was and how much money America was spending in the field (working on cyclotrons that cost DM 100,000,000). Word spread rapidly through industry, including the LBI, that Germany could catch up only if all interested groups worked together, and the industrialists orchestrated the cry that Adenauer create a Federal Ministry of Atomic Affairs for Strauß, to give the interested industry a cooperative negotiating partner of Cabinet rank.[31]

Strauß knew how to take care of his friends. The new minister acceded to most of industry's wishes, for example, that his new ministry be small, confine itself to coordinating and providing money, give industry wide-ranging autonomy and allow it to compete within a framework of state regulation (rather than manage or nationalize the atomic industry, as the Social Democrats wanted to do), and emphasize the construction of research reactors over reactors for power generation. When he created the German Atomic Energy Commission in December, 1955, he gave the strongest voices to the chemical, electric, and power generation industries (members included Karl Winnacker of Hoechst, Wilhelm Menne of the VCI, Hermann Josef Abs of the Bank Deutscher Länder, Gerhard Geyer of Esso, Ulrich Haberland of the public utility Bayernwerk, Hermann Reusch of Gutehoffnungshütte, Hans Reuter from DEMAG, and scientists such as Werner Heisenberg and Otto Hahn).[32] It is hardly too much to say that, rather than the Commission advising the Ministry, the Ministry functioned almost as an executive organ of the industry-dominated Commission. Strauß certainly endeared himself to industry when he said things like, Germany "hadn't done anything for a good ten to fifteen years, but 95 percent of what the Americans had accomplished in this time could be taken over for free. Lost time—saved money!" In an image calculated to resonate with industrialists, he referred to his policy as "reverse reparations."[33] The Ministry and the Commission proved ideal forums for Strauß to establish his reputation for spending government money in the interests of modernizing industry.[34]

As he did on defense issues, Strauß took advantage of basic circumstances of the German political system when he inserted himself into the gap between Adenauer's foreign policy and the interests of German industry. Adenauer and the CDU were completely invested in the Western alliance and rapprochement with France. They could ill afford to excite the suspicions and fears of the Allies by seeming too eager in atomic matters. Strauß and the CSU were under fewer constraints. While Strauß was too politic to articulate Germany's interest in developing the new technology against the French interest in holding Germany down, he invoked a Cold War "Battle of the Classrooms," appealing in a general way to patriotism and national pride; in his *Memoirs* he wrote of the founding of the Ministry of Atomic Affairs as the occasion whereby "the Fatherland returned to the ranks of the technological powers. What the army was in one field, atomic power was in another."[35]

The Euratom negotiations drew useful attention to the gap between Adenauer and industry. The idea of Euratom was to create a common European authority for atomic energy, analogous to the European Coal and Steel Community. While Adenauer supported the idea, German industry was quick to reject it, and Strauß took industry's side. German industry feared that Euratom would be based on the statist ideas prevalent in France, Italy, and the Benelux countries, which aimed to make atomic sciences and energy into a state-directed monopoly or nationalized industry, to control access to fuel and, of course, to make Germany a second-class member vis-à-vis France; lurking behind this was the French desire to develop nuclear weapons while shackling German science and industry and using the German contribution to Euratom to finance the French nuclear weapons program. German industry would not abide this but sought to build connections to the British and American atomic research and industry.[36] Strauß expressed his strong reservations about Euratom and worked with W.A. Menne, a Hoechst executive, president of the VCI, and chairman of the BDI's Working Circle for Atomic Matters, to frustrate a European atomic authority, claiming that Germany had to proceed by means of bilateral cooperation agreements with the United States and Great Britain, and that only after it had caught up with Britain and France could there be real European cooperation.[37]

Strauß seems to have had another ambition, which tells us much about his politics. There are indications that in early 1956 Strauß was planning to expand his Ministry of Atomic Affairs into a Ministry for Scientific Research, or into an Energy Ministry, or even beyond that into a kind of Ministry for Scientific Research and Nuclear War, as he privately assured Bavarian industrialists that Germany was going to acquire nuclear weapons and that his ministry would be responsible for them.[38] Many of those who had supported the creation of a Ministry of Atomic Affairs had done so hoping that it would eventually be transformed into a ministry for scientific research—that it would function as an opening wedge against the "cultural sovereignty" of the states. This had been exactly what the conservative federalists in the CSU had feared. Only the nomination of Strauß as Minister of Atomic Affairs had persuaded them not to denounce the creation of the ministry as a breach of the CDU/CSU parliamentary caucus agreement.[39] They had badly misjudged their man, who seems to have been willing to sacrifice a sacred tenet of federalism for a ministry from which industry would have benefited, as well as Strauß himself and the liberal wing of the CSU. Again we see that federalism was for Strauß more a means than an end.

Strauß's term as Minister of Atomic Affairs lasted only one year, but was considered a success on all sides. He made an impression as an energetic administrator, created interest and support for the new ministry, built up a staff, won points for modelling the ministry on America's Atomic Energy Commission, and gave it a sense of mission; he even purchased Germany's first atomic reactor. Overcoming hesitation on all sides, in June 1956 he convinced the state, banks, and businesses to found Atomic Reactor Construction and Operations, Inc. (Kernreaktor Bau- und Betriebs GmbH), a consortium for atomic research in Germany, with the money provided mostly by the federal government and the government of Baden-Württemberg and the benefit to be enjoyed mostly by industry.[40]

Strauß was quite clear that, as he told a gathering of Bavarian industrialists, "Undoubtedly the freedom of atomic energy from locational restrictions is a real chance for Bavaria and southern Germany to create an economic counterweight to the Ruhr." He made the most of the chance by sending atomic research and energy centers to Bavaria, and not only the Max Planck Institute for Physics and Germany's first atomic reactor, which he had built near Munich. He even attempted to circumvent Adenauer's ruling on the Atomic Reactor Station by making Karlsruhe a center for "general reactor research" and Munich the center for "reactor technology and reactor construction."[41] Though this proved beyond his means, it hardly mattered since the real action would be in research and Strauß saw to it that the federal government provided generous funding for the Munich

Research Reactor, while his ministry provided money to move Heisenberg's Max Planck Institute for Physics to Munich, to train scientists and technicians in Bavarian universities, and to pay for reactors.[42] In June 1956 Strauß moved the Munich Research Reactor to the head of the line of his ministry's projects and funded it generously. Though Strauß's systematic preference for Bavaria irritated some on his Atomic Energy Commission, industrialists saw that it was wise to become one of his constituents. Strauß lectured the Bavarian industrialists that in return he expected them to support the CSU against the Coalition of Four.[43]

But in retrospect we see that the issue was bigger than Bavaria's immediate interest in atomic research centers or in being among the first to develop atomic energy. Strauß's real success as Minister of Atomic Affairs was in the "the vision thing." He created and advertised a politico-industrial ideology to win the backing of leading industrial circles and secure the future of the CSU as the favorite party of those sectors of industry that looked to state contracts.

Strauß argued that there were industrial sectors in which Germany had once been a leader, such as aerospace, physics, and electronics, but in which it had fallen far behind, due to its defeat in World War II, the disruption of the postwar years, and the leap ahead that the other Western powers had made in the intervening decade. Germany could not secure its political or economic future without rebuilding its scientific and technical power in these sectors: if it failed to do so it would become hopelessly backward vis-à-vis those countries that dominated these technologies. Yet Germany could never rebuild its power in these sectors so long as the Christian-Democratic government bound itself to the ideology of economic liberalism: these sectors required extremely high capital start-up investments and often required investors to absorb many years of financial losses before they could compete with large, primarily American multinationals. Only the federal budget could carry the burden, in its magnitude and duration, of supporting these necessary industries until they became profitable. The nation depended on the state to get these industries going by providing them with capital, supporting their research (and, implicitly, absorbing their losses) until the industry became profitable (at which point, it was also implicit, the state would not share the industrialists' profits). "I was never a believer in the pure doctrine of Adam Smith," Strauß admitted.[44]

This was probably not yet a conscious plan for the industrial modernization of Bavaria. But it was something rather close. It was at least a political argument and tactic to promote science and technology, and there was little reason to think that as minister Strauß would be shy about preferring Bavaria. Though this "something rather close" was not integrated into a policy vision and stable set of political alliances and client relationships, it was more than enough to put Strauß out in front of other Christian Democrats on the issue of scientific, technological and industrial modernization. It didn't take much to be in front of the CSU's state parliamentary deputies, for there was little indication at the time that they were learning from the Social Democrats' challenge. Though the CSU opposition pointed out that Seidel had in effect done the preparatory work for the

Coalition of Four's atomic and scientific-educational politics, it tried harder to put the Social Democrats' ideas down as unrealistic than to co-opt them. Responding to the conservatism of his constituents, even Seidel scoffed that Knoeringen "had practically created a religion out of the atomic thing; I used to call him the 'atomic socialist,'" while Seidel's protégé Otto Schedl rejected the Rucker Plan as a "utopia," and Father Georg Meixner criticized Rucker's tendency to neglect the humanities and stressed the necessity of building more primary schools. The CSU deputies were skeptical and critical of the notion of a "second industrial revolution."[45] And the CDU's response was hardly better than that of the CSU state parliamentary deputies. Although the CDU was not inhibited by cultural federalism or a powerful Catholic reactionary element within its ranks, its dominant Weltanschauung connected poorly with the ideas promoted by the Social Democrats or Strauß: most of the CDU deputies were inclined to follow either Erhard's politically salable liberalism ("social market economy"), or an old-fashioned and self-conscious European humanism, or a sentimental Catholic progressivism. Adenauer himself was an old-fashioned humanist, culturally conservative, uninterested in science, technology, and even economics except as they connected to immediate political advantage or national defense, and was unable to take science and technology seriously as a political issue. As he told the CDU Federal Governing Council, "The Social Democrats have lately been making an effort ... to wrap themselves in the banner of science" and therefore the CDU "has to stick a few scientific bigshots in its buttonhole ... I guess we could also make use of a few movie actresses. That makes a good impression on young people. Herr Schröder [Gerhard Schröder, the handsome Interior Minister] will be responsible for recruiting a few movie actresses. (Merriment.)"[46]

It was fortunate for Strauß that he left the Ministry of Atomic Affairs in October 1956, after one year in office. In his final months in office it became apparent that, due to unanticipated scientific difficulties, cost-efficient atomic power would not come on line before the late 1960s, and the discovery of huge new oil fields in the Middle East promised to take additional pressure off the German energy market. The issue was no longer urgent for industry, and the Cabinet became suddenly resistant to funding requests. Strauß remained outwardly optimistic about the future of atomic power generation but directed the ministry's emphasis toward atomic research.[47]

It testifies to the importance of the Ministry of Atomic Affairs for Strauß's industrial politics that he did not part with the ministry entirely. He arranged for Siegfried Balke to succeed him, and in the coalition negotiations of 1957 and 1961 ensured that Balke continued to hold the ministry. There Balke faithfully continued his sponsor's policies, particularly those that benefited Bavaria and the chemical industry. Balke generously funded Heisenberg's Max Planck Institute for Physics and the Munich Research Reactor, and even seems to have tried yet again to revise Adenauer's 1955 decision in favor of Karlsruhe on the grounds of local opposition to the Atomic Reactor Station.[48]

Balke had a hard row to hoe. His program for the construction of small power-generating reactors (the so-called "Eltville Program," drawn up in a Hoechst office) proposed that the federal government generously support the reactors because if it did not do so there would be no reactor program at all and the ministry would lose its raison d'être. While Balke promoted plans to construct reactors in Bavaria, the Eltville Program stalled as the power companies quarreled with the federal government over who should pay: the federal government agreed to assist in the financing of a number of small power-producing reactors, but the power companies determined to make the federal government pick up the entire tab. [49]

Connecting Defense-Industrial Ideas and Interests

But Strauß was not strong enough to wrest the Defense Ministry from Adenauer. Despite the heavyweight fighting Strauß had done for Bavarian industrial interests, and despite his political and ministerial efforts to extend his connections beyond Bavaria into German industry in general, Adenauer remained unintimidated, and as loath as ever to give Strauß the Defense Ministry. To change Adenauer's mind Strauß would not only have to play his cards well, but pick up some new ones.

Strauß's play was made easier by his domination of the State Group. Strauß dominated the State Group in no small measure because nothing succeeds like success. He had consistently argued for the superior political strategy and made that strategy work. The State Group acquiesced in Strauß's challenges to Adenauer and the CDU because they paid off in ministries and in influence, and they appealed to their Bavarian particularism, and because Strauß had won most of his jousts. Though the other CSU deputies wanted to defeat the Social Democrats more than to joust with the CDU, behaved more conservatively, and would have contented themselves with the CSU's proportional share of positions, Strauß's successes had fully justified his strategy of confrontation. Under his leadership the State Group represented federalism, nationalism, and industry. But Strauß's federalism had little in common with that of the conservative Catholics; whereas the latter sought to protect the privileges of the Bavarian state, Strauß's challenged the other parties in order to consolidate the unity of the CSU delegates in Bonn. The nationalist undertones in his rhetoric got favorable attention for the CSU among voters across the political spectrum, many of whom wanted a policy more "national" than Adenauer's, and within the CSU membership, where it served as a clamp to hold together the CSU's conservative and liberal wings: the conservatives pretended to be more interested in Bavaria than Germany, yet their national feeling found its outlet in resentment of the Western powers, which Strauß played on expertly; as for the liberals, the nation had always been the object of their patriotism and they keenly felt its humiliation. As to industry, Strauß, like Seidel before him, had already found that he had nothing to lose by challenging the FDP and CDU claims to be its patron—there was no Left faction within the CSU's voting base. These three elements—federalism, nationalism, and industry—complemented each other. The other parties hesitated to invest themselves in the latter two. Yet Strauß speculated that a more nationalist climate of opinion and more modern industry would one day come to Germany. He invested deeply in both of them, so that when the time came the CSU would already own the issues.

Strauß had a personality ideally suited to this. The business of challenging the CDU was like the game of "chicken," in which two drivers race their cars directly at each other, the loser being the one who first swerves to avoid collision. In this game, it is irrational to allow one's opponent to think one is rational—rational play is to convince one's opponent that one is irrational, so that the opponent swerves first. In the same way Strauß worked to convince Adenauer and his advisors of his irrationality, or at least dangerous incalculability: that if Adenauer did not meet Strauß's demands Strauß might very well do something that would damage both of the Christian-Democratic parties.

Strauß did not have to put on an act: he was by no means risk-averse, and the impression that he was ready for anything was strengthened by the naked apparency of his ambition and will-to-power, and further reinforced by his imprudent and crude talk, bellowing, drunkenness, and womanizing. When in 1955 Adenauer decided to deny Strauß the Defense Ministry, he fully expected Strauß to do something drastic; perhaps to demand the chairmanship of the CDU/CSU parliamentary caucus and use Adenauer's refusal as a pretext to dissolve the CDU/CSU parliamentary caucus.[50]

Strauß's incalculability was indispensable to him in his struggle with Adenauer. For in the German parliamentary system the parties had quite stable relations with each other; within and between the parties, politics tended to be bureaucratic and managerial, rewarding prudence and policy over maneuver and personality. Strauß was often a rough stone in a bed of smooth pebbles, but never more than in 1955 and 1956, when he threatened to form a coalition with the Social Democrats—which really amounted to a threat to start a terrible public quarrel that would damage both Christian-Democratic parties. Strauß's threat preyed on the minds of Adenauer and his advisors. As Heinrich Krone, the chairman of the CDU/CSU parliamentary caucus, noted in his diary, "There is unfortunately no doubt of what is going on in some Bavarian brains. Everyone knows what end Strauß is pursuing. He will be reckless in choosing his means."[51]

Here we see Strauß flanking the CDU yet again. In the early 1950s Adenauer was driven by his responsibility for foreign policy to allow a gap to open between the CDU and industry. Now, in the EDC and NATO negotiations, Adenauer treated the possibility of producing weapons in Germany, particularly military aircraft, not as a right he must wrest from the Allies but as a bargaining chip. This alarmed Germany's potential defense industry, particularly Bavarian firms, since the French had designs to impose special restrictions on armaments production in "strategically exposed areas," of which Bavaria, bordering on Czechoslovakia and

East Germany, would have certainly been one. Though the agreement that brought Germany into NATO in 1955 gave German industry a reasonably fair deal, requiring only that Adenauer pledge not to produce on German territory nuclear weapons, long-range and guided missiles, and strategic bombers, Adenauer, Erhard, and Blank disappointed German industry in other ways. Adenauer did not object when in early 1955 Blank planned the construction of the aircraft industry as a purely private enterprise; nor did he object when Erhard resisted industry's demand for subventions and encouraged the federal parliament to do likewise, promising that "he [Erhard] himself is resolute in his wish that the aircraft industry enjoy the atmosphere of private enterprise."[52] An unsubsidized European aircraft industry was a chimera, and although Erhard admitted the political necessity of giving German industry some sort of investment credits, he continued to emphasize the free market. Industry could not have been pleased, for after the death of the EDC German industry was less interested in Erhard's crusade against French dirigisme than in large subventions from its own government.

From 1953 to 1955, when the gap was only a crack, one is struck by how little Strauß did to exploit it. Perhaps he recognized that he could not do so effectively; he certainly received little support from outside the CSU. His demand that Adenauer fulfill his 1953 promise to give him a Cabinet-level post in defense got him nowhere; it seems that Adenauer decided to stall, fobbing him off with lesser jobs, while Strauß appealed to Bavarian interests and Bavarian particularism.[53] Other members of the CSU State Group expanded their influence into a wide range of defense-related issues. As chairman of the Defense Committee, Richard Jaeger dedicated himself to the issue of parliamentary control over the new armed forces; in 1956 he led the CSU's successful fight to get the term of military service reduced. In 1955 and 1956 Hermann Höcherl and the other deputies called frequently for more defense contracts to be given to small and medium-sized firms (rather than to Ruhr-based heavy industry) and to areas far from the centers of industry and trade (i.e., to Bavaria).[54] All of the Bavarian parties shared the concern that Bavaria get its fair share of defense contracts, and both the Coalition of Four and the CSU organized their efforts for a just geographical distribution of defense contracts.[55] None of these moves garnered the CSU the support of the potential German defense industry.

But in 1956 events presented Strauß with a new opportunity. It became apparent that German military planning was outdated. By 1956 America had acquired the ability to destroy the Soviet Union overnight—while the Soviet Union was yet unable to strike the continental United States. This made possible the new American policy of massive retaliation: America would respond to a Soviet conventional invasion of Europe with a full-scale nuclear strike on the Soviet Union. This in its turn meant that conventional forces lost much of their importance in Europe.[56] Yet in 1956 Blank and Adenauer still planned German rearmament in general accord with an older NATO plan for the conventional defense of Western Europe, one that relegated Germany to providing ground troops while other allies led the war in the air, and to purchasing advanced weapons systems from its allies, lest higher ambitions awaken their allies' fears of German militarism. Strauß, the foremost German supporter of the new American policy, was quick to see its implications for German industry.

The implications were enormous. If Germany participated in the new strategic shift, it could sharply cut back on its planned conventional armies and spend the money saved on a smaller but modern air force. This might one day carry nuclear weapons, even control them. Germany would become more influential within the NATO alliance, a true partner rather than the object of the others' policy, pursuing a more independent foreign policy. In short, it might recover something of its place as a European great power.

Strauß was quick to perceive this, and that, since the earlier rearmament plans were made, industry's power within German politics had grown. Industry was less willing to accept a rearmament plan that took no account of its interests. In the summer of 1956 he took advantage of the issue, demonstrating his mastery of American strategic thinking and sharply distinguishing himself from Blank by arguing that Germany adapt fully to the new strategic realities by participating in nuclear deterrence, emphasizing, within the German force structure, the air force, and arming it with nuclear weapons. Much as this argument turned off the voting public, it spoke to the chemical and potential aircraft industries, and even to Adenauer, who, though not as advanced as Strauß, had been pursuing his own strategic education.[57] But if Adenauer's cultivated image as an inveterate civilian made it impossible for him to represent the new strategy, it also made it difficult for him to appoint someone like Strauß. Yet Blank had neither the inclination nor the weight to represent these ideas against a wall of public misunderstanding and opposition.

Blank persisted in rearming according to the outdated strategy, and in the course of 1956 both the BDI and the LBI turned on him. The BDI, long frustrated over its lack of influence with Blank, began to criticize Blank publicly on a number of counts: it wanted the army to be created more slowly, the draftees to serve a shorter term of service, and the army's final size to be substantially less than five hundred thousand men, lest, as Germany approached full employment, rising wages damage Germany's currency and position on world markets. It worried also about the cost of the army, particularly since early 1956 saw a downturn in economic activity.[58] Those sectors of German industry that anticipated defense contracts wanted contracts not for the mass manufacture of traditional materiel but high-technology weapons. They also wanted generous research and development contracts, in order to prepare them to withstand international competition in other fields. While Blank inclined to give in to Allied insistence that he purchase defense technology and major weapons systems like tanks and jet fighters abroad, the BDI obviously had in mind that Germany produce them at home.[59] While similar issues were being fought out in the United States, France, and Britain, German defense-industrial interests were weaker because Germany was in a weak position: it was the *demandeur,* asking its allies to defend it, allies who in any case had suffered greatly at its hands and thought that Germany should have the grace to defray the cost of its defense by buying their weapons systems.

The LBI outdid the BDI in boldness, perhaps because it had the closest connections to Strauß. The LBI's new president, Rolf Rodenstock, as willing as his predecessor Seeling to work with Strauß and the CSU, announced his "great anxiety" over defense-economic developments: insufficient planning and the lack of attention to technical questions, and the need, in order that Germany maintain its position in world markets, to develop atomic sciences and technology and to push defense-economic reforms. In early 1956 the LBI joined the campaign for more attention to defense technology and a greater role for industry in defense planning, claiming that "it was more and more apparent that due to the incomplete manner of defense-industrial planning the Federal Defense Ministry's mode of operation had conjured up a difficult situation."[60]

The flip side of dissatisfaction with Blank was support for Strauß. Other leading Christian-Democrats avoided defense issues—with Strauß having staked his claim against all comers and the issue of "going nuclear" on the horizon, they thought the Defense Ministry a political hot seat. Adenauer, well aware of Blank's failings, stood by Blank out of fear of Strauß.

So in the course of 1956 German industry looked at Strauß more closely, and it liked what it saw. We have already discussed Strauß's activity on behalf of industry as Minister of Atomic Affairs, and how the CSU was surpassing the CDU as a faithful promoter of industry's political wishes.[61] In 1956 Strauß publicized his desire for a rearmament that gave greater scope to the wishes of German industry and made it easier for industry to attach its cause to his by leading an active CSU opposition to Adenauer's government. The State Group's "Defense Coalition"—that is, the State Group and the CDU and FDP deputies who followed its lead on defense issues—launched a successful campaign to shorten the term of conscription to twelve months. This infuriated Adenauer, since the term had been set at eighteen months to satisfy the Allies, and the prominent role of CSU members in the "Defense Coalition" reinforced the impression that the CSU had special expertise in security policy and rearmament.[62]

In the summer of 1956 the political will to go through with Blank's rearmament program weakened. Though Blank began to come around to industry's point of view, supporting increased use of domestic industry to meet Germany's defense needs, his conversion was too little and too late. Even revised, his program relegated the air force to a supporting role.[63] In July Strauß and Seidel met with Adenauer to criticize Blank; "animated criticism indeed ... sometimes very animated criticism," remembered Adenauer. Strauß remembered the same meeting: "Konrad Adenauer remained unimpressed, unyielding, icy: 'Herr Strauß, I have heard you out. Mark my words: so long as I am Chancellor, you will never become Defense Minister!'" In a vain attempt to divide the CSU, Adenauer dangled before Seidel the prospect of becoming Justice Minister.[64]

Strauß seems to have sensed that Adenauer's rigidity masked weakness. In the middle of September the CSU launched a barrage of criticism against every imaginable aspect of the rearmament—the supposed discrimination against Bavarians in the personnel policy of the Defense Ministry, the failure to pass constitutional amendments resolving questions of conscription, supreme command of the armed forces, allied prerogatives to read Germans' mail and listen in on their telephone conversations, and Adenauer's failure to keep his promise of 1953 to the State Group. Then, on 16 and 17 September, Strauß called the State Group together for a weekend session in a Bavarian palace, where the deputies adopted a rearmament program artfully tailored to meet Germany's defense, foreign policy, and, most of all, its economic requirements.[65] It called for a drastically revised defense plan, demanding that Germany insist that it have a modern air force and carry high-technology and nuclear weapons, that the army's manpower be built up more slowly than the Allies had demanded, and that German industry get more high-technology defense contracts. That was the real import of the CSU's press release on the weekend:

> The State Group expects from the federal government a defense policy which is clear and suited to both the political situation and the state of technological development. Therefore it requests the federal government to undertake the following measures:
> 1. The federal government should come up with a defense program adapted to German realities and needs as well as to the common European-Atlantic defense policy. It should demand that in its general defense planning this program be taken into consideration by our allies, especially those Great Powers armed with nuclear weapons.
> 2. The federal government should in the working out of the defense program take the current scientific and technological revolutions and their strategic implications into consideration and at the same time demand that, in the event of revision of planning and strategic developments our allies give consideration to the views of the Federal Republic [of West Germany]; and furthermore that the security interests of the Federal Republic be given due consideration.
> 3. According to the suggestions of the CDU/CSU deputies Dr. Jaeger and Dr. Lenz it is intended that a general term of service of 12 months will be realized.
> 4. The construction of the Federal Armed Forces shall proceed organically, so that the housing, arming, training and compensating of the Federal Armed Forces results in the creation of high-quality forces.
> 5. The manufacture and provisioning of weapons and other military equipment must proceed in such a manner that German industry benefits from planned defense spending in the necessary measure and that corresponds to the current scientific and technological revolutions and their strategic implications. Above all it is necessary that an appropriate share of this defense spending goes to the scientific and technological fields in which Germany, despite its earlier dominant position, is no longer capable of competing with comparable nations.[66]

At the same time the State Group discussed the possibility of forming a coalition with the Social Democrats in Bonn. Such a coalition would seem to have been utterly incredible, but Adenauer took the talk as a sign that Strauß was prepared to take drastic measures. Heinrich Krone noted Adenauer's great "tensions and worries": "There are forces at work in the CSU that support a coalition with the Social Democrats at the federal level after the 1957 election. Then the same coalition in Bavaria. Franz Josef Strauß, party chairman Seidel and the vice chairman Dr. Eberhard are more or less actively thinking and working in this direction."[67]

Seeing that a showdown loomed, the press trumpeted Strauß's program and in the following two weeks Germany's industrial and financial elites came down in support of Strauß.[68] Adenauer had good reasons to give Strauß what he wanted: he needed to ensure that industry supported the CDU over the FDP in the upcoming 1957 federal election campaign.[69] He also needed peace with the CSU before that campaign; and must have been attracted by the prospect of putting Strauß in a position where he "would surely wear himself down in quarrels with the Social Democrats, so that the CSU would lose interest in a Grand Coalition [with the Social Democrats]." Yet, balancing his relations with industry against his relations with the Allies, who insisted that Germany stop dragging its feet and get its men in arms, and who would not be reassured by the appointment to the Defense Ministry of a deputy who appealed to nationalistic resentments against the Allies, Adenauer would not give up easily. In the last days of September he met with the members of his inner circle, frightened them by threatening to resign, and accused Heinrich Krone of lacking the aggressivity and nerve to control the CSU. Krone noted, "I have never had a discussion with the Chancellor so serious in word and substance as I had this morning." Krone wanted to move cautiously but Adenauer ordered him into "battle" against the State Group: "If this leads to a rupture with the CSU, then so be it."[70] Adenauer no less than Strauß knew how to play "chicken."

Several days later Fritz Berg, President of the BDI, wrote to Ludwig Erhard to press him with his conviction that Blank had failed and industry needed a strong voice in support of "the creation of a German defense industry." The chief spokesman of German industry argued aggressively for Strauß's defense program. Berg wanted the defense industry rebuilt, wanted contracts for research and development, and even argued that Germany should become a nuclear power.[71] Blank had not made his position clear on any of these matters, but Strauß had, and for over a year had been promoting his answers to industrialists behind closed doors.

Adenauer conceded defeat around 6 October 1956. Strauß transformed the occasion into a dubious anecdote, with himself surprised and reluctant to accept the Defense Ministry, and Adenauer eating humble pie with dignity: "Herr Strauß, do you want to take it amiss that an old man is still able to change his mind?" In agreeing to accept the ministry, Strauß secured agreement to his rearmament program and to a smaller army built up more slowly, and he even grandstanded by calling for postponing the first calling-up of soldiers. To satisfy the Allies, Adenauer had to insist on this unpopular measure. Within days Strauß told an interviewer that he intended to seek nuclear weapons from his NATO Allies.[72]

American diplomats, reporting to Washington that Strauß's approach to rearmament simply enjoyed greater popularity than Blank's, understood well the gap that Strauß was exploiting. And they understood Strauß's idea of saving money on troops by investing in the air force and nuclear weapons: the Eisenhower administration had pursued the same policy. The diplomats reported: "We must expect as a result of the atmosphere of an election year and of the attitude of Strauß a more national-minded approach to German defense planning," which meant not only keeping the draft as small as possible but also "advocating emphasis on new weapons, in particular, nuclear weapons." "In Germany this question is increasingly becoming involved with domestic political issues. Even though the election will not be held until September 1957, the campaign is already under way."[73]

Turning the Defense Ministry to Account

The amount of money the Defense Ministry spent in Bavaria provides one index of what Defense Minister Strauß did for Bavarian industry. Several months after he became Defense Minister Strauß reported to the parties of the Coalition of Four, still in power in Bavaria and convinced that Bavaria had gotten short shrift in Bonn, that as of 31 January 1957, 27 percent of the total value of all domestic defense contracts had gone to Bavaria, in absolute numbers more than in any other state—second-place North Rhine-Westphalia had gotten only 19 percent. Strauß wrote, "There is therefore no reason to speak, as you seem to do, about a preference for firms from the Rhineland; on the contrary, firms in other states, for example, the Rhineland-Palatinate, have every reason to speak of a preference for Bavarian firms. It seems to me, therefore, that we Bavarians have every reason not to raise this question of the distribution of defense contracts amongst the states, but to let sleeping dogs lie."[74]

Yet this crude index tells us little about Strauß's role. As of 31 January 1957 Strauß had held the Defense Ministry for only three and one-half months, so that these figures include contracts awarded by Blank to the Bavarian firms of Dornier and Krauss-Maffei (awards in which CSU pressure may have played a role), as well as highly lucrative contracts with Messerschmitt and BMW Triebwerkbau, which, as we shall see, involved both Blank and Strauß.[75]

A better index of Strauß's contribution to Bavaria's industrial modernization is his activity in support of major Bavarian firms. Here we must consider how remarkably free were the hands of a German Defense Minister in the 1950s. Public interest in the defense budget was low. The vested interests that in other western countries compelled defense ministries to award contracts to a limited group of firms had not vested in 1956. Germany had a clean slate: its defense industry, dismantled after the war, might have been rebuilt anywhere in the country. Though the German Empire, the Weimar Republic, and the Third Reich had concentrated it in North Rhine-Westphalia's Ruhr region, and though there were sound arguments and interests for rebuilding it there, in the first five or six years of the Defense Ministry's existence, the Defense Minister had enormous power to reshape German industry—if he knew how to use it. On the other hand, foreign countries jostled to involve themselves in the making of these decisions. And Blank had already begun to fill up Germany's defense-industrial "clean slate." In his seventeen-month term as Defense Minister, Blank had answered some important questions.

First, Blank had decided that rather than develop its own aircraft or buy fully built aircraft abroad, Germany would build other nations' aircraft on a license arrangement. Developing up-to-date aircraft was almost certainly beyond the capacity of the German firms, while buying fully built planes abroad would have sealed the fate of the German aircraft firms and condemned the country to buy its aircraft abroad for generations. But the decision to purchase licenses gave rise to a major question: with which country's firms should Germany make its license arrangement? France and the United States were the chief, and jealous, rivals. France considered German purchase of French planes almost a condition of Franco-German reconciliation; at the same time the United States was Germany's military protector, and had given Germany more than five hundred Korean-War vintage F-84s, with the intention of connecting West Germany to its own systems.[76] Second, Blank had decided which firms to support. Thirteen firms had sought contracts to produce aircraft but Blank decided that only four would be considered eligible to receive primary-producer contracts: Hamburger Flugzeugbau GmbH (Hamburg), Ernst Heinkel AG (Baden-Württemberg), Dornier-Werke GmbH (Baden-Württemberg and Bavaria), and Messerschmitt AG (Bavaria). The others might subcontract with or merge into the four majors. This was a wonderful decision for Bavaria, both of whose firms moved into the winners' circle. Nonetheless it was far from certain whether the southern firms would end up in Bavaria or Baden-Württemberg or relocate to northern Germany; as late as 1956, a foreign correspondent reported that the principal rivals for the aircraft industry were North Rhine-Westphalia and Baden-Württemberg.[77] Third, Blank divided the work between north and south, proposing henceforth to send contracts for transport aircraft and helicopters to the northern firms, while contracts for fighters would go to the southern. To the north would go the contracts for Piaggio (light trainer) and Noratlas (transporter), while the contracts for the Dornier 27 (reconnaissance and communications—the only contract awarded for a plane of German design) and the Fouga Magister (jet trainer) went to Bavaria and Baden-Württemberg, to Dornier and Flugzeug-Union-Süd GmbH (Aircraft Union South, Inc., a paper corporation created to allow Messerschmitt and Heinkel to cooperate yet preserve their separate identities).[78] This decision favored the northern industry, since according to Blank's strategic conception, the chief task of the air force was to support conventional ground forces (requiring many troop and equipment transporters), and since it set it up to make the transition from transporters to civilian jetliners. Fourth, Blank created a consensus in the federal government that German firms would have to merge to achieve economies of scale that would allow them to compete with British and French aircraft manufacturers. Withholding contracts from minor firms to encourage them to merge into the major firms was only a first step; the next step would be to encourage the four major firms to merge, and even to require merger as a precondition for future contracts.

Inheriting these decisions in October 1956, Strauß did nothing to reverse any of them but involved himself in the rescues of BMW and Messerschmitt, Dornier and Audi, and inspired Ludwig Bölkow's decision to move Bölkow Developments from Baden-Württemberg to Bavaria.

As soon as Strauß became Defense Minister Bavarian interests began pressing their cases with him. It fell to him to arrange deals for the rescue of BMW and Messerschmitt, two "especially difficult cases." The auto manufacturer BMW AG faced imminent bankruptcy—it had aimed its first generation of postwar cars at the top end of the market only to find that such hardly existed—but planned to resuscitate its fortunes through its wholly owned subsidiary BMW Triebwerkbau GmbH, which anticipated lucrative contracts to manufacture aircraft engines for the new German air force. Though inactive for over a decade, BMW Triebwerkbau had a plant, an engineering team, and the inside track on its possible competitors Daimler and Junkers, whose efforts to rebuild in North Rhine-Westphalia had already come to naught.[79] But when in the late summer of 1956, while Blank was still Defense Minister, the parent company's precarious financial position became known, the civil servants in the Defense Ministry, afraid to stuff the subsidiary with government money only to see it dragged under by the parent, enforced a regulation that no contract be awarded to insolvent firms. The subsidiary would have to be separated from the parent. But the parent resisted, and appealed to the Bavarian Economic Ministry to put pressure on the Defense Ministry. This failed; but as soon as Strauß became Defense Minister the parent firm, expecting favorable treatment from Strauß, dug in its heels. And indeed Strauß proposed a compromise which favored BMW's interests over the public interest: the Defense Ministry would merely withhold *development* contracts from BMW Triebwerkbau. Yet the quarrel dragged on, as BMW's rigid negotiating tactics so antagonized the responsible civil servants that Strauß finally had to step in and order them to award BMW the jet engine contract as well as work servicing allied airplanes, which kept BMW Triebwerkbau occupied through 1961 and brought in a great deal of money to the parent.[80]

Messerschmitt presented a similar problem. Blank had awarded the legendary Bavarian firm a contract to produce the Fouga jet trainer.[81] But in order to be able to produce the Fouga Messerschmitt needed money up front; but it was nearly bankrupt. The Coalition of Four agreed to lend a hand but, having lost confidence in Willy Messerschmitt (twice since 1950 the Bavarian state had paid off Messerschmitt's debts), it refused to recapitalize the firm unless recapitalization made the Messerschmitt family a minority shareholder. The family firmly rejected these terms, which led some directors and engineers to quit in protest. But the Messerschmitts, who owned 88 percent of the company's stock, called on their friends in the CSU. This infuriated Bavarian Finance Minister Friedrich

Zietsch (a Social Democrat), who determined to enforce his terms. Things looked bad for Messerschmitt. The Coalition of Four inquired whether the Fouga contract might be given to Dornier or Heinkel (if the latter firm agreed to build in Bavaria, perhaps in the plant of the by-then bankrupt Messerschmitt), or whether the Bavarian state might purchase Messerschmitt's properties from its creditors, take the Fouga contract itself, and then hire Willy Messerschmitt to produce the plane in his former factory as an employee of the Bavarian state.[82] Meanwhile, Dornier and Heinkel angled to steal the contract, the German air force hinted that it did not want the Fouga anyway, but preferred American trainers, and Fritz Schäffer's Federal Finance Ministry applied pressures to remove Messerschmitt from the contract.[83] Even within Strauß's Defense Ministry, many wanted to drop Messerschmitt and move on to other arrangements. Strauß, the only one of the dramatis personae bent on saving the Messerschmitt firm, once again offered a Bavarian industrialist a favorable arrangement. Assuming the role of an honest broker between the interests of the Bavarian firm and the Bavarian and German states, Strauß presided over negotiations the result of which was as follows. Messerschmitt AG transferred to Bavaria its wholly owned subsidiaries (its automobile- and bicycle-producing subsidiaries, Messerschmitt Leichtbau GmbH and Regensburger Stahl- und Metallbau-Werke GmbH) together with the debts that were dragging Messerschmitt AG toward bankruptcy. The Bavarian and federal governments then provided money for a recapitalization and the Messerschmitt firm issued new shares to the recapitalizers, so that Bavaria had 49.5 percent, the Messerschmitt family had 43.8 percent and the federal government held 6.7 percent in trust for the Messerschmitt family, who received an option to repurchase the shares in 1963. The federal government appointed neutral persons to dominate the board of directors and supervisory board. Strauß bent over backward to save Willy Messerschmitt's pride, making him honorary chairman of the board of directors and advisor to the republic on aerospace matters, for which he received a monthly honorarium.[84]

Nor did Audi go away empty-handed when it called on Strauß. Blank had ordered one thousand Audi jeeps but the firm, having a new plant in Ingolstadt, Bavaria, to pay for, wanted Strauß to buy more.[85] The firm wrote to Strauß offering to give him a DKW jeep to use for a week and shortly after this asked the Bavarian Plenipotentiary in Bonn to arrange a meeting with Strauß, confessing the firm's desperate need for follow-up orders. Strauß promised to help as soon as possible.[86] The Bavarian state lobbied Bonn before the final decision, threatening that if Audi didn't get another order the firm would be forced to close its Bavarian plant. The Defense Ministry ordered five thousand Audi jeeps for DM 42,000,000. A good deal of evidence indicated that Audi's jeep had nothing over its rivals, and at the time a strong current of opinion, given public voice by Erich Mende of the FDP, held that the contract proceeded from nothing more than Strauß's determination to keep Audi from closing its Bavarian plant—a plant that later led the economic development of the Ingolstadt area.[87]

Bölkow Developments KG presented the opposite case. Here it fell to Strauß to bring a successful firm to Bavaria. Ludwig Bölkow was the great design talent of the postwar German defense industry. During World War II an employee of Messerschmitt, after the war he opened his own engineering firm in Stuttgart and the nascent Defense Ministry awarded him contracts to develop helicopters, and antiaircraft and antitank missiles. In 1957 the Stuttgart airport authorities terminated Bölkow's lease upon learning that he was manufacturing antitank rockets on their premises, and the government of Baden-Württemberg fell down on the job, offering him nothing to remain in southwest Germany.[88] Bölkow might have settled his jewel of a firm anywhere in Germany, but looked to neighboring Bavaria, doubtless understanding that he could hardly go wrong in moving to the home state of the man who had installed himself in the Defense Ministry with all the aplomb of the pope in Rome. Bölkow liked to pretend that he had chosen Bavaria because it had the best site for his firm, or because the Coalition of Four was eager to help arrange the move. Yet several things indicate that Bölkow decided to move to Munich because Strauß wanted this. Bölkow himself wrote to his former landlord, "The suggestion for the relocation to Ottobrunn [a suburb of Munich] came out of the Defense Ministry." Bölkow was chronically short of capital and Strauß threw his weight around to arrange favorable financing.[89] Under pressure from Strauß, the Federal Economic and Finance Ministries agreed to give Bölkow an investment credit of DM 2,000,000.[90] Representatives of the Bavarian Economic Ministry then put pressure on Bölkow to move his entire firm to Bavaria; he did and received even more financial help from the state of Bavaria.[91]

A third index of Strauß's contribution to Bavaria's industrial modernization is provided by the Bavarian-industrial implications of his defense policy decisions. Strauß was by no means the only German politician who had an extraordinarily strong tendency to define Germany's defense needs so as to accommodate the German defense industry. But he probably was the only one to declare it publicly, carried it further than any of his successors, and, more than any of them, directed its benefits to his own home Land.

When Strauß took over the Defense Ministry, the big question was whether and how Germany should become a nuclear power. After all, in the Paris Treaties Adenauer had pledged only that Germany would not produce nuclear weapons and strategic bombers on German territory: this would not prevent Germany from importing them, producing them extraterritorially, or achieving a measure of control over nuclear weapons by means of agreements with other countries.[92] Strauß was convinced that, for the sake of its security and prestige, Germany *must* become a nuclear power. Only eight days after he became Defense Minister, Strauß told the State Group in camera that his goals included the rapid development not only of German aerospace research, but also rocketry and, most incredibly, that within five years he wanted Germany to become a nuclear power, the strategic equal of any other power on the continent.[93] Neither America nor France would agree willingly, though neither, as rivals for influence over Germany, could afford to say a definitive no, lest it drive Germany into the arms of the other; in fact the Americans were moving toward the position that Germans should carry nuclear weapons, though not participate in the decision to use them. This encouraged Strauß, and by 1957 it required little intelligence to read between the lines when he publicly referred to Germany's need for "modern weapons."[94] Much of Strauß's politics in the succeeding decade would be an attempt to manipulate one of these Allies into agreeing to something neither wanted.

Just as BMW was the preeminently qualified developer of rocket engines, only one qualified developer of German rockets presented itself: the newly Bavarian firm of Bölkow Developments, the only German firm with any experience in the field of rocketry and missiles. We cannot demonstrate but yet can hardly avoid the conclusion that when Strauß steered Bölkow toward Bavaria he had already in mind a great role for Bölkow in the design and construction of missiles and warhead-related devices.

Similarly, Strauß's program to reduce the size of the German army, to emphasize "quality over quantity," and to push toward nuclear weapons meant putting the accent on the new air force in a way that would benefit Bavaria. If Blank created a division of labor between northern and southern firms that on balance benefited the northern firms, Strauß turned it sharply to the benefit of the southern firms.[95] For the "quality" air force Strauß promised certainly did not feature a large stock of northern German troop transporters or helicopters, or even southern German close air support fighters, but Messerschmitt jet interceptors, made in Bavaria. So long as Germany planned to adhere to the earlier plans for rearmament Blank's division had seemed reasonably equitable: the large conventional army preparing to fight on its own soil required northern-German troop transporters as well as southern-German close air support fighters. But Strauß educated people to the changing strategic situation and the need for a fleet of interceptors, fast-climbing, high-flying fighters that could intercept incoming Russian bombers. His reorientation of the Defense Ministry away from conventional ground war to nuclear air war translated into a decisive edge for the southern firms, which would be building more expensive aircraft of a far higher technological level than the northern firms, while the enormous cost of a fleet of interceptors militated against the federal government supporting the northern firms in the production of commercial jetliners.

But the logic of Strauß's ideas pointed beyond interceptors to nuclear strike aircraft—even better for Bavarian industry.[96] It would have been impolitic to spell it out in the 1950s, but after thinking one's way past ground war to interception, the next step was to think past interception to nuclear deterrence. One had only to recognize that for a country the size of Michigan, bordering the Warsaw Pact countries, interception was a hopeless task. These were jumps that it took many people, including politicians and military men professionally involved in security issues, several years or more to make. Strauß, who in the early 1950s had made it his business to learn the intricacies of the new discipline of nuclear strategy, made them all before anybody else. Now it might be thought that bombers, that is, large planes, would be built by the northern firms. But the new American technology of nuclear miniaturization allowed nuclear weapons to be carried by "fighter-bombers," what was essentially an interceptor retooled for dual use, and which the southern German firms would produce, and which would be yet more technologically advanced, and the construction of which would further advantage the southern over the northern firms. But all this came later; in 1957 Germany did not even have permission from the Allies to carry nuclear weapons.

Strauß's strong political position going into the federal election of September 1957 foreshadowed the drama of the coming years. He had reached a peak of influence and respectability. He had worked well with the Coalition of Four, particularly with Wilhelm Hoegner, first in cooperative rivalry on atomic matters and then on defense matters. As Minister of Atomic Affairs he had succeeded in Europeanizing atomic questions in a manner that freed rather than further restricted Bonn.[97] As Defense Minister he had taken the Federal Armed Forces in hand, mastered uppity generals, and introduced a popular policy for "quality over quantity." And he dominated the State Group more securely than ever.

The question of arming Germany with nuclear weapons gave rise in 1957 and 1958 to the first great controversy that polarized opinion about Strauß. Prior to this controversy, his postures on national pride and national interests, on the Soviet threat and the failings of the Western allies, and on the need for conventional rearmament had not excited passionate opposition to him. Strauß had not acquired the image of a man of the Right, partly because the public image of him had been blurred by his opposition to Bavarian clericalism and particularism, and his promotion of technological and industrial modernization. But the emotional issue of Germany "going nuclear," combined with increasing journalistic attention to his aggressive, power-hungry personality, crystallized a new image of Strauß as a dangerous man, and publicists and politicians in other parties began to define themselves by their opposition to Strauß, a development that gained strength in succeeding years and changed the political dynamics around Strauß and the CSU.

And opposition to Strauß grew even within Christian-Democratic ranks, for Defense Minister Strauß confirmed some of Adenauer's greatest fears. A few weeks after becoming Defense Minister, Strauß responded to the Soviet invasion of Hungary by publicly criticizing American passivity and reassuring Germans they had nothing to worry about, for they were now members of an alliance strong enough "to wipe the Soviet empire clean off the map."[98] In the summer of 1957, several weeks after Strauß married the daughter of a prosperous Bavarian brewer, the East German *Berliner Zeitung* (Berlin Times) exposed Strauß's collection of girlfriends and his frequenting of brothels; the West German press then picked up the story and Alois Hundhammer, the leader of the CSU's clerical conservatives, denounced him and read the story aloud at a meeting of CSU politicians.[99] Strauß was humiliated. In Adenauer's judgment the revelations "cut him to the quick" and for several months he "withdrew completely into himself," muttering darkly about the dangers of believing communist propaganda. At about the same time he made some "extremely disparaging comments" about Generals Adolf Heusinger and Hans Speidel, postwar Germany's top generals, in the presence of fourteen journalists. No wonder Adenauer confided to President Theodor Heuss that, "the behavior of the Defense Minister (blustering manner, tactlessness, especially after consuming alcohol) gives him very great anxiety."[100]

Turning Point

By 1957 Strauß had become quite conscious of the desirability of promoting Bavaria's industrial modernization and was creating and putting into action something like a strategy.

The installation of Strauß in the Defense Ministry in October 1956 not only made this strategy possible, it signified the CSU's arrival as a force to be reckoned with in Bonn. Under Strauß, the CSU in Bonn was not only exercising unprecedented independence from the CDU, but was exerting considerable influence over the CDU. Prior to October 1956, the CSU had been trying to get into a position from which to do more for the Bavarian interests it represented. After this the CSU began to exercise disproportionate influence over the course of German Christian Democracy and bent its efforts toward making good use of the position it had won for itself. Getting the Defense Ministry proved the masterstroke that created the high-riding CSU—transforming a "have-not" into a "have" party. This southward shift in Germany's center of gravity was a novel experience for Bavarian conservatives. Little in Bavarian history had led them to expect success of this sort. But it also forced them to adjust to a more ruthless politics as the CSU became a more serious rival to the CDU and FDP.

For Strauß and the State Group were not satisfied to consolidate their new position. Rather Strauß tried to climb higher in Bonn. He set to work to turn the Defense Ministry into a CSU empire, and had ambitions to become chancellor. The State Group followed his lead. After all, he had nearly always been successful, not only for himself but also for the CSU and Bavaria. But we see in retrospect that Strauß had pushed CSU power in Bonn about as far as it could go: prior to 1956 the CSU had never held four ministries, and though it would continue to hold four until 1965, never again would it hold such a prestigious and powerful combination as Defense, Finance, Atomic Affairs, and Post. Yet Strauß thought that CSU power in Bonn might be pushed still farther. After 1956 Strauß became a fascinating spectacle to the German media, and much of the fascination of his personality came from the suspense of watching him try to push his power a bit higher, into a danger zone, wondering when his actions would call forth a reaction. Opposition was growing in the FDP and even in the CDU, whose leaders saw the CSU, with 20 percent of the total Christian-Democratic vote, take 27 percent of the Christian-Democratic ministries, and who saw their own policies undercut by CSU deputies who sat in on their councils; they resented it when, because of his defense-industrial "irresponsibility," Strauß was able to bind key industrial interests to the CSU. Here especially Strauß pushed ever farther. Adenauer's advisor Heinrich Krone asked himself: "Is Strauß trying ... through the demand that he be responsible for everything that touches on defense, to create a monopoly—a monopoly for himself? I categorically oppose such a concentration of power. That would be a bitter fight. If Strauß goes further down this road, it will be his undoing."[101]

Notes

1. Lanzinner, *Zwischen Sternenbanner und Bundesadler,* 374.
2. Wilhelm Hoegner address of 11.1.55, reproduced in *Dokumente zur Geschichte von Staat und Gesellschaft in Bayern,* Abt. III, Bayern im 19. und 20. Jahrhundert, vol. 9, *Die Regierungen, 1945-1962,* Karl Bosl, ed. (Munich, 1976), 197-225. Peter Jakob Kock, *Der bayerische Landtag: Eine Chronik* (Würzburg, 1996), 105.
3. Kock, *Bayerische Landtag,* 105.
4. BWA, LBI, Seidel to Seeling, 12.4.54; Aktennotiz. 27.7.55. Bößenecker, *Bayern, Bosse und Bilanzen,* 23.
5. ACSP, GFLVor, 8.1.55. Alf Mintzel, *Die CSU. Anatomie einer konservativen Partei 1945-1972* (Opladen, 1975, 1978), 274f, 286f.
6. Mintzel, *Anatomie,* 294f. Interview with Friedrich Zimmermann in *Geschichte einer Volkspartei.* Schlemmer, *Aufbruch,* 483. Herbert Riehl-Heyse, *CSU, die Partei, die das schöne Bayern erfunden hat* (Munich, 1979), 63-71.
7. Aline Marie Kuntz, "Conservatives in Crisis: The Bavarian CSU and the Ideology of Antimodernism" (Ph.D. diss., Cornell, 1987), 25f.
8. Alf Mintzel, *Die CSU-Hegemonie in Bayern: Strategie und Erfolg; Gewinner und Verlierer* (Passau, 1999), 43-72, 97ff.
9. Schlemmer, *Aufbruch,* 482.
10. Arnold Toynbee, *A Study of History,* vol. 1, Somervell abridgment (New York, 1947), 63.
11. Interview with Richard Stücklen in *Geschichte einer Volkspartei.* QQ
12. Irvin C. Bupp and Jean-Claude Derian, *Light Water: How the Nuclear Dream Dissolved* (New York, 1978), 21. Susan Boenke, *Entstehung und Entwicklung des Max-Planck-Instituts für Plasmaphysik, 1955-1971* (Frankfurt a.M., 1991), 46; Peter Weilemann, *Die Anfänge der Europäischen Atomgemeinschaft: zur Gründungsgeschichte von EURATOM 1955-1957* (Baden-Baden, 1983), 53.
13. Franz Josef Strauß, "Deutschland im friedlichen Atomwettkampf," *SZ,* 10/11.12.55.
14. BHA, StK, 114004, Ministerratssitzungsprotokoll, 15.12.54. Walter Stain, cited in Manfred Treml, ed., *Geschichte des modernen Bayern. Königreich und Freistaat* (Munich, 1994), 489f. Hoegner's address of 11.1.55, in *Dokumente,* 205. "Weniger Stromhandel—mehr Stromproduktion!" *CSU-Correspondenz,* 1.7.55. "Vernachlässigte Energiewirtschaft," *SZ,* 2./3.7.55.
15. Deutinger, *High-Tech-Staat,* 141.
16. IFZ, NL Hoegner, Ministerratsprotokolle vom 11.1.55. NL Heisenberg, Korrespondenz, Heisenberg to Meinzolt, 7.12.54. Strauß, *Erinnerungen* (Berlin, 1989), 221. Joachim Radkau, *Aufstieg und Krise der deutschen Atomwirtschaft 1945-1975: Verdrängte Alternativen in der Kerntechnik und der Ursprung der nuklearen Kontroverse* (Reinbek bei Hamburg, 1983), 43f. Alistair Horne, *Return to Power: A Report on the New Germany* (New York, 1956), 319. Boenke, *Entstehung und Entwicklung,* 94. BWA, LBI Geschäftsbericht 1955, 20ff.

17. IFZ, NL Hoegner, Ministerratsprotokolle vom 21.2.55, 22.3.55, 28.3.55, 5.4.55, 19.4.55. Deutinger, *High-Tech-Staat,* 137ff. Boenke, *Entstehung und Entwicklung,* 94f. Wilhelm Hoegner, *Der schwierige Außenseiter. Erinnerungen eines Abgeordneten, Emigranten und Ministerpräsidenten* (Munich, 1959), 330. Staudt, "Anfänge Bayerischer Atompolitik," 45ff.
18. Winnacker, *Nie den Mut verlieren,* 309. Radkau, *Aufstieg und Krise,* 43. Staudt, "Anfänge Bayerischer Atompolitik," 51f., 65.
19. Balke, "Chemiewirtschaft in Bayern," 23f. Boenke, *Entstehung und Entwicklung,* 45, 53ff. Horne, *Return to Power,* 317ff.
20. "Kulturpolitische Aufgabe in Westdeutschland," *NZZ,* 22.1.57 (Fernausgabe). Hoegner, *Schwierige Außenseiter,* 331. See also Hoegner's "Erklärung über die Ziele seiner Regierung—17-Punkte-Programm" of 17.1.56, reproduced in *Dokumente,* 227-244. Kock, *Der Bayerische Landtag,* 113.
21. Strauß, *Erinnerungen,* 230-231. "Kulturpolitische Aufgabe in Westdeutschland," *NZZ,* 22.1.57 (Fernausgabe). Bernd-A. Rusinek, "Das Porträt Leo Brandt (1908-1971)," *Geschichte im Westen* 6, no. 1 (1991): 87. Deutinger, *High-Tech-Staat,* 147.
22. "Kulturelles Schwerpunktprogramm," *MM,* 31.10.56. CSU-Fraktion im Bayerischen Landtag, ed., *In Verantwortung für Bayern. 50 Jahre CSU-Fraktion im Bayerischen Landtag 1946-1996* (Munich, 1996), 143. Kock, *Bayerische Landtag,* 115.
23. Speech of Dr. Hildegard Hamm-Brücher, released in 12.56, can be found at BHA, MK, 66042. "Kulturpolitische Aufgabe in Westdeutschland," *NZZ,* 22.1.57 (Fernausgabe). Burghard Freudenfeld, "Die Forschung und der Föderalismus," *SZ,* 3/4.11.56.
24. BHA, MK, 65981, Niederschrift, 18/19.6.56. "Kulturpolitische Aufgabe in Westdeutschland," *NZZ,* 22.1.57 (Fernausgabe).
25. ACSP, Protokolle der Landesgruppe, 2. Wahlperiode, 20, 21.5.55. Krone, *Tagebücher,* vol. 1, 168, 171, 174. "Atom-Ministerium vorläufig vertagt," *MM,* 7.10.55. Hans Ehlert, "Innenpolitische Auseinandersetzungen um die Pariser Verträge und die Wehrverfassung 1954 bis 1956," in *Anfänge westdeutscher Sicherheitspolitik,* vol. 3, 437.
26. ACSP, NL Strauß, 211, Strauß to Adenauer, 9.7.55, Adenauer to Strauß, 13.7.55; 245, Jaeger to Strauß, 15.6.55; Büro BMVg, 899, Limmer to Strauß, 16.5.55. Krone, *Tagebücher,* vol. 1, 183, 186. *Die Welt,* 16.9.55.
27. ACSP, NL Strauß, 211, Adenauer to Strauß, 19.9.55. Ammann, "Haltung der CSU," 62ff.
28. ACSP, Protokolle der Landesgruppe, 2. Wahlperiode, 34, 27.9.55. Krone, *Tagebücher,* vol. 1, 190.
29. Radkau, *Aufstieg und Krise,* 176, fn 1065, 40, 43, 138. Catherine McArdle Kelleher, *Germany and the Politics of Nuclear Weapons* (New York and London, 1975), 40. Christian Greiner, "Die militärische Eingliederung der Bundesrepublik Deutschland in die WEU und die NATO 1954 bis 1957," in *Anfänge westdeutscher Sicherheitspolitik,* vol. 3, 690f.
30. ACSP, NL Strauß, Büro BMVg, VI, 210, Strauß to Adenauer, 5.5.56. ACSP, Rep. Landesgruppe, 2. Wahlperiode, 88, Für *Bayernkurier,* 24 or 25.10.55. Ammann, "Haltung der CSU," 74.
31. BWA, LBI, Sitzung des Präsidiums, 22.9.55. Winnacker, *Nie den Mut verlieren,* 314. Radkau, *Aufstieg und Krise,* 137, 138, 170, 506 fn. 734. Karsten Prüß, *Kernforschungspolitik in der BRD* (Frankfurt a.M., 1974), 38. Boenke, *Entstehung und Entwicklung,* 47.
32. ACSP, Protokolle der Landesgruppe, 2. Wahlperiode, 31, 10/11.9.55. BA, NL Höcherl, 170, Pressekonferenz of 28.10.55. Winnacker, *Nie den Mut verlieren,* 315. Radkau, *Aufstieg und Krise,* 27. Boenke, *Entstehung und Entwicklung,* 51. Müller, *Geschichte der Kernenergie,* 154. Weilemann, *Die Anfänge der Europäischen Atomgemeinschaft,* 50, 54-57. Staudt, "Anfänge Bayerischer Atompolitik," 13.
33. Strauß, *Erinnerungen,* 234ff. Winnacker, *Nie den Mut verlieren,* 315. Boenke, *Entstehung und Entwicklung,* 49f. Radkau, *Aufstieg und Krise,* 133ff, 146.
34. Radkau, *Aufstieg und Krise,* 37, 101ff, 163ff.
35. Franz Josef Strauß, "Der Kampf der Klassenzimmer," *Schweinfurter Volksblatt,* 27.1.56. ACSP, Rep. Landesgruppe, 2. Wahlperiode, Rede, 26.1.56. Strauß, *Erinnerungen,* 232.
36. ACSP, NL Strauß, Büro BMVg, VI, 210, Strauß to Adenauer, 21.9.56. Weilemann, *Die Anfänge der Europäischen Atomgemeinschaft,* 22f, 37ff, 68, 103ff.

37. ACSP, NL Elsen, 4.2.6, Sitzung, 20.2.56. BA, NL Höcherl, 170, Pressekonferenz, 28.10.55. Strauß, *Erinnerungen,* 230f. Weilemann, *Die Anfänge der Europäischen Atomgemeinschaft,* 50, 57f, 67, 93-94. "Plan Euratom," *Der Spiegel* 9, no. 44 (9.11.55): 11f.
38. Andreas Stucke, "Die Raumfahrtpolitik des Forschungsministeriums. Domänenstrukturen und Steuerungsoptionen," in *Technische Visionen - politische Kompromisse: Geschichte und Perspektiven der deutschen Raumfahrt,* ed. Johannes Weyer (Berlin, 1993), 41. ACSP, NL Elsen, 4.2.6, Referat Strauß, 20.2.56.
39. BHA, MK, 66924, Bemerkung Abt. I, 9.3.56.
40. Strauß, *Erinnerungen,* 226, 232.
41. ACSP, NL Elsen, 4.2.6, Referat Strauß, 20.2.56.
42. ACSP, NL Elsen, 4.5.5, Forschungsvorhaben/Niederschrift, 15.5.56. BHA, MK, 66924. Lanzinner, *Zwischen Sternenbanner und Bundesadler,* 378.
43. BHA, MK, 66924, Rucker to Strauß, 23.6.56. ACSP, NL Elsen, 4.2.6, Referat Strauß, 20.2.56. Hoegner, *Schwierige Außenseiter,* 331. Deutinger, *High-Tech-Staat,* 145f. Staudt, "Anfänge Bayerischer Atompolitik," 66ff.
44. Strauß, *Erinnerungen,* 222ff.
45. ACSP, LVor, 22.6.56. Otto Schedl, "Die Stimme der Opposition in Bayern," *AZ* (Munich), 29.11.56. CSU-Fraktion im Bayerischen Landtag, ed., *In Verantwortung für Bayern. 50 Jahre CSU-Fraktion im Bayerischen Landtag 1946-1996* (Munich, 1996), 145. Hanns Seidel, *Weltanschauung und Politik* (Munich, 1961), 117. Staudt, "Anfänge Bayerischer Atompolitik," 16.
46. *Adenauer: "Wir haben wirklich etwas geschaffen": die Protokolle des CDU-Bundesvorstands 1953-1957,* ed. Günter Buchstab (Düsseldorf, 1990), 1095.
47. "Neue Atom-Probleme," *MM,* 14.3.56. See also ACSP, Protokolle der Landesgruppe, 2. Wahlperiode, 17, 29.5.56; NL Elsen, 4.2.6, Protokolle/Sitzung, 6.6.56. Radkau, *Aufstieg und Krise,* 83f.
48. ASCP, Protokolle der Landesgruppe, 2. Wahlperiode, 32, 13.11.56. Staudt, "Anfänge Bayerischer Atompolitik," 55.
49. BA, B102, 41037, Gesellschaft für die Entwicklung der Atomkraft in Bayern, Projektplanung, and Schwarz to Westrick, 11.10.57. BWA, LBI Geschäftsbericht 1956; LBI Tätigkeitsbericht 1957. BWA, LBI, Ordner, 1.55-6.56. ACSP, NL Strauß, Büro BMVg, III, 182, Balke to Strauß, 14.12.56; Strauß to Balke, 15.12.56; Rep. Landesgruppe, 2. Wahlperiode, 68, Atomfragen, Landesgruppe CSU, Pressestelle, 9.5.57. Winnacker, *Nie den Mut verlieren,* 314, 324. Manfred Pohl, *Das Bayernwerk, 1921 bis 1996* (Munich, 1996), 379. Staudt, "Anfänge Bayerischer Atompolitik," 33f. "Nase verloren," *Der Spiegel* 11, no. 25 (10.7.57):13.
50. Krone, *Tagebücher,* vol. 1, 158.
51. Krone, *Tagebücher,* vol. 1, 158.
52. BA, B102, 15551, H2, Aktennotiz, 10.2.55. Kelleher, *Politics of Nuclear Weapons,* 9f, 20f, 26f, 30, 133ff, 143. Andres, *Luft- und Raumfahrtindustrie,* 140ff, 147ff, 170ff, 187.
53. ACSP, NL Strauß, Büro BMVg, VI, 190, Strauß to Erhard, 9.7.55. BWA, LBI, Niederschrift, 12.1.55. ACSP, LVor, 4.7.55. Krone, *Tagebücher,* vol. 1, 155, 161, 171, 174.
54. ACSP, Rep. Landesgruppe, 2. Wahlperiode, 87. MILITÄR, BV3, W II, 11802, Höcherl to Strauß, 30.7.57; 13953, Vermerk, 18.7.57. Ammann, "Haltung der CSU," 59, 69-70.
55. ACSP, Rep. Landesgruppe, 2. Wahlperiode, no. 89, Landesgruppe CSU, Pressestelle, 4.5.56; Donat to Karl-Heinz Sottong, 25.5.56. BHA, BBbB, 1048. Hoegner Regierungserklärung, 23.3.55, in *Dokumente,* 226-227. *CSU-Correspondenz* 6, no. 99 (16.9.55): 2ff. BHA, BBbB, 1048. "Die Länder schalten sich in das Rüstungsgespräch ein," *FAZ,* 4.12.54. Abelshauser in *Anfänge westdeutscher Sicherheitspolitik,* vol. 4, 141.
56. Marc Trachtenberg, *A Constructed Peace: The Making of the European Settlement, 1945-1963* (Princeton, 1999), 146-201. John Lewis Gaddis, *Strategies of Containment: A Critical Appraisal of Postwar American National Security Policy* (Oxford, 1982), 127-197.
57. Gerhard Brandt, *Rüstung und Wirtschaft in der Bundesrepublik* (Witten and Berlin, 1966), 161. Kelleher, *Politics of Nuclear Weapons,* 40.

58. BWA, LBI, Präsidialsitzung, 30.1.56; Rundschreiben, 9.2.56; Präsidialsitzung, 3.5.56; Hauptausschußsitzung, 3.5.56. 5. Abelshauser in *Anfänge westdeutscher Sicherheitspolitik,* vol. 4, 153. Brandt, *Rüstung und Wirtschaft,* 164-170, 186.
59. Andres, *Luft- und Raumfahrtindustrie,* 151. Kurt Johannson, *Vom Starfighter zum Phantom* (Frankfurt a.M., 1969), 11. *Wehrtechnisches Monatsheft,* 3/1957, p. 86 and BDI-Jahresbericht, 1955/56, Köln 1956, pp. 181, 184. Abelshauser in *Anfänge westdeutscher Sicherheitspolitik,* vol. 4, 155.
60. BWA, LBI, Sitzung des Präsidiums, 22.9.55; Geschäftsbericht 1955. "Wehrwirtschaftliche Sorgen," *MM,* 3.2.56. "Bayerns Industrie kritisiert Blank. Landesverband vermißt wehrwirtschaftliche Planung," *SZ,* 4.5.56. "Wirtschaft verschuldet sich beim Staat," *MM,* 4.5.56.
61. BWA, LBI, Sitzung des Präsidiums, 10.7.56.
62. "Für eine Qualitätsarmee," *Die Zeit, 10.5.56. Johannson, Vom Starfighter zum Phantom,* 9ff. Andres, *Luft- und Raumfahrtindustrie,* 180f. Brandt, *Rüstung und Wirtschaft,* 188. Rilling, *Kriegsforschung,* 14. *Adenauer: "Wir haben wirklich etwas geschaffen,"* 1126.
63. Brandt, *Rüstung und Wirtschaft,* 187. Johannson, *Vom Starfighter zum Phantom,* 14.
64. *Adenauer: "Wir haben wirklich etwas geschaffen",* 1125. Strauß, *Erinnerungen,* 272. Rudolf Morsey and Hans-Peter Schwarz, eds., *Unter Vier Augen: Gespräche aus den Gründerjahren/ Konrad Adenauer; Theodor Heuss* (Berlin, 1997), 206f. Volker Hentschel, *Ludwig Erhard: ein Politikerleben* (Berlin, 1998), 372.
65. "CSU kritisiert das Verteidigungsministerium," *SZ,* 13.9.55. Johannson, *Vom Starfighter zum Phantom,* 9ff.
66. ACSP, NL Strauß, BMVg, 669, Landesgruppe CSU, Pressestelle, 18.9.56. ACSP, Protokolle der Landesgruppe, 2. Wahlperiode, 26, 16/17.9.56 (Strauß emphasized that, "the policy of the government must be changed, above all it must fulfill the demands of the CSU for a better coordination of industrial and defense policy.... The CSU has to press very vehemently for the realization of these goals. Above all it must maintain its unity, as it remains the only political group capable of taking action on this issue"). *Bayern-Kurier,* 22.9.56, p. 1 ("In its meeting at Kirchheim palace in September 1956, the CSU State Group demanded that German industry be given its share of the manufacturing and provisioning of weapons and other military equipment. An appropriate share of this defense spending should go to the scientific and technological fields in which Germany once led but is no longer capable of competing, in order to be able to measure up to new technical and strategic challenges."). Brandt, *Rüstung und Wirtschaft,* 190. Kelleher, *Politics of Nuclear Weapons,* 45ff.
67. Krone, *Tagebücher,* vol. 1, 229. *WBH,* 2, nr. 38 (20.9.56). Schwarz, *Adenauer,* vol. 2, 275.
68. Ehlert in *Anfänge westdeutscher Sicherheitspolitik,* vol. 3, 542. "CSU entwickelt ein eigenes Wehrprogramm," *SZ,* 19.9.56.
69. Daniel Koerfer, *Kampf ums Kanzleramt: Erhard und Adenauer* (Stuttgart, 1987), 118ff.
70. Morsey and Schwarz, *Unter Vier Augen,* 210. Strauß, *Erinnerungen,* 271-279. Krone, *Tagebücher,* vol. 1, 230. *WBH* 2, no. 40 (4.10.56).
71. BA, B102, 76252, Berg to Erhard, 1.10.56. Milosch, "Die Rolle von Franz Josef Strauß," 28ff.
72. Strauß, *Erinnerungen,* 274. Krone, *Tagebücher,* vol. 1, 231. Morsey and Schwarz, *Unter Vier Augen,* 215. *FAZ,* 18.10.56.
73. FRUS, 1955-1957, vol. XXVI, Beam to Sec'y of State, 20.10.56, p. 170, and "Progress Report on U.S. Policy toward the FRG," 181ff.
74. Strauß further wrote that "An examination of the statistical data reveals that Bavarian industry has done very well indeed from defense contracts, as we can see from the following official numbers (reflecting the position as of January 31, 1957), and which I pass on to you confidentially: with a total of DM 462,000,000 in contracts (27% of the total domestic contracts) Bavaria marches *absolutely* at the head of all the states of the Federal Republic. In second place and a considerable distance behind comes North Rhine-Westphalia with DM 326,000,000, or 19%. Per capita, DM 50 is being spent in Bavaria, as opposed to DM 23 in Hesse, DM 22 in North Rhine-Westphalia, and DM 7 (!) in the Rhineland-Palatinate, while the average for the

Federal Republic is DM 37. Approximately 20% of all Bavarian contractors go to firms owned by exile Germans, firms along the Iron Curtain and other privileged firms. Approximately 28% of all Bavarian defense contractors are small- or middle-sized firms with fewer than fifty employees. I must say that I myself was surprised by these numbers, especially that Bavaria has received more contracts than North Rhine-Westphalia." MILITÄR, BW 9, 4202, Strauß to Bayerischen Staatsminister für Arbeit; Rentrop to Sottong, 12.3.57; Letter to Strauß, 14.2.57.

75. BA, NL Schäffer, 60, 20.5.57 (from 1951 to 1954 only 13% of the German defense budget had flowed to Bavaria). Andres, *Luft- und Raumfahrtindustrie,* 202f.
76. Andres, *Luft- und Raumfahrtindustrie,* 186.
77. Horne, *Return to Power,* 321-322. Abelshauser in *Anfänge westdeutscher Sicherheitspolitik,* vol. 4, 168.
78. Andres, *Luft- und Raumfahrtindustrie,* 103, 189ff.
79. ACSP, NL Elsen, 2.11, Elsen to Strauß, 19.11.56; 2.12, Elsen to Strauß, 2.1.57, Elsen to Strauß, 16.1.57, Strauß to Elsen, 22.11.57, Dornier-Werke to Elsen, 15.1.57. BA, B102, 15367, Vermerk, 29.11.56; B136, 1570. Jürgen Seidl, "Schwieriger Neuanfang—Wiederaufbau und Expansion der BMW AG unter besonderer Berücksichtigung der Unternehmensbeziehungen zum Staat (1945/48-1969)" (Ph.D. dissertation, Regensburg, 2001), 199-204.
80. Seidl, "Schwieriger Neuanfang," 212ff.
81. Alfred Mechtersheimer, *Rüstung und Politik in der Bundesrepublik: MRCA Tornado: Geschichte und Funktion des größten westeuropäischen Rüstungsprogramm* (Bad Honnef, 1977), 23.
82. MILITÄR, BV 3, 11784, Betr. Messerschmitt, 9.10.56; Zietsch to Bundesverteidigungsministerium, 8.11.56; Besuch Münemann, 7.12.56; 12156, Stellungnahme, 24.10.56. "Im Schatten der Aufrüstung," *Der Spiegel* 10, no. 48 (28.11.56): 17.
83. MILITÄR, BV3, WII, 12156, Kiefer to Goetze, 17.11.56; Kiefer to Bezold, 8.11.56; Vermerk, 7.2.57; Vermerk, 18.2.57; 12157, Vermerk, 11.4.57.
84. MILITÄR, BV3, WII, 12156, Brief, 21.12.56; 11784, Zietsch to Strauß, 3.12.56; 11742, Besprechungsergebnis, 10.1.57; Notiz, 20.7.57. These numbers come from "Neuordnung der Messerschmitt AG," *Industriekurier,* 15.1.57. Different numbers are given in "Die Messerschmitt AG ist neu geboren," *Handelsblatt,* 20.2.57. BHA, MWi, 25928, Strauß Fernschreiben, 4.1.57; Notiz, 30.1.57.
85. BHA, BBbB, 1048.
86. BHA, BBbB, 1048, Auto-Union to Strauß, 5.3.57; Schmidt to von Dessauer, 6.5.57; Schmidt to Leusser, 15.10.57; Leusser to Schmidt, 17.10.57.
87. BA, Bundeskanzleramt, 6896, Vermerk, 20.5.57, Betr. Artikelserie. Peter Miska, "Das Geschäft mit der Rüstung (IV)," *Frankfurter Rundschau,* 17.4.57.
88. BA, B102, 015485, Vermerk, 12.6.57.
89. BA, B102, 015485, Boecker to Benecke, 10.7.57; Bölkow to Flughafen Stuttgart, 14.1.58; Niederschrift 31.10.57. BHA, MWi, 25927, Bölkow to BMVg, 1.10.57; Bölkow to BMWi, 8.10.57; Niederschrift 22.8.57; Teicher to Fernmeldeamt.
90. BA, B102, 015485, Niederschrift, 6.12.57; Bölkow to Bundesvermögenstelle, 9.12.57; Bölkow to BMW, 18.12.57; von Coelln to Strauß, 21.12.57.
91. BA, B102, 015485, Niederschrift 28.1.58; Bölkow to Wahl, 18.3.58; Boecker to Engelmann, 1.4.58; Engelmann to Boecker, 9.4.58; Boecker, 29.4.58; Darlehensantrag, 30.5.58.
92. Kelleher, *Politics of Nuclear Weapons,* 9f, 26ff. Walter Schwengler, "Der doppelte Anspruch: Souveränität und Sicherheit. Zur Entwicklung des völkerrechtlichen Status der Bundesrepublik Deutschland 1945 bis 1955," in *Anfänge westdeutscher Sicherheitspolitik,* vol. 4, 493f.
93. ACSP, Protokolle der Landesgruppe, 2. Wahlperiode, 29, 23.10.56; NL Seidel, 10, Rundfunkansprache, 17.4.57.
94. ACSP, Rep. Landesgruppe CSU, 2. Wahlperiode, 88, Geschäftsstelle, 9.12.57.
95. Andres, *Luft- und Raumfahrtindustrie,* 206.
96. Johannson, *Vom Starfighter zum Phantom,* 17.

97. Hoegner, *Schwierige Außenseiter,* 323. Peter Kritzer, *Wilhelm Hoegner. Politische Biographie eines bayerischen Sozialdemokraten* (Munich, 1979), 336. Krieger, *Strauß: barocke Demokrat,* 31.
98. Strauß, *Erinnerungen,* 298-299.
99. "Kriegsminister als Heiratsschwindler," *Berliner Zeitung* (East Berlin), 12.6.57. *Der Spiegel* 11, no. 25 (10.7.57): 18-20. Wolfram Bickerich, *Franz Josef Strauß: Die Biographie* (Düsseldorf, 1996), 132.
100. Morsey and Schwarz, *Unter Vier Augen,* 222, 233.
101. Krone, *Tagebücher,* vol. 1, 276.

CHAPTER 3

THE GREAT LEAP FORWARD, 1957–1962

A Window of Opportunity

One of the great circumstances that the CSU took advantage of in the years from 1957 to 1962 was the years themselves. Never was that window of opportunity that the defeat and division of Germany had created for Bavaria open so wide as in this half decade. Before 1957 the country was too busy getting up and running again to relocate its industries or its scientific research institutes. After the early 1960s its industries were rooted in new networks of connections and its research institutes anchored in new locations, so that politicians who would improve the relative position of their states by promoting their relocation found the inertial weight of the existing state of affairs increasing fast.

The other great circumstance was that the years from 1957 to 1962 were also those in which the CSU reached its maximal power position in German politics. Never again would the CSU's overall political position be as strong as it was from its great triumph in the 1957 federal election and the subsequent breakup of the Coalition of Four to the end of 1962. Never again would the CSU be so well-positioned to both benefit from the social market economy and make the federal budget work for Bavaria. Strauß was the Defense Minister, one of the three or four most powerful politicians in Germany, and firmly in control of the State Group, which had a ministerial contingent of four. Meanwhile, in Munich, Hanns Seidel and his liberal lieutenants dominated the political landscape. For the CSU's victory in the 1957 federal election had consequences in Bavaria: the nonsocialist parties deserted the Coalition of Four, and the CSU formed a token

Notes for this section begin on page 119.

coalition with the FDP and the Alliance of the Homelandless and Wronged, giving them minor posts, in which they were unable to profile themselves and quickly found themselves dragged under in the CSU's wake. The Bavaria Party was left out in the cold, and then its destruction brought about in the sordid "Casino Affair" ("Spielbankenaffäre"). All of these developments tended to harmonize the priorities of the CSU leaders in Bonn and Munich.

We have kept up with Strauß and the State Group in Bonn; now it is time to catch up with Hanns Seidel and the CSU in Munich. Seidel seemed the right man to bring Bavaria through the window of opportunity. His earlier contribution to Bavaria's industrial modernization had been to elevate economic policy and the Economic Ministry, and to promote the idea that for the common future of Bavaria and the CSU Bavaria had to modernize its industrial base and that the Bavarian state support scientific research and industrial modernization. In his first state of the state speech in November 1957 he offered a Ten Point Program calling on his government to address Bavaria's energy problem, which he described as Bavaria's "fundamental problem," and to support industry-oriented research (that is, the Fraunhofer Foundation, aerospace research, and atomic research). He wanted his ministers to continue some of the policies of the Coalition of Four that had been popular with industry, such as increased spending for technical training, and, even more, to pick up some of the policies he had pursued as Bavarian Economic Minister from 1947 to 1954: both the Fraunhofer Foundation and aerospace research had been neglected by the Coalition of Four, caught up as it had been in the race for the now-dissolving atomic mirage.[1]

Seidel proved popular with voters and remained so with industry. His "cool" style, moderate, tolerant, cooperative, objective, and earnest, provided a healthy contrast to Strauß's polemics and anticipated by several years a general movement away from ideology, confrontation, and polemic in German politics. His moderate line helped to defuse the controversy over Catholic education that had embittered Bavarian politics for years.[2] Certainly Bavarian industry was satisfied that with Seidel as Minister-President Bavaria was in "the best hands."[3] Seidel had maintained his close relationship with industry, but, like Strauß, signaled his determination to maintain a decent independence. This was evident in the dispute over the "Bavaria Calls Industry" advertising campaign. The Coalition of Four had initiated this campaign to puff Bavaria to industry—its cheap land, its large labor pool, and its "well-balanced" wage structure (a charming euphemism, certainly). Rolf Rodenstock, the President of the LBI, had voiced his angry objections to the Coalition of Four's FDP Economic Minister. Rodenstock's plain concern was to keep wages down. The response of the Coalition of Four had been defensive but insistent. The CSU likewise refused to terminate the campaign, but did agree to direct its advertising away from American industry, which had a reputation for paying high wages.[4]

But Seidel's role came to an early end. Shortly before the 1958 election he suffered a spinal injury in a head-on collision and he never recovered. Unable to participate actively in his government, he resigned as Minister-President in January

1960 and as party chairman in February 1961, and died in May 1961. Strauß easily won the party chairmanship, and to fill the Minister-Presidency the CSU turned again to Hans Ehard, its conservative but not clericalist Minister President from 1949 to 1953, whose political weakness within the CSU translated into greater scope of action for his ministers.

Black Politics and Red Oil

Seidel's torch for the industrial modernization of Bavaria was picked up by Otto Schedl, his protégé, who henceforth figures as a major player in our story. Appointed to Seidel's old position as Bavarian Economic Minister in 1957, he promoted Bavaria's move into the age of oil. As historian Paul Erker held, this set the switches in Bavaria for further industrial modernization.[5] Schedl's life epitomized the CSU's liberal wing. During the Third Reich a young journalist, scholar, member of the Nazi party (as were more than a few of the CSU liberals), and soldier on the Russian front, after the war Schedl joined the CSU and associated himself with Chairman Josef Müller, who appointed him CSU party secretary.[6] Conservative machinations denied him a safe seat in the federal parliament, and in 1950 he was elected to the Bavarian parliament, where Seidel relied on him as the media voice of the CSU state parliamentary deputies (during the Coalition of Four he wrote a regular column for Munich's *Abendzeitung*, or Evening News), to address economic questions, and to conduct the negotiations that broke the Coalition of Four.

Like Strauß and Seidel before him, Schedl succeeded because he found levers with which he could move players far bigger than the CSU and take advantage of circumstances and events that were far beyond his party's control.

Most beyond its control was a rapid change in the world economy of energy, which made and broke industries and energy policies throughout the industrialized world. In the mid 1950s the major international oil companies discovered a series of "elephants," gigantic oilfields, in the Middle East. At the same time they developed pipelines to transport the oil. This led to price wars for the European market, and, since the British, French, and Italian governments protected their national markets for their national firms, above all for the German market.[7] Oil prices in Germany collapsed: whereas in 1957 the price of heavy heating oil in Hamburg stood at DM 146 per ton, by 1958 it fell to DM 88 and by the end of 1959 to DM 66. Light heating oil and gasoline told a similar story. In 1957 light heating oil was 242 DM/ton; 1958 155 DM/ton; end of 1959 133 DM/ton.[8] This encouraged German industry and homeowners to switch from coal to heating oil for the generation of heat, and in some cases even for generating electricity.

This had implications for Bavaria. Bavarian industry had long compensated for its high energy costs by paying low wages, but by the mid 1950s Bavarian industrialists began to feel the pinch of a labor shortage.[9] Industrialists feared that, in the approaching era of full employment, the large pool of available labor in Bavaria would dry up, wages and production costs would rise, Bavarian industry would no longer be competitive, and that this would be the end of the postwar Bavarian economic recovery. By the time Hanns Seidel formed his government in 1957, after the discrediting of the hopes that had been placed in atomic energy, many in industry and government believed that many Bavarian industries would have to migrate northward and that there was no way but that Bavaria would lose more ground.

For it was by no means clear that the turn to oil was good news for Bavaria. Just as coal had to be transported to Bavaria from the distant mines of North Rhine-Westphalia, oil had to be transported from northern German seaports, and petroleum products cost 50 percent more in Bavaria than in Hamburg.[10] Although pipelines had recently been developed and when used to capacity were by far the cheapest way to transport crude oil to refinery locations, the powerful lobbies of the Federal Railway and inland waterways argued against them, and the oil companies were reluctant to make the enormous initial investment. Only a few short oil pipelines were built in Germany: in 1957 the oil companies decided to build one from Wilhelmshaven to Cologne; and in 1958 another from Rotterdam to the Rhine; in 1958 the oil companies tentatively projected to build one from Marseilles to Karlsruhe.[11] No one planned to build a pipeline anywhere near Bavaria, at least not until the Marseilles-Karlsruhe line was extended to southeast Germany, which was vaguely expected to happen in the late 1960s or early 1970s.

Whether or not oil solved the problem of relative prices within Germany, oil was absolutely cheaper than coal and German consumers turned to it en masse. In the early and mid 1950s, the federal government, seeing that coal production could not keep up with energy demand and acting in accord with its trade liberalism, had removed taxes and tariffs from oil. The coal interests did not protest. Then in 1957, only one day after the federal election in which the CDU/CSU won an absolute majority, the coal industry raised its prices, creating the impression that industry, which had supported Adenauer, had pulled a fast one on consumers. But this was followed by the recession of 1957–1958 and the collapse in oil prices followed. Coal stockpiles grew and the coal industry laid off miners for the first time since World War II. Industry representatives met with Adenauer and Erhard in late 1958; Adenauer, worried about votes that would go to the Social Democrats in the event of layoffs, expressed his sympathy but Erhard did not. Erhard and many others saw the sudden decline of the coal industry and the rise of oil as a worldwide "organic development," a stroke of luck for Germany as the wave of oil would solve Germany's present and future energy problems, and Erhard let the representatives of coal know that his priority was to encourage the growth of the whole economy by securing its energy at the cheapest possible cost. Many in Adenauer's cabinet shared Erhard's view, and the coal industry, for all of its storied influence in the capital, got no legislative relief. [12] The most the coal interests could achieve in 1958 was a permit for a cartel with the oil interests. This seems to have lulled the coal interests into a false sense of security—false because the big oil companies saw in the agreement merely a way to prevent a price war among themselves. The cartel's list of minimum prices put heating oil in Hamburg, Bremen, and Wilhelmshaven at DM 87.80 per ton, but over DM 133 per ton in Munich—the most expensive city in Germany.[13]

As in other cases we have seen, the CSU was prompted into action more by Bavarian industry than voters. The Bavarian chemical industry was strongly in favor of oil because it was an enormous energy user, and because it required oil in order to make the transition from a coal-based chemical production to petrochemicals, which were at this time revolutionizing the chemical industry around the world. Particularly Hoechst's Bavarian empire was too far from Germany's northern seaports to remain competitive. CSU circles, worried that the Bavarian chemical firms would gradually move their operations northwards, were frightened by Hoechst's 1958 acquisition of 50 percent of Wacker-Chemie, Bavaria's traditional chemical giant, and Wacker's construction of a plant near Cologne.[14]

By late 1958 some Bavarian governmental insiders were in touch with pipeline companies and financiers, trying to get an oil pipeline built to Burghausen, the major city in Bavaria's "chemical triangle" (Chemie Dreieck). They tried, for example, to convince the speculator Rudolf Münemann to build an oil pipeline; he seems to have wanted a Bavarian state guarantee and the state government was cautiously interested.[15] Otto Schedl made at least one direct approach to the oil companies. But they rebuffed him rather rudely. Pipelines led to substantially lower prices, but the initial capital investment was enormous, so that if one oil company built a pipeline, the others would have to follow: in the end no firm would gain a price advantage over any other and all would be saddled with the investment.

Again as in other cases we have seen, it was an impulse from outside Bavaria that got things moving. This time the outsiders were Hjalmar Schacht and Enrico Mattei. Schacht, the famous president of the Reichsbank under the Weimar Republic and the Third Reich, had been acquitted of war crimes at the Nuremberg trial and set up as a private banker in Düsseldorf. He became an advisor to Enrico Mattei, president of ENI (Ente Nazionale Idrocarburi), the Italian national oil company, and through Josef Müller, with whom Schacht had been imprisoned at Dachau concentration camp, arranged for Mattei to meet Schedl. The idea they wanted to propose to Schedl: an oil pipeline to Bavaria, originating not at a northern German but at a Mediterranean seaport.[16]

Mattei, with his willful originality, personified the contingency of this story. His image as a Che Guevara of the boardroom made the Bavarian pipeline a major news story, and, in the perception of the Bavarian public, an adventure and a heroic achievement. Though rarely remembered outside of Italy, from 1958 to 1962 Mattei was one of the most important actors on the world stage. He exercised enormous political power in Italy through the judicious distribution of political contributions and his genius for propaganda, and ran ENI and its vast array of subsidiaries as if they were sole proprietorships. His goal was to build ENI into one of the world's major international oil companies. In the mid 1950s Mattei believed that the major international oil companies were about to come to a new agreement for the division of Middle Eastern oil concessions, and demanded that

ENI should be given an equal share. Dismissed, he was infuriated and resolved either to force the majors to recognize ENI as a member of their cartel, or to force the American government to order them to do so. He pursued his goal by making himself into a nuisance. He toured the Middle-Eastern capitals, offering much better concessionary terms than the majors; a number of countries granted him minor concessions in unprospected territory, and he magnified the effect of these concessions by conducting an aggressive publicity campaign against the majors, claiming that his terms proved how the others exploited the downtrodden of the world. Although Mattei became a hero to many in Italy and the anticolonial movement, he was an egomaniac saddled with a nationalistic inferiority complex, particularly toward America and Britain, which dominated the international oil industry. He was obsessed with his dream of building ENI into an "eighth sister"—it was Mattei who coined the term "the Seven Sisters" as a term of abuse for Exxon, Mobil, Chevron, Texaco, Gulf, Shell, and British Petroleum.

Bavaria was for Mattei only a part of his larger game against the Seven Sisters. By building a pipeline from Trieste or Genoa northwards, he would gain the edge over the majors, whose tankers had to go around Spain to Hamburg. His pipelines would be the first into northern Italy, Switzerland, Austria, and Bavaria, putting him in a position to win price wars throughout the central European market. They would increase his nuisance value, and help him to force his way into the club. Whether or not Schedl suspected the true scope of Mattei's game, he liked Mattei, whose Robin Hood posturings on behalf of southern Europe and the Third World appealed to the resentments the Bavarians felt toward northern Germany, and he recognized that the savings to Bavarian consumers would be enormous.[17] Things started moving in the spring of 1959, when ENI studied the possibility of a pipeline and Schedl hinted vaguely at the possibility of a state financial guarantee.

Events soon proved that even in oil "the market works"—though it didn't have to, for there were barriers to market entry. One of them was uncertainty about the size of the Bavarian market and another the cost and technical difficulties of building a pipeline over the Alps. The major oil companies maintained that these factors made a pipeline unfeasible. Schedl created an authority to say otherwise. In March 1959 he founded Transalpin, an expert commission that would conduct a feasibility study and build up public interest. Schedl appointed civil servants from his ministry, professors of engineering, Bavarian economists, and prominent Bavarian industrialists, above all from the chemical industry, including the commission's chairman, Herbert Berg, General Manager of Wacker-Chemie.[18] Schedl and Transalpin appealed to Bavarian public opinion by implying that northern German interests were holding up energy prices (playing the Prussian card) and to Bavarian industrial opinion by stressing that the state would not finance the pipelines. But they baited their hook for other oil industry renegades. Most of the respondents were on fishing expeditions of their own: a Saudi Arabian sheik, J. Paul Getty and an Italian road-building company.[19] The only serious interest was shown by Mattei, and he still hoped to receive a state guarantee.[20] Schedl jetted around central Europe with him, gave him full encouragement, and kept up a public show of confidence, though it is impossible to know whether he thought Mattei's plans would become a reality, for, in his struggle against the majors, Mattei had stretched ENI's resources to the breaking point.[21]

Politics presented a potentially higher barrier to entry. Here the CDU and the Social Democrats, representing the interests of coal industrialists, miners, and North Rhine-Westphalia, set themselves against the CSU, the CDU liberals, and Ludwig Erhard, who represented the interests of the states that did not produce coal and of household and industrial consumers. The two sides were well-matched and some sort of compromise was inevitable.[22]

Events worked in favor of oil. Already in August 1959 the oil companies, finding themselves undercut by independent wholesalers, cancelled the coal-oil cartel. At that time the economy was picking up and the coal stocks being worked down, so that it was not easy for the coal interests to convince their legislative allies to tax oil.[23] The CDU proposed a tax on heating oil of only DM 30/ton, but, though this would have left heating oil substantially cheaper than coal, the CSU resisted vigorously.[24] As *Der Spiegel* commented, "The Bavarian CSU deputies rose up, without taking much concern for the politics of the coal crisis, as fanatical defenders of oil. Led by the former judge Hermann Höcherl, the chairman of the CSU State Group, they went onto the offensive...Höcherl, the good-old-boy from Brennberg near Regensburg, thundered, 'There is absolutely no doubt that the heating oil tax, as it has been proposed to us, is one nasty piece of work.'" The CSU forced a reduction in the tax to DM 15/ton for heavy heating oil (used by certain industries) and DM 10/ton for light (used by residential consumers and other industries), with part of the tax income to be used for freight subventions for coal.[25]

So in 1959 high barriers to entry could not be erected. Rather the opposition of the special interests, as well as the presence of the controversial Mattei and a fascination with the new pipeline technology, gave the CSU what amounted to free advertising. In late 1959 not only the Bavarian but the national and the industrial press began to follow the story, and Schedl cast himself as the defender of Bavarian interests against northern Germans, as well as of consumers against producers and new industries against old industries. "I haven't found any verse in the Bible where it says that Bavaria must pay the highest prices for coal, gas, heating oil and electricity until the end of time, as it does today." The press picked up his tone: Bavaria had launched a "Counter-Reformation" against the egoism of coal, and cheap energy was the "highest interest of the economy."[26] Schedl became the first and probably last state Economic Minister in postwar Germany whom the national press could identify to its readers by his last name alone.

Events continued to break well for Bavaria. The next attempt to raise a barrier to entry proceeded from the major oil companies, who addressed themselves to Mattei. In December 1959 Eugene Holman, the president of Esso, invited Mattei to meet him in Monte Carlo, where Mattei seems to have expected an invitation to join the international cartel. But Holman treated Mattei like a representative of an inconsequential European oil company and dickered about prices and pipelines, proposing that Mattei and the majors agree to raise prices in Italy and hold off on any central European pipelines. Mattei responded by boasting that his pipeline to Bavaria would also feed refineries in Switzerland and near Stuttgart and that he was planning to establish a dense network of gas stations; Holman countered that if Mattei built his pipeline, the majors would proceed to extend their projected Marseilles-Strasbourg pipeline into Bavaria (this pipeline had been announced in 1958, but then delayed, and there was much uncertainty as to whether it would actually be built). Mattei lost his temper and blustered that his shorter pipeline would allow him to undersell the majors. He left the meeting resolved to build his pipeline.[27]

Mattei's resolution broke the cartel's united front against a Bavarian pipeline. In January 1960, one month after the Mattei-Holman meeting, Schedl officially announced a pipeline—standing next to not Mattei but representatives of Esso and Shell, who would build a joint pipeline and separate refineries. Indeed, there was soon talk of five refineries: British Petroleum, Mobil, and Gelsenberg expressed interest in joining Esso and Shell, and Mattei promised to proceed with his independent pipeline. But most observers thought Mattei would soon be forced out, allowing the majors to leave their pipeline forever on the drawing board. Months after the announcement, the Esso/Shell project was regarded skeptically by industry experts.[28]

But not only did Mattei go forward with his pipeline, he stepped up his campaign against the majors. He seems to have believed that his Arab concessions, price wars, and press war had shaken up the cartel so that it was nearly ready to come to terms with him. To his way of thinking, this was no time to back down in Bavaria; rather a final heave was needed. To scare Washington into brokering a new division of interests, Mattei flew to Moscow in October 1960 and signed a five-year trade agreement to buy Russian oil, which he would get for 40 percent under world prices and pay for with steel pipes and synthetic rubber products produced by SNAM, another company in his empire; the Russians would use his pipes to build their own giant "Friendship" pipeline from central Asia to Bratislava.[29] American and European Cold Warriors saw the Friendship pipeline as the start of a communist "oil offensive," a conspiracy to sabotage and spoil the market. The communists would, so the thinking went, enter the European market from Bratislava, undersell the majors on that market, and cultivate a dependency that could later be politically exploited. When Washington and other NATO capitals accused Mattei of buying "red oil," he responded, plausibly enough, that the Americans had denied his country oil and forced him to secure its supply elsewhere. He also reopened price wars in Italy, and gave interviews to major international newspapers charging that the Anglo-Saxon cartel had kept prices artificially high and held back the development of the European economies.[30]

Meanwhile the coal crisis returned. By mid 1961 it was clear that coal was in the throes of a long-term decline, and Germany was swept by a wave of coal protectionism. The federal government gave subventions to coal and it appeared inevitable that it would soon raise the heating oil tax. Legislative moves were soon under way to get tougher on air and water pollution caused by oil (though not that caused by coal), to raise the costs of the oil companies by requiring the oil industry to hold unnecessarily large oil stocks, and to require long notice and approval procedures for oil pipelines and refineries.[31]

"Red oil" was a dream come true to the coal protectionists. In the months after the erection of the Berlin Wall and the 1961 federal election, coal-friendly journalists and politicians charged in hundreds of newspaper articles that Mattei meant to refine "red oil" in Bavaria and even that he planned to connect his pipeline to the Soviet Friendship pipeline, which would terminate in Bratislava (only ninety miles from the Bavarian border), and to flood central Europe with "political oil." The campaign reached its ridiculous peak in early 1962 when Ludwig Erhard, traveling in America, said in response to a question from the press, "the project for a Soviet refinery near Ingolstadt [in Bavaria] is dead," the decision having been made right before he flew out of Germany.[32] But Erhard had no idea what he was talking about. The project was nothing more than a rumor launched in the press by interested circles. But this led to a spate of articles on Soviet refineries in Bavaria, and the rumor ran in the *Süddeutsche Zeitung* (South German Times), the *Frankfurter Allgemeine Zeitung* and the *Industriekurier* (Industry Courier) that Bavaria was going to extend a guarantee to a Russian refinery. Chancellor Adenauer urgently requested of the CSU ministers in his Cabinet that Schedl be "whistled back" from any such move.[33]

Schedl's tactic was not to deny coal's claims outright but to redirect them. Schedl protested that he sympathized with coal and was willing to help it; the question, he said, was how it should be helped.[34] He argued that Germany should take advantage of the low "political price" of Mattei's Russian oil, but keep imports limited (though later he was forced to request a letter from Mattei, solemnly promising that no Russian oil would flow to Bavaria), and that the greater danger was protectionism and dirigisme, quotas, a concession system, and the attempt of special interests to damage Bavaria by erecting regulatory trade barriers using as pretexts desulphurization, water cleanliness, and the desirability of putting pipelines under the regulatory jurisdiction of the Federal Transport Ministry, requiring the oil companies to maintain large stocks. Though Schedl moderated his tone so as not to agitate the other parties into making use of the northern Germans' anti-Bavarian resentments, the story, with its north-south and east-west angles, played very well in Bavaria, where even the Social Democrats unreservedly supported Schedl.[35] Of course the other energy-poor states, such as Lower Saxony, supported Schedl, but they kept a much lower profile on the issue than the CSU.

While the weight of the publicistic battle was carried by Schedl and the CSU, within the councils of the federal government Ludwig Erhard argued quietly for free trade in energy. Under the political cover provided by Schedl and the CSU, Erhard did not promote Bavarian interests, of course, but the principle of free trade in energy and the benefit that the national economy drew from the oil boom.[36]

The results exceeded expectations. When Esso's and Shell's refineries near Ingolstadt in central Bavaria went into operation in 1963 and 1964, oil prices in Bavaria plummeted.[37] Though they rose again in the mid 1960s, at the end of the decade, Bavarians, who at the end of the 1950s had paid 50 percent more than Hamburgers for petroleum products, paid almost the same price. Bavarian industrial and household consumers rapidly switched from coal to heating oil and the decline in prices had all sorts of collateral effects. The oil refineries made possible the construction of power plants driven by heating oil.[38] A small petrochemicals industry grew up around Ingolstadt, though the refineries near Ingolstadt were not close enough to Burghausen to serve the Wacker and Hoechst plants, which had to wait until the late 1960s for another pipeline to be built over the Alps to refineries near Burghausen.[39] Though it was of little concern to the CSU, ENI was slow to cross the finish line. Mattei's company had problems getting permits from Swiss and Austrian authorities, and from Bavarian municipalities, problems that, it darkly hinted, were due to the machinations of the majors. ENI's pipeline was not completed until 1966. By that time Mattei was dead, having been killed, or possibly murdered, in an airplane accident in 1962. The ENI pipeline and refinery fell miserably short of Mattei's ambitions, as for many years the firm lacked a sales network in southern Germany.

Schedl's personal achievement was overblown in the 1960s, as the press gave credit to his claim to have brought oil to Bavaria almost singlehandedly. It will be easy for future historians to minimize his achievement for the Bavarian economy by arguing that oil pipelines were bound to come to Bavaria eventually.[40] In any case, though Mattei's arrival on the scene probably speeded up the construction of the Marseilles-Karlsruhe pipeline and its extension into Bavaria by five to ten years, the fact remains that it was Mattei who found Schedl, and it seems likely enough that any Bavarian Economic Minister, whether from the CSU or Social Democrats, would have seen the value of Mattei's proposal.

Schedl's contribution was rather the energy and flair with which he took up oil's cause. He made himself a major actor in the contest over energy policy, for four years putting himself and the CSU in the German spotlight as the determined and effective pursuers of an independent economic policy. Schedl's achievement had parallels with some of Strauß's and Seidel's earlier achievements. As in other cases, an initial impetus came from Bavarian industry, magnified by the Bavarian feeling of being "permanently on edge," so that the Bavarian opinion united strongly behind the project and made it politically worthwhile. Whereas the CDU had been weighed down, on other issues, by its responsibility for foreign affairs and its dependence on the Western powers, this time its ball and chain was the working-class Catholic vote of North Rhine-Westphalia, unstably linked to the CDU, whose interests ran contrary to the general interest of German consumers and industry in cheap energy. And again the CSU represented the policy that moved toward the future, polishing up its image in industrial circles. In short, for four years newspaper articles reminded German industry that much had changed in the neglected southeast of Germany.

Big Science

"Big science" was also built up in Bavaria between 1957 and 1962. In biochemistry, atomic research, and aerospace research, Bavaria became the home of the large research institutes on which modern science depends and that create synergies with universities and attract a highly educated labor force and modern industries.

"Personnel is policy," as the saying has it, and Bavaria began to land prize scientific research institutes because during these crucial years it had powerful supporters within the Max Planck Foundation (MPF). This was not just a fortuitous circumstance, as we have seen, and Strauß and Seidel and the CSU-led Bavarian government continued to cultivate scientific friends. Though the MPF was funded by the state and federal governments, politicians had little influence over its decisions, which were made by its Senate and president. The Senate was dominated quite overwhelmingly by scientists (of over thirty senators, the federal government nominated only two and the states together only three), who decided how and where its money would be spent, and elected the president, who was responsible to propose general policies to the Senate—including proposals for new institutes and their locations.[41] As supporters of Bavaria among the senators we may number Siegfried Balke and Theodor Maunz, who as Minister of Atomic Affairs and Bavaria's Culture Minister, respectively, held two of the five government-appointed seats. Two other senators oriented to Bavaria's interests were Werner Heisenberg, and, though with important qualifications, Karl Winnacker.

But Bavaria's biggest supporter was the MPF's President, biochemist Adolf Butenandt. This was the man whom the Bavarian government had lured away from Baden-Württemberg, whose Max Planck Institute for Biochemistry had opened in Munich in 1957. He was elected the president of the MPF in the fall of 1959 and this began a new relationship between Bavaria and the MPF. Shortly after his election, in 1960 and 1961 Butenandt moved his presidential offices from Göttingen into the old royal palace in Munich (though the foundation's headquarters remained in Göttingen for several years).[42] From 1961 to 1964 the network of Max Planck Institutes in Bavaria grew rapidly and by the end of the 1960s Munich had the most important concentration of Max Planck Institutes in all of Germany.[43] As Stephan Deutinger, the historian of Bavaria's postwar research boom, observed: "Since the late 1950s Bavaria and the Max Planck Foundation developed 'a partnerlike relationship of a special sort,' as Butenandt put it...the institutes that were transferred to Munich kept spawning new institutes and drew after them new Max Planck Institutes from other disciplines, so that Munich came to have a more important concentration of Max Planck Institutes than Göttingen and Tübingen."[44]

If this was Bavaria's payoff for supporting Butenandt, its "atomic" payoff for supporting Heisenberg and Balke was almost as great. In fact, the CSU had done more than court and support Heisenberg's Max Planck Institute for Physics and put Balke in a ministerial position. Strauß and Balke had given Bavaria the Munich Research Reactor and had built up atomic sciences in the physics department at the Munich Technical University. They had also supported others proponents of Bavarian interests, such as Heinz Maier-Leibnitz, within the German Atomic Energy Commission's Working Group for Atomic Physics, which made recommendations (effectively, decisions) on which research areas to support.[45]

But more than anything it was Balke's support for Heisenberg's Max Planck Institute for Physics and Astrophysics that made the difference for Bavaria, though not in the way it had been expected to. Heisenberg and Balke built up this institute so that it led Bavaria into other research specialties, first of all into the fusion research center that became the "nucleus" of a German Oxford.[46]

If fission research was practical, about nuclear weapons and power generation, fusion research was close to "pure science." It had been the possibility of controlled fusion reactions that drove the atomic euphoria of the mid 1950s: dreams of inexhaustible, ridiculously cheap power that would power airplanes and automobiles, desalinate the oceans, irrigate the world's deserts, and turn Antarctica into a tropical paradise. The idea that Munich be made the center of German fusion research originated in the mid 1950s, before Adenauer decided that the Atomic Reactor Station would be built near Karlsruhe. But nothing was done about fusion until after the second Geneva Conference in September 1958, when it became clear to all that fusion reactions were extremely difficult to control, and that controlled reactions would not be possible for many decades, if ever. Thereafter industry took little interest in fusion. But the fascinating results obtained from early experiments and publicized at the second Geneva Conference created great scientific interest in fusion. This was especially true in Germany, one of the world's leaders in fusion research. Munich was positioned to benefit, not only because Heisenberg and his Max Planck Institute for Physics and Astrophysics were there, but also many of the other leaders of the "fusion community," including Rudolf Mössbauer, Germany's first postwar Nobel prizewinner, were working in the area, supported by Balke's Ministry of Atomic Affairs.[47]

Balke's attitude toward fusion research was "entirely positive" and he was prepared to make Munich the center of German fusion research.[48] His idea was to expand Heisenberg's Max Planck Institute for Physics and Astrophysics into an institute for research in plasma and fusion physics. Heisenberg's institute had moved from Göttingen to Munich in the fall of 1958 and by 1959 the Max Planck Foundation, the leaders of the Max Planck Institute for Physics and Astrophysics, the Ministry of Atomic Affairs, and the Bavarian Culture Ministry were at work on the creation of an Institute for Plasma Physics (IPP), a "fusion center" on the grand scale.[49] It would be a research center comparable to the biggest in other countries, located near the village of Garching, immediately north of Munich. There was some difficulty about the form of organization, for the Max Planck Foundation was reluctant to get involved in such a large, expensive project, particularly since the founders wanted to get Euratom involved in its financing, and the MPF feared Euratom's pretensions to supervise research and encroach on the autonomy of science. Their objections were overcome by Balke, Heisenberg, and Butenandt, who convinced the foundation's members that they would defend the autonomy of science, and in the end it was agreed to set the IPP up as a Max Planck Institute, but that this would be only a temporary solution. The oddness of the final arrangement—the initial costs of nearly DM 100,000,000 were paid entirely by the Ministry of Atomic Affairs but when the IPP was founded as a Max Planck Institute in June 1960 the founding partners were the Max Planck Foundation and Heisenberg himself—testifies to Balke's and Heisenberg's determination.[50]

With the IPP it became possible to realize the dream of making Munich into a new Dahlem. Dahlem had been the German Oxford, the Berlin neighborhood in which German scientific research institutes had been concentrated prior to World War II, in an effort to create an atmosphere of research excellence attractive to the best scientists and to industry. Dahlem had been destroyed in the war, after which it found itself in the Soviet sector of Berlin, and its scientists dispersed throughout Germany, Western Europe, America, and Russia, but many of Germany's top scientists longed to recreate the Dahlem environment somewhere else—early candidates had been Göttingen and Tübingen, but neither had materialized. The development of Garching toward the Dahlem model had begun before the IPP, with the Munich Research Reactor, which project, having been carried by the Coalition of Four and Strauß's Ministry of Atomic Affairs, was opened by Hanns Seidel in 1957. The Munich Research Reactor was followed by an Institute for Radio Chemistry and an Institute for Low Temperature Research, which, like the Munich Research Reactor, were affiliated with the Munich Technical University. In 1958 Siemens decided to create its own reactor research group, complete with a mini-reactor, in Garching.[51] With the creation of the IPP in 1960 developments in Garching attained "critical mass." The IPP, with its over seven hundred employees, was decisive for Garching: the idea quickly became current that it was definitely slotted to become the "new Dahlem."[52] Balke himself suggested, at the first meeting of the IPP Governing Board, that the board "take up very close contacts with the city of Munich, and pointed to the possibility of creating a 'new Dahlem,' complete with apartment blocks, schools, subways and roads." The Bavarian ministries were naturally eager to cooperate. Garching approved initial building plans in late 1959, and between 1960 and 1965 it became one of Germany's largest research centers.[53]

Yet if Balke and others provide another story of a successful CSU effort to bring modernity to Bavaria, a companion failure story also teaches us something about the CSU.

Though interest in atomic power generation had declined, it had not collapsed. There remained a circle of firms in the chemical and electric industries that continued to position themselves to play a role in a future atomic industry. The most important were Hoechst, which was heavily involved in Bavaria, and Siemens, which was headquartered in Bavaria, where it was the region's largest industrial employer.

Balke kept his ministry involved in atomic power generation by reorienting it toward supporting small, experimental reactors that would prepare Germany to move into large reactors as soon as they became cost-efficient power sources. But atomic power generation was a minefield of technical questions with political implications. For the decision between types of reactors had to be made before it was possible to make informed judgments about them. The power generating industry preferred enriched uranium, light-water reactors, since they were relatively cheap to construct. German physicists, industrialists, and the nationally-minded much preferred the uranium, heavy water (or graphite) reactors. Though the latter were much more expensive, Germans had developed the uranium, heavy-water technology themselves during World War II, and they could "breed" so that Germany could soon free itself of dependence on American suppliers (the American and Soviet governments had between them acquired almost complete control of the world's uranium) and would have its own supply of plutonium (a by-product of "breeder" reactors) for nuclear weapons. Uranium/heavy water reactors also meant that the chemical and electric industries would receive contracts to develop atomic fuel reprocessing plants, heavy water plants (heavy water was extremely expensive to produce and in anticipation of contracts Hoechst had already built a heavy water plant), and breeder reactors (which produced plutonium as a by-product).[54]

Balke mishandled the politics of this choice, which led to the rapid decline of his ministerial influence. From 1957 to about 1960 Balke, naturally oriented toward the interests of the chemical industry (from which he came) and electric industries, generally promoted uranium, heavy water reactors.[55] But because he could not contribute enough to their financing, his budget being held in check by the Finance Ministry, he failed to unite the power-producing industry behind his plans, or even to broker any compromise between the power producers and the chemical and electric industries.[56]

This was too bad for Bavaria, for Balke was eager to turn his ministry to account for his home state. From 1957 to 1961 Balke reported the details of his plans and hopes for helping Bavaria to the State Group's Hermann Höcherl. In 1958 Balke could report granting practically all of the financial assistance applications of the Bavarian universities, as well as his intention to support the construction of a center for fusion research (which became the Institute for Plasma Physics), "although for political reasons I don't emphasize this very much," and that he had nullified earlier plans to concentrate Germany's atomic research in Karlsruhe and Düsseldorf. In 1960 he reported that "in the years 1956 to 1959 approximately fifty million marks flowed to Bavaria from the Ministry of Atomic Affairs," with the biggest sums going to the universities and technical universities, the Max Planck Institute for Physics and Astrophysics, and the Munich Research Reactor.[57]

Yet while Balke farsightedly pointed to the benefits that "big science" would one day bring to Bavaria, the State Group seems to have had its eyes fixed on the short-term "porkbarrel." Taken as a whole, the Bavarian deputies were underwhelming in their support for Balke's plans or in their appreciation for his efforts on Bavaria's behalf. They did not even support his budgetary requests, so that Balke was driven to complain to Hermann Höcherl that he was not treated with respect by his fellow CSU deputies, who worked "to undermine my prestige." Strauß had to take Balke by the hand and soothe his feelings.[58] Nor were Balke's problems with his party limited to the State Group. Even as he sent to Bavaria atomic reactors that other states wanted, Balke found himself having to apologize for his largess, reassuring CSU conservatives that his support of atomic research did not undermine the federalism of the Basic Law, that he had no intention to take over Bavarian state prerogatives, and that his ministry sought to cooperate with Bavarian authorities. Sometimes Balke even had to fight against the Bavarian state government in order to bring his projects to Bavaria—and lost. He complained that Bayernwerk, the Bavarian state utility company, had "by means of massive pressure on the Bavarian state government," brought to naught his plans to erect a multipurpose atomic research reactor in Bavaria.[59] And when Balke's ministry financed the cooperation of Bayernwerk and RWE (the North Rhine-Westphalian power utility) on the first atomic power plant to produce power for the German grid, the Bavarian State Government, responding to local citizen concerns, rejected the choice of a construction site near Bertoldsheim, Bavaria. Balke wrote to Minister-President Hans Ehard, Interior Minister Alfons Goppel, and Economic Minister Otto Schedl, begging them to accept the atomic power plant that other states would have been only too happy to have.[60] But the CSU-controlled State Government only grudgingly permitted the plant to be built at Kahl am Main, in a less-populated area right on Bavaria's northern border. The entire controversy was a humiliation for Balke.[61]

Much of the reason for the CSU's lack of enthusiasm for Balke lay in Balke himself. He was a political weakling. This was not entirely his fault, as Strauß had selected him for ministerial office in order to cement the relationship between the State Group and Bavarian industry—remember that when Balke became Post Minister in 1953 he was not even a member of the CSU. And so he found himself derided as the minister without influence ("ohne Ellenbogen"), and without a political base in his own party ("onhe Hausmacht"). But Balke did little to build up his political position: he prided himself on being a responsible and objective technocrat, played the role of a nonpolitical politician, spoke disparagingly of politics and politicians, and trusted too much in his connections to industry and Strauß, as well as his technical knowledge, to see him through. His resulting political isolation did not please industry.[62] And the CSU deputies who despised him understood correctly enough that Balke served not so much their party's interests as industry's. However their attitude toward Balke may have been magnified by bigotries (Balke came from North Rhine-Westphalia, hence was a "Prussian," as well as a Protestant of Jewish extraction), he was treated just as badly by Adenauer—one Catholic from the lower Rhineland justly famous for his openness to Protestants and Jews.

Yet the lack of interest most CSU deputies took in industrial modernization points up the effectiveness of those few CSU leaders who did give thought to a strategy for Bavaria's industrial modernization. Strauß, Seidel, Schedl, Balke, and a handful of others were certainly in a minority within their party, but, holding the party and governmental positions they did, were enough to make the difference for Bavaria.

Aerospace research presented the CSU with a different challenge altogether. Here the task was less to bring research institutes to Bavaria than to hold onto the institutes Bavaria already had. The CSU had to steer them through a period of institutional consolidation driven by the federal government, which threatened to withhold its financial support from the variety of small aerospace research institutes unless they agreed to merge into the German Aviation Research Institute (DVL, Deutsche Versuchsanstalt für Luftfahrt), which was concentrated in and dominated by North Rhine-Westphalia. We have already seen how the DVL leadership and North Rhine-Westphalia worked hand in glove to draw Germany's scattered institutes under the DVL and to concentrate them in North Rhine-Westphalia. In 1957 Bavaria had one DVL institute, the FFO (Flugfunk-Forschungsinstitut Oberpfaffenhofen, Aerospace Communications Research Institute in Oberpfaffenhofen) in Oberpfaffenhofen, as well as the Institute for Fuel and Lubricants in Munich, the Test Bed for Thermodynamic Investigations in Grainau, and the Central Collection of Aviation Documentation and the German Research Institute for Glider Flight, which were both in Munich, and sought to draw two institutes to Oberpfaffenhofen, the DVL's Microwave Institute and Institute for Control Engineering.[63] The Bavarian state government supported the small institutes in their resistance, though not in order to prevent consolidation, since Bavaria could not support its institutes. Rather Bavaria's plan was to support the merger as soon as the DVL gave sufficient guarantees that Bavarian institutes would never be transferred to North Rhine-Westphalia.

The negotiating and jostling on this point dragged on for half a decade. Though the DVL was a considerable burden on North Rhine-Westphalia's budget, that state drove a hard bargain, insisting that, in view of its early and continuing financial contributions to the reconstruction of aerospace research, this science remain concentrated within its borders. Between 1957 and 1962 the DVL and the federal government put increasing financial pressure on the small aerospace research institutes to join the DVL, and most of them did. The issue between North Rhine-Westphalia and Bavaria was joined over the German Research Institute for Glider Flight (DFS, Deutsche Forschungsanstalt für Segelflug). The DFS was in crisis, its researchers old, its field of research seemingly obsolete. But the CSU-dominated State Government was willing to abandon DFS only if it could extract a promise from the DVL. It took years to work out, but in 1961 Bavaria agreed to deny the DFS further financial support, which would force it to dissolve itself into the DVL, and promised considerable financial support for the building up of the FFO research center in Oberpfaffenhofen, Bavaria, which would be fully integrated into the DVL.[64] In return the DVL agreed to make Oberpfaffenhofen an aerospace research center equal ("gleichberechtigt") to Porz-Wahn in North Rhine-Westphalia. As a result of the cooperation some Bavarian aerospace research institutes were transferred to Porz-Wahn and others from Porz-Wahn to Oberpfaffenhofen.[65]

What kind of a deal was this? Bavaria got its Oberpfaffenhofen center elevated to the status of "DVL-South" (DVL-Süd), responsible to conduct research in Aerospace Communications, Steering and Controls Technology, Jet Fuel and Lubricants, Flight

Technology, Flight Mechanics, Atmospheric Physics, and Measurements Technology (Flugfunk and Mikrowelle, Steuer- und Regeltechnik, Flugtreib- und Schmierstoffe, Freiflugtechnik, Flugmechanik, Physik der Atmosphäre, and Meßtechnik). As we will see, all this led into Bavaria's long-term goal, the concentration of German aerospace in the Munich area. For Bavaria, this was an excellent return on investment since even as late as 1960 Bavaria spent only about DM 700,000 annually on aerospace research, while North Rhine-Westphalia still spent nearly DM 3,000,000.[66] While both were tiny figures compared to the aerospace budgets of France and Britain, let alone the United States, the point, in the early 1960s, was for Bavaria to hold its own within Germany, not against the world. Later, when through European cooperation in military and civilian aircraft, the German industry took its place alongside the French and British, it would be the Bavarian industry that would be the great beneficiary—hence an even better return on Bavaria's modest investment.

Strauß played an indirect but vital role in this—instructive of how the politics of industrial modernization works through multiplier effects. Though the Bavarian Economic Ministry drove a very active policy in aerospace research, pushing relentlessly for the Bavarian advantage and involving itself in more than five aerospace research institutes, more than any other state or federal ministry, it could never have forced North Rhine-Westphalia to give up its ambition of exercising hegemony over aerospace research and settle for a "draw."

Strauß reined in North Rhine-Westphalia's ambitions simply by occupying the Defense Ministry. The chief reason that North Rhine-Westphalia had invested in aerospace research institutes had been to use them to draw the aircraft firms within their borders. With Strauß in the Defense Ministry, North Rhine-Westphalia had obviously lost the struggle for the aircraft industry, and the "game" having been lost, North Rhine-Westphalia had every reason to seek to spread the burden of supporting aerospace research.

And Strauß's own ministry soon became an important financial supporter of aerospace research. Though the Transport Ministry maintained formal ministerial responsibility for this field, in 1957 Strauß started taking direct interest in aerospace research, kept the Bavarian Economic Ministry well informed of his intentions, and in January 1958 made a proposal to the Cabinet on financing its reconstruction, arguing that "It is therefore necessary to definitively abandon German aerospace research, or build it up to a level at which it can function.... If we abandon it ... I would have to give decisively important tasks in defense-technical research to friendly foreign countries, and the equipping of the armed forces would depend on the research results of foreigners. And with that the government would definitively deprive the German aerospace industry of the preconditions and foundation of its competitiveness." Strauß was speaking about airplanes but also about antitank and antiaircraft missiles—and here one thinks of the firm that would almost inevitably have manufactured them, Bölkow Developments near Munich.[67] Strauß argued that the aerospace research institutes lacked proper equipment to enable them to conduct useful research; he also argued that if Germany had its own aerospace industry it would pay less for its arms. This was a very dubious proposition, but Strauß's goal was not to make valid arguments. Of course Strauß had no interest in pure science: the aerospace research institutes would do applied research in the service of the aerospace industry and the Defense Ministry. He proposed that the states put up DM 6,000,000, the Defense Ministry DM 5,000,000, and the Transport Ministry DM 1,000,000. Since several states hosted aerospace research institutes, Strauß's ministry would become the effective leader in aerospace research.

Strauß's proposal was accepted, and came as a great help to Bavaria, reducing the pressure on the Bavarian government to come up with more money. Money for aerospace research had always been scarce in Bavaria—in 1957 the Bavarian Economic Ministry could only manage to get DM 360,000. But in early 1958 the Defense Ministry began picking up the burden that North Rhine-Westphalia had carried: in 1956/57 the federal government paid for 21 percent of the support for aerospace research, North Rhine-Westphalia 72 percent, but the following year the numbers were 72 percent and 20 percent respectively, and remained approximately the same through the early 1960s. In all these years, Bavaria's contribution remained between 6 percent and 4 percent.[68]

NATO Nuclear Strategy and Bavarian Interest Solidarity

From 1957 to 1962 Strauß created and acted on a conscious and complex strategy that used the issue of NATO's nuclear defense plan to promote Bavaria's industrial modernization. For in these years strategic decisions were made that had far-reaching consequences for Germany—and strategic armaments programs were adopted that had far-reaching consequences for Bavarian industry.

Strauß pushed hard for a German military buildup in "modern weapons," a euphemism for nuclear weapons, missiles, and advanced fighter-bombers—precisely the sort of weapons that, if Germany produced them or cooperated in producing them, would almost certainly have been produced by the Bavarian firms of Bölkow and Messerschmitt.

Soon after taking office, Strauß threw himself into the national and international debates as to whether and how Germany might participate in an Allied decision to use nuclear weapons. Strauß was by 1957 much more than a Defense Minister. He had considerable influence within the German Cabinet, but also with German industry (especially the defense industry), and dominated the CSU, whose federal deputies oriented themselves increasingly to his positions and tactics.[69] Moreover, he enjoyed a high public profile and a reputation as a powerful and dynamic minister, a formidable political tactician of outstanding intelligence, and an authority on world politics with genuine expertise in defense, weaponry, and strategy. It is not too much to say that Strauß's ideas carried weight in all of the Allied capitals and that he was growing into the role of one of the chief actors on the European stage.

Strauß determined to make the most of his influence. He stood out as the German politician most vocally seeking German control and even production of nuclear weapons and delivery systems (when West Germany became a sovereign state and entered NATO, Adenauer had only committed the country not to *produce* such weapons *on German soil;* hence some other country could give Germany nuclear weapons or Germany could produce them on foreign soil or Germany could make decisions regarding some other country's nuclear weapons). Strauß was the German politician least likely to duck and cover on the issue, and the only one who consistently and openly argued that a decision to use nuclear weapons stored on German soil could not be left to the Americans.

Strauß represented not just a policy of how to defend Germany from Soviet attack, but a foreign policy vision pointed toward improving Germany's international position. Since at least the mid 1950s Strauß had wanted Germany to step out of the shadow of the Third Reich and to pursue its interests as determinedly and openly as any other country. Believing that there was no hope for even partial agreement on German goals with the communist countries and that West Germany had to commit itself completely to NATO, he argued that Germany's goal must be to acquire a more powerful voice within the alliance, and that to do this Germany would have to make a major military contribution to that alliance. It could not accept the role of providing the alliance with its infantry but must, at a minimum, participate fully in any decision to use nuclear weapons. Strauß's pursuit of this goal often seemed erratic but, as a scholar of nuclear politics wrote, his operational principles never varied: "test the limits of the possible; keep all possible options open; and try to anticipate if not shape the future."[70]

One of Strauß's chief tactics was to play France and America against each other—a tactic that had profound implications for Bavaria's industrial development, as we will see. Both countries refused to say a clear yes to German control of nuclear weapons; but neither could afford to say a definite no lest it drive Germany into the arms of the other. At the end of 1957, even before the NATO decision that the European allies, including Germany, could carry—though not control—American nuclear weapons, the French government secretly offered to cooperate with Germany in developing "the most modern weapons."[71] France sought Germany's financial assistance, in return for which it was willing to give Germany a certain shared control over some nuclear weapons, though how much control appears not to have been decided. Strauß, intensely annoyed by the American desire to perpetually put off any decision as to whether the Germans might control nuclear weapons, could hardly believe his luck, and in the spring of 1958 he secretly agreed to jointly fund French nuclear weapons production. A few months later Charles de Gaulle returned to power and rudely overturned the agreement. Outraged, Strauß gave orders to shelve all defense-technical cooperation with France and to hold no more talks about the purchase of French materiel. He later wrote, "My cancellation hit Paris like a bomb, all hopes for close cooperation with the Germans and for big defense contracts for the French defense industry were dead."[72] The French were soon trying to mend fences but to give Germany even limited control of nuclear weapons remained unthinkable for de Gaulle. It was a loss for Bavaria, for there were indications that Germany's role was to have been in missile development, and the only conceivable contractor was Bölkow.

Thrown back onto the Americans, Strauß began pressing them to permit joint production of a missile to carry a nuclear warhead. But he found Washington less likely than ever to permit German production or control of nuclear weapons. This had to do with renewed tension over Berlin. If the Berlin blockade were renewed, and if Germany controlled nuclear weapons, Strauß would be able to launch a nuclear strike on the Soviet Union, drawing his allies in behind him. Whether or not the American government was willing to launch a nuclear war in response to moves on West Berlin, it was not willing to put any German in a position to force its hand.

In fact, as the Berlin crisis became more or less permanent and the Soviets developed rockets capable of striking American cities, the Kennedy administration began looking for a modus vivendi with the Soviets. This had tremendous implications for Germany, and for the Bavarian defense industry. For the easiest way to achieve a modus vivendi with the Soviets was to sacrifice Germany, to steer it away from nuclear decision-making, prevent it from taking control of American weapons, reduce its role in carrying American nuclear weapons (even under ostensible American control), and centralize command and control over nuclear weapons in Washington. Decreasing reliance on American nuclear threats to protect Europe also implied increasing reliance on allied conventional forces, which would therefore have to be built up. This was the policy that came to be called "flexible response."

"Flexible response" fell heavily on Germany, and heaviest of all on Bavaria and Strauß. Strauß had planned Germany's force structure around massive retaliation, presuming that Germany would get increasingly free access to nuclear weapons, and allowing the buildup of Germany's conventional forces to fall far behind schedule. Strauß now began to come under pressure to give up *his* defense program of a low-manpower, high-technology army—the program had won him the backing of German industry, carried him into the Defense Ministry, and become synonymous with his name, and in it he had invested all of his political prestige and capital. To accept the new American strategy would mean giving up the demand for nuclear-weapons control-sharing, and, in Strauß's military-political logic, agreeing to relegate Germany to the status of a minor power, subordinate to France and Britain. It would also mean giving up the high-technology projects by admitting, implicitly, that missiles, advanced fighters, and nuclear-capable equipment were not for Germans to possess—or Bavarians to produce.[73]

Strauß would not have been Strauß had he accepted this. Rather he pushed forward with his plans to build up the defense-industrial complex that a "modern," low-manpower, nuclear-armed military force would require. He also threw himself into a bitter struggle to force America to reverse the course of its defense policy—something even Chancellor Adenauer could not do. As we shall see,

Strauß's drive became so determined and ruthless that it led to his forced resignation from the Defense Ministry at the end of 1962. But though he could not dictate NATO nuclear defense policy, German defense-industrial policy was another matter entirely. Denied control of nuclear weapons, on warning that American defense policy was moving away from "massive retaliation" nuclear warfare toward "flexible response" conventional warfare, and that America would be increasingly reluctant to allow Germany to merely carry nuclear weapons, Strauß could and did continue to construct an armed forces that made sense only if armed with nuclear weapons. Yet since through 1962 nothing could stop Strauß from creating his "massive-retaliation" force (*sans* nuclear weapons!), he did succeed in creating a concentration of high-technology industry in Bavaria, oriented to defense and aircraft production, and to research and development.

Strauß was able to create this force and its supporting industry because he had developed his rearmament program into a political program, a remarkable political tour de force.

Deeply conscious that decisions on what armaments to buy from whom shaped a national economy, Strauß made his procurement decisions part of an openly declared plan to recover Germany's prewar industrial position—and an undeclared plan to recover it as much as possible in Bavaria. Refusing pleas to use his budget to prop up dying industries, Strauß directed his attention to industries in which Germany had formerly led and in which it would be worthwhile to lead again, to growth industries and key technologies that seemed likely to shape the future, and that would prepare German industry to withstand international competition.[74] And he pitched his plan so as to appeal to industrial interests that were not even involved in defense contracting. Conceding that the defense industry was unproductive, at least because it took factors of production away from civil production, he argued tirelessly that the entire economy received "stimulations and impulses" from the defense industry.[75]

This pointed to defense research and development, and indeed the laboratory interested Strauß as much as the factory. Yet Strauß had to approach this carefully. Germany could not move directly into military research and development, since its firms, out of work since 1945, had fallen far behind, and lest such a move alarm and disappoint its allies, who hoped to support their own defense industries through large sales to Germany. Yet precisely for this reason the German government could advocate alliance cooperation in defense production without threatening the interests of German industry.[76] Before Strauß became Defense Minister, Adenauer and Blank had pronounced against autarky in defense production; but they had meant to purchase arms from their allies, and to do so for foreign policy reasons. Strauß promoted joint production of arms, not for reasons of foreign policy, but to turn it to Germany's technical advantage. As he told industrialists who preferred a national autarkic approach to rearmament, if Germany cooperated intelligently with its allies it could quickly and cheaply pick up the key technologies that others had spent a great deal of money to develop.[77]

Strauß made aircraft development and production his top priority. The aircraft firms would be the core of his new German defense industry and he had in mind an ambitious program for high-speed aircraft, small and medium-sized transport aircraft, helicopters, trainers, and the development of aircraft that could take off and land vertically and guided missiles. In 1956 the idea of German production of missiles lay beyond the dreams of avarice, but already in February 1958 Strauß informed the representatives of the southern German aircraft firms that he would soon have them building not only an interceptor on license but also a missile, and by 1960 Strauß publicly avowed his interest even in space flight.[78] He was speaking aggressively indeed, being far ahead of his allies' and Adenauer's public positions.[79]

In order to move forward against the opposition to which his plans gave rise, Strauß began to manage a "solidarity of interests" between military and political desiderata and economic and political interest groups.[80] In the interest solidarity there was, first, the Bavarian defense-industrial complex that Strauß was supporting. This consisted of the industrial beneficiaries of an armed services dominated by its air force and emphasizing state-of-the-art technology in its jets, missiles, and nuclear weapons. Specifically, featured among the industrial beneficiaries were Bavarian aircraft firms, such as Messerschmitt and Dornier; Bavarian aerospace development firms, such as Bölkow Developments; the Bavarian jet engine firms of BMW Triebwerkbau and MAN; and such Bavarian suppliers as Siemens. Second, there was the CSU, which benefited from this industry's financial contributions and reaped the political benefits of having brought these industries to Bavaria. Third, there were the Bavarian voters who benefited from the presence of these industries in their state. Fourth, there were those non-CSU politicians, analysts, and pundits attracted to a military posture less dependent on the United States and more aggressive vis-à-vis the Soviet Union, whether out of intellectual conviction, nationalism, anticommunism, or anti-Americanism. Fifth, there was the German air force. And, sixth, there was Strauß himself. The prosperity of any member of the interest solidarity was related to the success of the others. Each had an interest in supporting the others against their detractors or any potential rival solidarities—say, a solidarity of Rhenish defense industry producing more traditional weapons such as tanks and artillery, the CDU, Rhenish voters, more NATO-oriented politicians and opinion-shapers, and the German army. This interest solidarity became the pivot of the German military-industrial complex, and all of its members looked to Strauß for leadership.

But Strauß had to do more than lead his interest solidarity where it wanted to go: he had to dominate it in order to move it in directions in which it was sometimes reluctant to go. For Strauß's plan sacrificed the short-term interests of the defense industry (which were to produce as many of Germany's weapons as possible, of whatever sort and on whatever level it could do so) and the military (whose interest was to expand rapidly, in accord with NATO timetables) in order to create a more internationally competitive defense industry and a more powerful military force over the long term. Already in his first meeting with the defense industrialists who had pressured Adenauer to elevate him into the ministry, Strauß let them know he was boss, flatly denying some of their requests, refusing to commit himself to fulfilling others, while yet showing a general openness to their ideas.[81] He would do what he could for the defense-industrial complex so long as its demands pointed in the direction in which he wanted to go. Strauß could declare his partial independence from his sponsors because he convinced many of them that in the end they would get more of what they wanted from him, a politician "with elbows," someone who could deliver, than they would from a more pliable but politically weaker Defense Minister.

Starfighter, Space Flight, and Military R & D

There is no question but that Bavaria benefited more than other states from Strauß's tenure in the Defense Ministry. After Strauß's tenure came to an end, the State Contracts Office for Bavaria reported that, regarding defense contracts awarded in the period from 1 October 1955 until 31 December 1962, "Bavarian industry came out quite far ahead. Excluding the specially situated city-states of Hamburg and Bremen, Bavaria marches, with 22,889 contracts of the BWB and a total contractual value of DM 5,463,000,000 today as yesterday at the head of the states. On a per capita basis, Bavaria received DM 574.21, compared to DM 415.87 in Schleswig-Holstein, DM 350.00 in Baden-Württemberg, DM 271.59 in North Rhine-Westphalia, DM 245.58 in Hesse, DM 237.83 in Lower Saxony."[82]

But to understand these numbers we must look to the most important defense-industrial programs, contracts and initiatives.

No element of Strauß's program promised to be more important for Bavaria than his jet interceptor. He had decided that Germany should produce one, and to him belonged the final decision between available foreign models. It would be the biggest defense-industrial decision he made. Because of the interceptor's advanced technology, the German firms expected to learn much more from this plane than the others. It would be by far the most expensive and important weapon in Strauß's modern armed forces.

In fact, everything having to do with the interceptor decision was influenced at least as much by the needs of German industry as of the German air force. Strauß admitted to the federal parliament in July 1958 that, "Urgent here is not the provision of airplanes for the air force; we have a supply of usable airplanes that will suffice for a very long time. Urgent is that the start that we have made toward reconstructing the German aircraft industry, which is of considerable significance for the economy of the Federal Republic [West Germany], for its ability to compete on the world market and for Germany's prestige...does not prove to be all for naught due to a period of unemployment in which the development teams and the skilled workers will find employment elsewhere."[83]

But the needs of German industry and the German air force were not in conflict, except in the short term, and this was not a matter of luck but the result of Strauß's success in constructing his "interest solidarity." The aircraft industry wanted to construct an expensive high-tech aircraft and the military supporters of Strauß's "quality army" concept wanted a high-spec aircraft, two demands that were by no means difficult to reconcile. Between May 1957 and the summer of 1958, the Defense Ministry tested candidates, narrowing the choice to the American (Lockheed) F-104 Starfighter or the French (Dassault) Mirage. And so an great Franco-American lobbying battle reverberated through Strauß's Defense Ministry.[84]

There was never much of a battle within German industry. German industry was solidly, though not unanimously, behind the American Starfighter.[85] Representatives of the aircraft industry and the Federal Office for Defense Technology and Procurement created a working group "Interceptor," and in July 1958 the group reported to Strauß that the Starfighter was the world's most modern, technologically advanced airplane. This went to the core of Strauß's "interest solidarity": Germany was building an interceptor on license in order to catch up, to learn what the state of the art was; and so the aircraft industry naturally wanted to work with the world's most advanced aerospace industry and to build the most technologically advanced fighter available.[86] And German engineers considered the engines of the French Mirage to be merely an improved version of the jet engines BMW had produced during World War II, its electronics unsophisticated—while aerospace electronics was the area in which the German aircraft firms had fallen farthest behind.

Even less was there a battle within the German air force, which considered the Starfighter the ne plus ultra of jet fighters.[87] It was foreign policy that created the battle. The decision to construct a foreign airplane was bound to create military and defense-industrial relations between Germany and the licensing firm's country that would be hard to break and would influence German foreign policy for a decade or more.[88] The French put enormous diplomatic pressure on Germany, making the German decision into a crucial test of Franco-German reconciliation. The Americans had already established defense-industrial relations with Germany, having given the German air force American fighter jets of Korean-War vintage and hired the German aircraft firms to perform the maintenance on American military aircraft in Germany. And the American government put on pressure in favor of Lockheed, intimating privately that if the Mirage were chosen, Germany could forget about American nuclear weapons for its air force.[89] This consideration alone must have weighed heavily in favor of the Starfighter. For in the course of 1957 and 1958 Germany's political and military leaders, most emphatically including Strauß and Adenauer, were in the process of concluding that Germany could not be defended from nuclear attack with interceptors. Germany would have to deter attack by carrying nuclear weapons—in effect, by constructing interceptors for use as fighter-bombers.

But other factors complicated the decision-making process, and the final decision was delayed. For one thing, the Germans had every interest in not letting the French down too hard. There is some reason to think that delays were a ploy to get a better deal from Lockheed, which was confident Germany would have to buy American and unwilling to offer the same deal sweeteners as did Dassault. Already in February 1958, long before de Gaulle cancelled Strauß's deal to cooperate with the French in nuclear weapons production, Strauß confided to Ludwig Bölkow and Willy Messerschmitt that he was drawing out the decision for Starfighter as a negotiating tactic: "As soon as we commit ourselves to a certain model we'll come under pressure. We have to let the American firms know that we have other options, for example, the Mirage."[90] Another factor may have been kickbacks paid by Lockheed to Strauß or the CSU. Though this has never been proven, in the mid 1970s a Lockheed scandal, in which it emerged that over a course of years Lockheed had paid kickbacks as a matter of business policy, raised questions as to whether kickbacks were paid to the CSU or to Strauß. It was impossible to find any real evidence against Strauß, but suspicions ran high, for Lockheed had hired Ernest F. Hauser, an old pal of Strauß from the days of the American military occupation of Bavaria, to be its representative in West Germany. There were cries for an investigation, but the crucial documents having to do with the Starfighter purchase negotiations were missing from the Defense Ministry, together with their duplicates.[91] In any case, on 24 October 1958 Strauß announced that Germany would purchase a license to construct the Starfighter.

Strauß served the industry in other ways. The aircraft industry, which desperately needed money, pressed Strauß for a decision. Strauß probably made his decision in 1958 in order to cooperate with the industry, since the German air force held that no decision was necessary, it being years away from having either pilots qualified to fly the Starfighter or airfields from which it could take off and land.[92] Quantity was also vital to the aircraft industry. By mid 1958 the Defense Ministry had adopted the principle that the industrial capacities that had already been built up (especially at Dornier and Messerschmitt) must be maintained "under any circumstances."[93] Naturally, the firms wanted the government to order as many planes as possible, and naturally, the Bavarian Economic Ministry, lobbying for Bavarian jobs, recommended that Strauß order more reconnaissance aircraft and jet trainers from Dornier and Messerschmitt, and even set up a meeting between Strauß and Claudius Dornier to discuss possible ways to help the Dornier firm.[94]

But Strauß preferred to order more Starfighters. At the end of 1959, after the German air force declared that 250 Starfighters would meet its needs and while the northern German aircraft industry was running out of work, Strauß insisted on ordering an additional 364 Starfighters from the Bavarian aircraft industry, and the parliamentary Defense Committee, a CSU stronghold, approved. It is true that Strauß helped the northern German aircraft manufacturers when they faced similar troubles—it appears that the construction of transporters (Transall and Noratlas) was hurried and more were ordered—but not to the same extent. Answering his critics in the federal parliament, Strauß said that Germany either must build the Starfighter or the southern German firms would go bankrupt. Helmut Schmidt, the Social Democrats' expert on defense issues and later federal Chancellor, responded that the issue was not maintaining current capacities, but expanding the capacities of the southern firms. And so it was that the opposition to the Starfighter, which often enough came from within the CDU, essentially opposed the reestablishment of a sizable German aircraft industry in Bavaria, one that would have no work after the Starfighter contract ran out and would require follow-on contracts from the federal government.[95]

Strauß came up with a strategy to silence critics and further strengthen the German aircraft industry—more than that, to maneuver it into a position from which it could compete with its French and British rivals. After Strauß selected the Starfighter over the Mirage, Italy and Belgium followed suit and joined in production, while Denmark, Norway, Greece, Turkey, and Spain purchased them (all of which embittered the French, derailing their plans to concentrate the European aircraft industry under their dominance). Strauß invited these countries to work together with the German Starfighter program, and, due to the small number of Starfighters each of these counties required and the small size of their domestic aircraft industries, they were happy to accept. Strauß's likely intent was to draw the Italian, Belgian, and Dutch aircraft industries into a dependent relationship with the German: the Starfighter program would create in these countries industrial capacities which could be kept working only by follow-up defense contracts from Germany. Germany could then work with them on advantageous terms, since, once industrial capacities were created, the governments of these countries would be under great pressure to keep their nationalized industries working; if all went well, this situation would pressure them to concentrate with the German industry under conditions that would ensure German dominance.[96]

Yet this meant short-term sacrifices. When in 1960 Italy, Belgium, and the Netherlands joined Germany to build the Starfighter, the second round of Starfighters did not go to Bavaria, but to the northern German firms, which were in need of more work at that time, and, disproportionately, to Italy, Belgium, and the Netherlands.[97] As a result of the expansion of the Starfighter program, by 1961 Strauß's ministry had become, as one German civil servant remarked, "the largest source of government contracts on the continent … far and away the biggest source of public contracts in Germany … a factor in politics and commerce that can no longer be ignored."[98]

The Starfighter project was a great boon, in some cases even a lifesaver, to key Bavarian firms. The chief contracts were awarded to Messerschmitt and BMW Triebwerkbau. As we saw earlier, Messerschmitt's financial situation had been catastrophic and through 1957 and 1958 the firm teetered on the edge of bankruptcy, until rescued by the Starfighter contract.[99] The Starfighter's jet engines, developed in America by General Electric, were built on license in Germany by the Bavarian firms of BMW Triebwerkbau and MAN. Other industries also benefited. Strauß had hoped that the Starfighter's electronics would be built in Bavaria by Siemens, but though Siemens did get Starfighter work, and though Honeywell and Litton guarded their secrets by founding German subsidiaries which worked on the German Starfighter, these subsidiaries were for the most part located near Munich. Furthermore, the American electronics firm of Bendix worked with AEG-Telefunken in Teldix and Hughes Aircraft worked with AEG-Telefunken in Eltro. Bavarian firms also received important work in new metals.[100]

The Starfighter contract re-created the German aircraft industry within reach of the European standard, ready to cooperate if not compete with French and British firms, and it re-created it in Bavaria. Neither the northern German aircraft industry nor Heinkel in Baden-Württemberg ever caught up. And Strauß's strategy of using the Starfighter program to concentrate the central European aircraft industries around the German was to be of long-term benefit. It was one of those short-term sacrifices Strauß asked of his industrial clients in order that together they realize greater long-term gains. In these years Strauß was working several other long-term strategies.

Strauß led the industrial interests that wanted the federal government to create a German space industry. In these years space, succeeding to the glamour and fascination that atomic energy had enjoyed in the mid 1950s, seemed the very horizon of the future. But German advocates of space flight had special obstacles to overcome: Nazi Germany had been the great pioneer of military rocketry and its V2 rocket attacks on London were very much in living memory; after World War II the victors sequestered Germany's rocket scientists abroad and banned research in rocketry. When in the early 1950s Germans showed some interest in rocketry, the federal government had kept it quiet, kept support for researchers low, and carefully framed any discussion of it in terms of space travel and the research of outer space rather than rocketry. But after Strauß became Defense Minister in 1956 and the Russians launched Sputnik in 1957, the question was "up." The whole logic of Strauß's defense-political ideas and his defense-industrial "interest solidarity" pointed beyond missiles to rocketry and space flight. And, although Strauß kept a low profile on the issue, he was in fact resolved to build rockets and arm them with nuclear warheads—despite the official denials, this was no small part of the impetus behind the creation of the Ministry of Atomic Affairs and in developing an atomic industry. Strauß's interest was unmistakable. He used the same arguments that had justified support for the aircraft firms to justify a space program: that a highly industrialized state like Germany, if it wanted to remain technologically competitive, had no choice but to participate in the development of space-flight technology and the research of outer space.[101]

Strauß had to maneuver his plans through two obstacle courses: the problems of ministerial jurisdiction and those of international cooperation. The first admitted of no easy solution, since the issue involved ministerial jurisdiction over quite different things, each one seeming plausible to belong by right to different ministries: rocketry (Defense), space flight (Transport), satellite development and the research of outer space (the proposed Ministry of Scientific Research feared by federalists), in addition to the claims of the Interior Ministry and the Foreign Ministry. In early 1960 the Defense Ministry dominated matters relating to space flight, since it was responsible for military rocketry and no other ministries had devoted much attention to these matters. But when later in that year the country began to take up the issue publicly, there began a "quite passionate" debate over which ministry should be responsible for space flight and how this responsibility would be institutionalized.[102]

Strauß tried to keep the new rocketry and space flight activities within his range of influence, or at least out of the hands of his enemies, so as to increase his own influence in the government and with the industries concerned. No doubt he would have liked to claim rocketry and space matters for the Defense Ministry, but once the debate began he recognized that, "in order not to create any false impressions abroad," this was quite out of the question.[103] In his 1961 speech to the Federation of the German Aircraft Industry, Strauß admitted that the Defense Ministry couldn't be "responsible for the whole field of aerospace research and for the whole field of space flight technology or even research," or even claim an important say in these fields, but insisted that it could be active in it.[104] He was certainly one of the most active participants in the debate.

This debate involved him in complex machinations with other Cabinet members. In 1960 and 1961 Siegfried Balke and Gerhard Schröder, the CDU Interior Minister and Strauß's political enemy, competed for jurisdiction over space flight.[105] While Balke was a minor nonpolitical minister, Schröder was a formidable figure in the CDU, so that Strauß did the former's fighting for him. On Strauß's insistence it was finally decided to create an Interministerial Committee for Questions of Outer Space (Interministerielle Ausschuß or IMA), but when in early 1961 Schröder was given lead responsibility within the IMA, Strauß moved to cut Schröder out.[106] He tried to reclaim the issue by setting himself up as the industry's most devoted advocate, associating himself completely with its desire, for example, that the federal government exercise "tight central control" over the field (as opposed to permitting scientists their cherished self-regulation and autonomy) and create a special Federal Authority (Bundesoberbehörde) with an "energetic personality at the head of this authority," to be given powers that previous federal authorities had not enjoyed, and "money, money and more money."[107]

The situation improved with the Cabinet reshuffle of November 1961, which took the Interior Ministry away from Schröder and gave it to CSU deputy Hermann Höcherl. But Strauß continued to support Balke's claims. On 29 January 1962, Adenauer decided to transfer lead responsibility for space flight research, space flight technology, and space research, as well as chairmanship of the IMA to Balke's Ministry of Atomic Affairs.[108] Strauß was happy with the decision, since Balke's ministry was part of the military-industrial-research empire beholden to the CSU and he seems to have hoped that a strong Ministry of Atomic Affairs would allow his Defense Ministry to exercise influence on "civil production."[109] He lent Balke one of his advisors from the Defense Ministry, Theodor Benecke, a high-level civil servant and a consistent promoter of the Bavarian defense and aerospace industries. Strauß emphasized at the time that the transfer of leadership in space flight to the Ministry of Atomic Affairs was only the beginning; the goal was to transform the Ministry of Atomic Affairs into a "technical ministry" that would be responsible for all of applied research and technology. But though Balke did try to stretch his powers beyond what Adenauer had given him, and though Strauß continued pushing for a ministerial centralization of responsibility for aviation, they got little support from Adenauer or their ministerial colleagues, who certainly saw the need to restrain the CSU's power in this field.[110]

If Strauß barely and belatedly surmounted the first obstacle, he stumbled through the second, international cooperation. He tried but failed to steer a substantial German program into fruitful cooperation with European and American programs. France and Britain took the initiative. Determined not to get left too far behind by the huge American space program, in 1960 they proposed to cooperate with each other in a European rocket and satellite development program, and invited Germany to participate. Strauß understood that they intended to reserve to themselves the tasks most valuable for national technology development, and that they believed Germany to be so far behind them that its participation would amount to little more than a financial contribution. Strauß responded by promoting a grandiose vision of European-American cooperation in space ventures, proposing that the Europeans together carry half the burden of a joint European-American space program.[111] Strauß thought that as part of a European team Germany could get work more valuable for national technology development than it could as the outsider faced by a Franco-British front. But the Americans never took Strauß's overture seriously and the German government accepted the Franco-British offer.[112]

With the support of Strauß and the other CSU members of the Cabinet, in 1962 the German government signed two treaties for a European space program. The first, ELDO (European Launcher Development Organization), agreed to develop rockets to act as satellite launchers, and the second, ESRO (European Satellite Research Organization), to develop satellites. At the same time and also with the concurrence of the CSU the federal government began funding a national space program, albeit a small one, making only DM 11,000,000 available for space-related projects, and created the German Commission for Space Research (Deutsche Kommission für Weltraumforschung). Both the European and German programs faced many problems: in ELDO, the other governments assigned Germany the third stage of the European rocket—from the point of view of rocketry the least important stage, though from the point of view of electronics the most interesting; in ESRO the French and British rejected Germany's attempt to make Munich its technical center; and Germany's national program was too ridiculously small to achieve anything worthwhile.[113] The Germans were really too deeply split among themselves to make anything of European cooperation or of their national program. Strewn with rivalries between Strauß, Schröder, Balke, Erhard, and Seebohm, the latter the Transport Minister, the field was not susceptible of a national goal more specific than not being exploited by the French and British.[114]

Strauß and the CSU State Group supported all space flight initiatives, objecting only that the initiatives should have gone farther. The beneficiaries of any German space program were clear enough from the beginning: they would include Strauß himself, the CSU, Bavaria, where the space industry would likely have been concentrated, as it was the second home of the DVL and the home of the most important potential contractors: above all Bölkow Developments, but also Messerschmitt, BMW, and Siemens (particularly Bölkow and Messerschmitt would be in need of work as soon as the Starfighter contract ran out).[115]

But there were political pressures in favor of the northern firms, who together formed the Northern Development Ring (Entwicklungsring Nord, ERNO) and demanded a share of the ELDO work. In the fall of 1961 Balke handed responsibility for the decision on a contractor to a committee of experts, who, after studying Bölkow's and ERNO's proposals for the third stage of the European rocket, recommended giving it to a working group of both. Bölkow and ERNO formed Satellite Launcher Working Group (ASAT, Arbeitsgemeinschaft Satellitentraeger), though Bavaria likely got the better of the deal, since ASAT's coordinating office was in Munich and Bölkow seems to have gotten the choicer work.

Beyond space flight, Strauß supported a range of initiatives that built up an infrastructure of defense- and aerospace-related research and development in Bavaria. They are often forgotten because some of the boldest of them seemed to produce more smoke than fire. Yet most of them did produce fire, if only years later.

The Defense Ministry's biggest research and development project was for vertical-takeoff aircraft (V/STOL, Vertical/Short Take-Off and Landing). With V/STOL, Strauß was again thinking big.

Despite its technical dubiety, the V/STOL project had plausible justifications. It was justified, on the military side, by geography: the few runways from which the German air force operated were so close to the Warsaw Pact counties that they could be destroyed within minutes of a Soviet attack, and most of Germany's expensive Starfighters thereby grounded. Vertical-takeoff aircraft, which could be dispersed through small pads located in forests throughout Germany, would be more survivable, which would enhance deterrence. On the industrial side, which drove the project, the project would keep the German aircraft industry working between the end of the Starfighter production and the production of the next generation of fighter-bombers. If the V/STOL project failed, the development contracts would nonetheless have contributed to the survival of the industry. If it succeeded, the German aircraft industry would have startled the French and British with its capacities, and positioned itself for a more substantial role in European cooperative projects, and would have technological leadership in a potentially important field—V/STOL aircraft would be marketed to countries in a strategic position similar to Germany's, and to countries that couldn't afford long runways.

In its initial phase, the project benefited chiefly the Bavarian aircraft industry. Strauß awarded to the Southern Development Ring (Entwicklungsring Süd, EWR, a cooperative venture of Messerschmitt, Bölkow, and Heinkel) the prize development contract, that for a supersonic V/STOL interceptor. Dornier, the other Bavarian firm, received a contract to develop a V/STOL transporter, and the northern German firms settled for a contract to develop a V/STOL tactical-reconnaissance fighter. Though the German aircraft industry stunned the French and British by producing a functioning prototype, it was unable to perfect the technology and never proceeded to production. In fact, V/STOL was treated like an employment program, work being shifted around to whichever of the German firms needed it the most at any given moment. The only V/STOL airplane to proceed to production in the 1960s, the British Harrier, was produced later, and independently from the German aircraft industry.

The Industrial Facilities Business Corporation (IABG, Industrieanlagen-Betriebsgesellschaft) was Strauß's other major research and development initiative. The IABG was a development and testing facility by which Strauß proposed to underwrite the Bavarian aircraft firms' research and development. Germany's numerous small aircraft firms were unable to afford research and development equipment comparable to that used by the major American, British, and French firms. Strauß proposed that the federal government finance a development facility where the firms would share access to such equipment. The development facility would be built in Bavaria—a justifiable decision, given the presence there of Bölkow, Germany's leading development firm, and the southern German concentration in jet fighters.

In fact IABG was tailor-made for Bölkow. After Ludwig Bölkow moved his firm to Bavaria in 1958, he asked Strauß to pay for a development facility out of his research budget. As early as 1957 and 1958 Strauß's ministry refined the idea in conversations with Bölkow, Messerschmitt, and Dornier.[116] This indicates Strauß's will, from the earliest days in the Defense Ministry, to make Munich the heart of the most industrially modernizing elements in the German aircraft industry. The site would be in the Munich suburb of Ottobrunn, Bölkow's backyard. Strauß approved the final concept in March 1960, IABG was set up in 1961, and it began operations in 1962.

Yet if Strauß and Bölkow had reason to be satisfied, many others were not. Certainly the non-Bavarian firms were unhappy, as well they had reason to be. A leading historian of the postwar German aerospace industry wrote that IABG, "created in the northern German firms the by no means false impression that they had been passed by in one of the most important decisions in the reconstruction of the German aircraft industry."[117] Strauß had not only spent the money his ministry received from the United States military assistance program in Bavaria, but even sought to give research and development money that had originally been destined for northern German firms Weser Flugzeugbau and Hamburger Flugzeugbau to the development facility in Bavaria.[118] Nor was Strauß entirely satisfied, for he had wanted IABG to be run by his ministry, and therefore part of his defense-industrial empire. But in the interministerial bargaining that went into its creation, the Federal Economic Ministry, which saw the whole thing as pork for Bavaria, successfully resisted this. In the end IABG was created pursuant to an agreement between the Corporation for Flight Technology (GfF, Gesellschaft für Flugtechnik), founded by the southern German aircraft industry in July 1959, the state-owned Industrial Management Corporation (IVG, Industrieverwaltungs-Gesellschaft), and the

Defense Ministry. Naturally, the aerospace research institutes saw IABG as a rival and a threat to their own budgets.[119]

IABG illustrates a more general move on Strauß's part to provide the Bavarian defense firms, which were almost all on financially shaky ground, with money to tide them over until they were paid for their work on the Starfighter and other projects. The Bavarian firms' applications for Mutual Security Act funds (MSA, an American program for military assistance to allies) tell the story. While IABG was preparing its application for MSA funds, similar applications were pending from the Bavarian firms of Messerschmitt, Dornier, BMW Triebwerkbau, and Siebel ATG (a Bölkow subsidiary) for a total of DM 28,422,000, not a staggering sum within the American military budget, but a great deal of money within the MSA program as well as for the Bavarian firms trying to finance their initial round of defense production; the non-Bavarian firms of Klockner-Humboldt-Deutz and Arbeitsgemeinschaft Nord had applied for a total of DM 14,000,000. The German Defense Ministry decided which firms got how much money, and preferred to put its money into IABG, indicated that it "entertained doubts over the justifiability of these applications, especially those of Klockner-Humboldt-Deutz and the Northern Group." And in fact, Dornier received DM 2,500,000, Messerschmitt DM 4,260,000, Siebel ATG DM 2,000,000, and BMW Triebwerkbau DM 12,015,000, while IABG received a whopping DM 21,000,000. The only non-Bavarian firm that received MSA money, the venerable Rhineland giant Klockner-Humboldt-Deutz, received DM 8,000,000.[120]

Strauß also set up the Defense Ministry as a patron of the Fraunhofer Foundation. Strauß's Defense Ministry rescued Fraunhofer after Erhard's Federal Economic Ministry, which had funded Fraunhofer's work in the early 1950s, drastically cut its funding in 1955. Five Fraunhofer Institutes were founded on the initiative of the Defense Ministry: the Institutes for Aerobiology, for Fuel and Explosive Chemistry, for Electrical Conductors, Radiometeorology and Maritime Meteorology, and the Ernst Mach Institute (Aerobiologie, Chemie der Treib- und Explosivstoffe, Institut für Elektrowerkstoffe, Radiometeorologie and maritime Meteorologie, Ernst-Mach-Institut). By 1959 Fraunhofer had four institutes working almost exclusively for the Defense Ministry, while six others worked partly for the Defense Ministry. Strauß became a member of Fraunhofer's Senate (the Fraunhofer Foundation was organized much like the Max Planck Foundation).[121] And by 1962 Balke's Ministry of Atomic Affairs looked to begin supporting three Fraunhofer institutes to work on space flight research. Hence the Fraunhofer Foundation became partially dependent on the CSU, a part of Strauß's "interest solidarity."

Were it not for the lack of vision in the Bavarian state government, the relationship between the Defense Ministry and the Fraunhofer Foundation might have worked much more to Bavaria's advantage. For most of Fraunhofer's new institutes were located in Baden-Württemberg, which, unlike Bavaria, was willing to contribute money to their support—Bavarian contributions to Fraunhofer increased only very slightly from the mid 1950s through the end of the 1960s.[122]

The practical abandonment of the Fraunhofer Foundation by the CSU-controlled Bavarian state government demonstrated once again that the CSU's politics of industrial modernization did not proceed from any integrated and agreed-upon CSU strategy, or even a strategy common to the leading CSU liberals, to modernize Bavarian industry. It proceeded rather from individuals working with their own ideas about how to improve Bavaria's position within Germany and, with that, their own political position. Though Hanns Seidel had been a cofounder of the Fraunhofer Foundation and passages in his 1957 inaugural address boded well for Fraunhofer, the new Bavarian Economic Minister, Otto Schedl, had concentrated on oil pipelines and "Strukturpolitik" and was too much a liberal to provide state funding for industrial research. While we do not know whether Strauß undertook to persuade the Bavarian state government or Schedl to work more closely with the Fraunhofer Foundation, Schedl seems to have believed rather firmly that firms should pay for their own research and that anyway the benefits industrial research institutes offered to Bavaria were too speculative to justify the expense.[123]

Two other research and development projects deserve mention, the Air Force Testing Site and an initiative to fund civil aircraft development. Germany's new Air Force Testing Site (Luftwaffenerprobungsstelle) was built in Bavaria on Strauß's order. The German air force had been using the Dornier firm's company airstrip in Oberpfaffenhofen, Bavaria, but in the late 1950s that arrangement was deemed unsuitable and the Defense Ministry began looking for a new site. The Bavarian state government lobbied Strauß to keep the Testing Site in Bavaria, but many in the Defense Ministry and in industrial circles preferred that it be moved to Speyer in the Rhineland-Palatinate. In 1959 Strauß decided in favor of Manching, a small town north of Munich, since, in the words of the Bavarian state government, "[Strauß] very much wants the Testing Site to be here, in the closest relationship with the Bavarian aircraft industry."[124]

Strauß also took up the cause of federal subsidies for the development of a civil aircraft industry. Arguing that the dependence of the aircraft industry on defense contracts was dangerous, on which point all were agreed, Strauß persuaded Economic Minister Ludwig Erhard to cooperate with the Defense Ministry in sponsoring a design competition for civil aircraft.[125] The Bavarian firm of Siebel ATG won with its SIAT 223, and in August 1962 Erhard's Federal Economic Ministry agreed to support production of the SIAT 223 with a credit of DM 1.2 million. Erhard prepared a supportive Cabinet presentation for 15 November 1962, though by that date the Spiegel Affair had put Strauß's position in question and the Cabinet postponed its decision.[126]

By late 1962, Strauß had constructed a defense-industrial empire, with a considerable network of defense industries and defense research and development fields dependent on him and the CSU State Group for support: and much of the empire was in Bavaria. As Strauß admitted to Fritz Berg, President of the BDI, "It would be superfluous to maintain that I have nothing to do with these factories [of the defense and aerospace industries in Bavaria] and that, taking the narrow view of my ministry and its official task, their fate could be of no consequence to me. I am not only a minister responsible to create an army, but also a politician, who has a certain responsibility for the economic future of his home state."[127]

As we have seen, large parts of this defense-industrial empire were not directly governed by Strauß, but influenced through proxies, allies, and relations of dependence. The empire had its center of gravity in Bavaria, but geographically it extended far beyond Bavaria. Politically, it extended through the federal government into areas involving other ministries, some held by members of the CSU State Group, some not, and through the major industries that looked to the government for contracts and funded research. But its importance in German politics and industry was undeniable, and it gave rise to opposition, resentment, and resistance.

Strauß's Fall

From 1957 through 1962 Strauß's political influence grew enormously, and he found himself in the thick of the struggle to succeed Adenauer. In this period he consolidated his control over the CSU, in 1961 receiving 546 out of 572 votes to become chairman of the CSU, then leading the CSU to victory in the 1961 federal elections, in which the CSU received 54.9 percent of the Bavarian vote and fifty deputies—10.5 percent of the national vote, up from 8.8 percent in 1957 and 5.8 percent in 1953. Strauß went into coalition negotiations in a strong position—in fact he intrigued with the FDP to replace Adenauer with Erhard, in exchange for which Strauß was to become Foreign Minister and Vice-Chancellor. Adenauer fought them off but in coalition negotiations the CSU held the Defense Ministry for Strauß, Atomic Affairs for Balke, and Post for Stücklen, and won the Interior Ministry for Höcherl (Fritz Schäffer, Justice Minister since 1957, retired). This was nearly equivalent to its previous position, a remarkable achievement considering that, due to the decline in the CDU's vote, the two parties had lost their absolute majority in the federal parliament and had to make room in their coalition for the FDP.

But resistance to Strauß's power also grew. A large block of CDU leaders were determined to block Strauß from the Foreign Ministry or chancellorship. Adenauer, long acquainted with Strauß's aggressiveness, brutality, and hostility to anyone who criticized him or trespassed on his territory, quite agreed with them, though in the early 1960s he seemed to fear Strauß—he even warned Federal President Heuss of the danger that Strauß might use the army to stage a coup d'état. This resistance was encouraged by developments in Strauß's public image, which seemed to darken as his power grew. His quest for German control of nuclear weapons and the bluntness with which he spoke of nuclear warfare strongly colored his image and from the years 1957 through 1962 the worst aspects of his personality became notorious even among the general public. Rudolf Augstein, the publisher of *Der Spiegel,* the leading national newsmagazine, had conceived an intense dislike for Strauß, whom he considered a

German McCarthy, all the more dangerous for his great intelligence, eloquence, and ruthless ambition. Augstein opened his pages to anything that tended to discredit Strauß—and material to use against Strauß existed in abundance, much of it relating to drunkenness, abuse of power, and corruption, which, though never perfectly substantiated, became proverbial.[128] In 1962 *Der Spiegel* made the "Fibag Affair" into a major national news story: Strauß had recommended the American government contract with a fly-by-night development company, Fibag, to build housing for American servicemen and their families in Germany. Hearings were conducted in the parliament and the developers testified that they had taken a Bavarian newspaper publisher as a partner, solely for his connections to Strauß, and that the publisher had remarked to them that he had to share his profits with Strauß. Strauß denied it, of course, but few believed him. By mid 1962 the political climate in Bonn had turned against Strauß, and the road to higher office there seemed blocked by his enemies in the CDU and FDP.[129]

But in Munich the road remained wide open, or at least it seemed to. In the summer of 1962 Strauß expressed his interest in running for the Minister-Presidency of Bavaria. Strauß's idea was probably to withdraw from the Bonn arena, where everyone was getting bloodied in the fight to succeed Adenauer, and at the opportune moment to use the Bavarian Minister-Presidency as a springboard into the chancellorship. The moment certainly seemed opportune to move back to Munich. Bavarian politics were quite tranquil at this time. Hans Ehard, the compromise candidate who had succeeded Hanns Seidel in 1960, was seventy-five years old and ready to retire. The CSU needed a candidate. Though the CSU's conservative wing had no candidate that could stop Strauß, it wanted to keep him out of Munich, and many who were not of the conservative wing felt that a Strauß Minister-Presidency would overthrow the balance between CSU conservatives and liberals and provoke a party crisis.[130]

When Strauß failed to get his candidacy accepted by the CSU Managing Committee, the party had to find a compromise candidate, as it had to in 1949 and 1960, and turned to Alfons Goppel, the little-known Bavarian Interior Minister. Augstein responded to the news that Strauß would remain in Bonn by launching a new affair in *Der Spiegel*, "Uncle Alois" ("Onkel Aloys"), accusing Strauß of promoting the defense-industrial career of a friend of his wife's family.[131]

But the affair that brought Strauß down—or rather, the affair that was the occasion for Strauß bringing himself down—was the "Spiegel Affair." On 8 October 1962 *Der Spiegel* published an article, "Conditionally Ready to Defend" ("Bedingt abwehrbereit"), that revealed weaknesses in German defense planning in surprising detail—essentially revealing the weakness of Strauß's "massive-retaliation" force *sans* nuclear weapons. The article was part of Augstein's anti-Strauß campaign, and it claimed to demonstrate the inability of Strauß's expensive military armed with "modern weapons" to either turn back or deter a Soviet attack. It appeared to be based on secret government sources, and raised questions of what other information the publisher might have, of who had provided the information, of whether the magazine had operated in conjunction with Soviet-bloc intelligence services and, in the eyes of the magazine's critics, of whether Augstein had compromised national security and committed treason.

On the night of 26/27 October 1962, the police searched *Der Spiegel's* offices and arrested Augstein and the article's author, who was vacationing in Spain. Though the government probably had sufficient grounds to take the actions it did, it soon appeared that the arrests were not ordered according to proper legal procedure. Strauß denied that he had a hand in ordering them—but it later became evident that he had. Publicists and intellectuals opened a campaign to force Strauß to resign, claiming that he had abused his power to punish a hostile journalist and was an imminent threat to German democracy.

This was the chance Strauß's rivals had been waiting for. Many in the CDU, tired of being outmaneuvered by Strauß, were happy to see him cut down to size. The FDP was even more eager to strike a blow against Strauß. Opposition to Strauß had been growing within the FDP for several years, as Strauß stole its nationalist thunder, proposed that Germany should move to an electoral system of proportional representation, which would have destroyed the FDP, and served the anti-Catholic FDP, notwithstanding his own battles against conservative Catholics in his party, as a convenient symbol of Catholic Bavaria. This opposition crystallized in 1962 as the FDP saw a blow against Strauß as a way to redeem its failure to keep its campaign promise to drive Adenauer from office. On 19 November the FDP ministers resigned from the Cabinet, saying they would return only when Strauß was no longer in the government. Then the CDU/CSU ministers resigned, opening the way to a Cabinet reshuffle. Since Strauß was willing to go to almost any length to hold onto the Defense Ministry, the renegotiation of a new government was put off until after the Bavarian state parliamentary election, scheduled for 25 November 1962. This election took on the character of a Strauß-plebiscite, with the idea that when the CSU vote declined and the FDP vote increased, Strauß would lose face, the FDP's anti-Strauß stand would be confirmed, and Strauß would have to resign. But in fact the CSU increased its vote by 1.9 percent to 47.5 percent, enough to give the party its first absolute majority in the Bavarian parliament. Strauß declared that the Spiegel Affair had led to an "astonishing solidarity of the Bavarian voters with a *paesano* under attack by Prussian intellectuals ... Bavaria stood to a certain extent against the rest of the world; and it stood with me."[132]

Still this was not enough to save Strauß. When Strauß realized this he fought to install Höcherl to hold his place in the Defense Ministry for him until things cooled down, but Adenauer refused, insisting that the ministry had been given to Strauß, not the CSU. All his power notwithstanding, Strauß could not force the CSU to bring down a government led by the CDU and CSU in order to save the Defense Ministry for him. The CSU's standing with Bavarian voters would have been too gravely damaged. On 30 November 1962 Strauß resigned as Defense Minister. When on 14 December Adenauer assembled his new government the only CSU ministers to retain their posts were Höcherl (Interior Minister) and Stücklen (Post Minister). Strauß was out, as was Balke (who learned that he lost the Ministry of Atomic Affairs from the ministry's doorman, which rude ouster did nothing to separate the LBI from the CSU).[133] In a poor return for the loss of Defense and Atomic Affairs, Werner Dollinger became Federal Property Minister and Alois Niederalt Minister for Affairs of the Federal Senate. The Spiegel Affair was a devastating blow for the CSU: not only were Defense and Atomic Affairs far more powerful and useful to Bavaria than the Treasury and Affairs of the Federal Senate, but Strauß's defense-industrial empire was now a ship without a captain, or at least without a CSU captain. The political atmosphere had turned sharply against the CSU, and consequences for Bavaria were predictable. For if Strauß had done much to rebuild Germany's defense and aerospace industry in Bavaria, he left this industry in a precarious position. His "Bavarian economic miracle" within the "German economic miracle" was not a liberal one: it required the power of the federal government, and making that power work to Bavaria's interests meant having Bavarians in power in Bonn—or so it would seem.

If the CSU had so often and so skillfully, in the previous fifteen years, taken advantage of circumstances and events, now, after the Spiegel Affair and Strauß's resignation, the problem was how to get around this most unfortuitous circumstance. How could the CSU defend and consolidate Bavaria's gains without controlling the Defense Ministry and the Ministry of Atomic Affairs?

Notes

1. BHA, StK, 112561, 26.11.58. Regierungserklärung, 26.3.58, and Erklärung, 5.11.57, reproduced in, *Dokumente,* 282ff, 251–277.
2. Lanzinner, *Zwischen Sternenbanner und Bundesadler,* 395f. Groß, *Hanns Seidel,* 186ff.
3. BWA, LBI, Ordner, 1957/58, Rede Seidel to LBI; LBI Tätigkeitsbericht 1957, "Vor schweren Aufgaben," 12.11.57; Otto Eberle, "Staatspolitik," 15.
4. BHA, MWi 21820, Bayern ruft Industrie. BHA, MWi, 21820, Rodenstock to Bezold, 20.5.57; Bezold to Rodenstock, undated; Schedl Brief, 11.12.57, 4.12.57; 21821, Werbung für Industrieansiedlung; 21822, Errichtung von Industriebetrieben in Bayern.
5. Erker, "Keine Sehnsucht": 509.
6. BHA, NL Schedl, Bearb. Kart., 17.
7. BHA, NL Schedl, I, 1, 19, Vortrag Schedls 24.9.58. Daniel Yergin, *The Prize: The Epic Quest for Oil, Money and Power* (New York, 1991), 499f. Anthony Sampson, *The Seven Sisters: The Great Oil Companies and the World They Shaped* (New York, 1975), 176. Immo Stabreit, "Internationale Zusammenarbeit auf dem Gebiet der Energie: ein Gebot der wirtschaftlichen und politischen Vernunft," *Europa Archiv* 33 (1978), 145. Werner Abelshauser, *Der Ruhrkohlenbergbau seit 1945. Wiederaufbau, Krise, Anpassung* (Munich, 1984), 92.
8. BA, B102, 33486, Entwicklung der Preise. Different prices (though similar proportions) can be found at BA, B136, 7701, Vermerk vom 1.7.58. Sampson, *The Seven Sisters,* 182.
9. BHA, MWi, 21820, "Bayern ruft Industrie."

10. Rainer A. Roth, *Freistaat Bayern, die politische Wirklichkeit eines Landes der Bundesrepublik Deutschland*, 4th ed. (Munich, 1986), 383.
11. *Mineralöl* 8 (1958), 13.
12. Abelshauser, *Ruhrkohlenbergbau*, 88f, 92ff, 103f (quoted is Westrick).
13. *Bundesanzeiger*, 6.2.59.
14. ACSP, NL Elsen, 2.13, Elsen to Aradi, 22.12.58; Elsen to Aradi, 24.10.58. "Diskussion um den Bau einer Alpenpipeline," *SZ*, 25/26.7.59. *Erdöl-Informationsdienst* 12, no. 38 (8.4.59). Winnacker, *Nie den Mut verlieren*, 210, 271f.
15. ACSP, NL Elsen, 6.7.13. Otto Barbarino, *Ein Lebenslauf im 20. Jahrhundert* (Munich, 1998), 74–81.
16. BHA, NL Schedl, Karton 62, 16, "So floß Öl nach Bayern." John Weitz, *Hitler's Banker: Hjalmar Horace Greeley Schacht* (Boston, 1997), 331–341. Italo Pietra, *Mattei, la pecora nera* (Milan, 1987). Leonardo Maugeri, *L'arma del petrolio. Questione petrolifera globale, guerra fredda e politica italiana nella vicenda di Enrico Mattei* (Florence, 1994). Paul H. Frankel, *Mattei: Oil and Power Politics* (New York, 1966), 130. Josef Müller, *Bis zur letzten Konsequenz: Ein Leben für Frieden und Freiheit* (Munich, 1975), 266, 268. Renate Höpfinger, ed., *Josef Müller—der erste Vorsitzende der CSU* (Munich, 1998). There were other connections between the protagonists and with Winnacker. BA, NL Schacht, 9. "Mattei am ersten," *Der Spiegel* 12, no. 32 (6.8.58): 34–41. Winnacker, *Nie den Mut verlieren*, 272f.
17. Frankel, *Mattei: Oil and Power Politics*, 23.
18. BHA, NL Schedl, II, 2, 52.
19. "Bayern prüft transalpines Ölleitungs-Projekt," *Oberbayerisches Volksblatt*, 10.6.59. BHA, NL Schedl, Karton 52, 2. BHA, NL Schedl, II, 2, 52, 6.10.59. BHA, NL Schedl, II, 2, 52.
20. BHA, NL Schedl, II, 2, 52.
21. BHA, NL Schedl, Leitzordner 65, Schedl to Mattei, 1.8.59, 18.7.59; Karton 52, 2, Schacht to Schedl, 25.6.59, 17.7.59. "Interesse für Ölleitung Bayern—Mittelmeer," *FAZ*, 16.7.59. "Pipelines nach Bayern erwogen," *SZ*, 13.3.59.
22. "Diskussion um den Bau einer Alpenpipeline," *SZ*, 25/26.7.59. *Erdöl-Informationsdienst* 12, nr. 38 (8.4.59). "Schildbürgerstreich mit Staatshilfe, Bayern auf dem Wege zu einer grotesken Fehlinvestitionen," *Verkehrs-Wirtschaft*, 3.10.59; "Donauschiffahrt hat Bedenken gegen Pipeline," *Mittelbayerische Zeitung*, 22.7.59.
23. BHA, NL Schedl, I, Vortrag 14.3.60. "Bayerns Kohlehalden nehmen ab," *SZ*, 3–4.10.59.
24. ACSP, Rep. Landesgruppe, 4. Wahlperiode, 22.2.60, 7.3.60; LGF - V 29.1.60 (1-) lfd. 1. BA, B102, 33487, Ehard to Adenauer, 16.3.60; Adenauer to Ehard, 4.60; 33492, Bert. Gesetzentwurf, 28.3.60; 33486, Brief, 10.3.60; Vermerk 8.3.60; Adenauer to Ehard, 3.60.
25. BA, B102, 33500, Westrick to Strauß, 27.9.60; 33487, Ehard to Adenauer, 16.3.60; Adenauer to Ehard, 4.60. "Durchhöcherlt," *Der Spiegel* 14, no. 10 (2.3.60): 20–22.
26. "Wenn das Öl über die Alpen kommt...," *Der Bayernspiegel*, 24.7.59 (quote from Schedl). "Eine Pipeline vom Mittelmeer nach München? Pläne einer energiepolitischen Gegenreformation," *Junge Wirtschaft*, 9.59. "Billige Energie—oberstes Interesse der Wirtschaft," *SZ*, 25.9.59.
27. Maugeri, *L'arma del petrolio*, 238. Luigi Bazzoli and Riccardo Renzi, *Il miracolo Mattei* (Milan, 1984), 217–219. *100 Jahre Esso* (Esso AG, 1990).
28. BHA, NL Schedl, II, 2, 52, Fetzer to Schedl, 15.2.60. Hermann Bößenecker, "Zwei Raffinerien für Bayern," *Die Welt*, 27.1.60. Maugeri, *L'arma del petrolio*, 241.
29. BHA, NL Schedl, Karton 52, 2. Giorgio Galli, *La sfida perduta: biografia politica di Enrico Mattei* (Milan, 1976), 181. Maugeri, *L'arma del petrolio*, 232.
30. Maugeri, *L'arma del petrolio*, 233, 237.
31. BA, B136, 2508, Betr.: Kohlenbergbau, 26.6.61. "'Aktion 'Eichhörnchen' für Rohöl?" *Handelsblatt*, 2.5.62. Abelshauser, *Ruhrkohlenbergbau*, 107.
32. "Keine Sowjet-Raffinerie in Bayern," *FAZ*, 11.1.62. "Keine Russenöl-Raffinerie in Bayern," *SZ*, 11.1.62.

33. Bayerischer Landtag, Stenographische Berichte, 7.2.62, p. 3489f. "Kein russisches Öl für Ingolstadt," *FAZ*, 8.2.62. "Russisches Öl hat in Bayern wenig Chancen," *SZ*, 8.2.62. "Kanzler-Attacke gegen bayerische Ölpolitik," *Intern: Vertrauliche Informationen - Unternehmen und Wirtschaftspolitik*, 29.1.62.
34. Bayerischer Landtag, Stenographische Berichte, 29.11.61, p. 3170.
35. BHA, NL Schedl, Karton 52, 2, Mattei to Schedl, 10.3.62; Schedl to Mattei, 29.3.62. Maugeri, *L'arma del petrolio*, 240. "Bayern gegen Kohle-Protektionismus," *FAZ*, 23.9.61. "Absage an Energiemarkt-Dirigismus," *SZ*, 23–24.9.61.
36. "Absage an eine Heizöl-Kontingentierung," *SZ*, 1.5.62. "Bayern befürchtet Kohlepreiserhöhung," *Industriekurier*, 1/2.5.62.
37. BHA, NL Schedl, I, 1, 24.
38. BHA, NL Schedl, Leitzordner 80, Bayerischer Wirtschaftsbrief, 29.5.64. Roth, *Freistaat Bayern*, 383. Werner Disko, "Die bayerischen Pipeline- und Raffineriepläne," *Mineralöl: Eine Zeitschrift für die Mineralölwirtschaft* 7, no. 11 (11.62): 5.
39. BHA, NL Disko, Karton 3, "Welche Zukunftsaussichten hat die chemische Industrie?" 4.70.
40. BHA, NL Schedl, Leitzordner 20/21, Etatrede für die Haushaltjahre 1960 und 1961.
41. Boenke, *Entstehung und Entwicklung*, 37, 40ff.
42. Deutinger, *High-Tech-Staat*, 48, 126.
43. BHA, MK, 66005.
44. Deutinger, *High-Tech-Staat*, 47f (quoting Butenandt). Boenke, *Entstehung und Entwicklung*, 154.
45. Boenke, *Entstehung und Entwicklung*, 53.
46. Deutinger, *High-Tech-Staat*, 148.
47. Boenke, *Entstehung und Entwicklung*, 92, 107ff, 113ff. Radkau, *Aufstieg und Krise*, 67–71, 80. E. Telschow and G. Lehr, "Das Institut für Plasmaphysik in Garching," *Die Atomwirtschaft* 8, no. 5 (May 1963): 302–306.
48. Boenke, *Entstehung und Entwicklung*, 115–121.
49. IFZ, NL Hoegner, Bd. 10, Sitzung, 16.7.59. Deutinger, *High-Tech-Staat*, 147.
50. IFZ, NL Hoegner, Bd. 79, *Nucleus*, 46/60. Ministerialdirigent Dr. Henninger, "Kernforschung und Kerntechnik in Bayern," in *Atom - reaktoren - energie - forschung in Deutschland - Situation 1965, Überblick 1966* (Frankfurt a.M.: Heinz P. Conté, 1966), 45. Boenke, *Entstehung und Entwicklung*, 23, 106, 122f, 134, 124–147.
51. Müller, *Geschichte der Kernenergie*, 257. Michael Eckert, "Anfänge der Atompolitik in der BRD": 141. Deutinger, *High-Tech-Staat*, 217.
52. Henninger, "Kernforschung und Kerntechnik," 45.
53. Boenke, *Entstehung und Entwicklung*, 156. Deutinger, *High-Tech-Staat*, 216f.
54. Radkau, *Aufstieg und Krise*, 39, 48ff, 56ff, 130.
55. Radkau, *Aufstieg und Krise*, 140.
56. IFZ, NL Hoegner, Bd. 79, *Nucleus*, 3/59. Radkau, *Aufstieg und Krise*, 27, 120ff, 141, 198.
57. BA, N1407, 170, Balke to Höcherl, 26.8.58. ACSP, Rep. Landesgruppe, 3. Wahlperiode, 101, "Atomministerium fördert Wissenschaft und Forschung in Bayern," 2.2.60; 2, Balke to Höcherl, 27.2.62.
58. ACSP, Rep. Landesgruppe 3. Wahlperiode, 101, Balke to Höcherl, 26.8.60. ACSP, Rep. Landesgruppe 3. Wahlperiode, 101, Balke to Höcherl, 10.4.60. ACSP, NL Strauß, Büro BMVg, VI, Balke to Strauß, 14.12.56; Strauß to Balke, 15.12.56.
59. BA, N1407, 170, Rede am 3.2.58; Rede am 3.60; B136, 6099, Balke to Vialon, 13.9.60.
60. BA, B138, 5102, Balke to Ehard, 5.6.62; Cartellieri to Goppel, 7.6.62; Cartellieri to Schedl, 7.6.62. Henninger, "Kernforschung und Kerntechnik in Bayern," 45.
61. BA, B138, 5102, Vermerk, 15.6.62; Vermerk, 18.6.62.
62. IFZ, NL Hoegner, Bd. 79, *Nucleus*, no. 8 (1959). Radkau, *Aufstieg und Krise*, 141f.
63. BHA, MWi, 12871.

64. BHA, MWi, 12946; 12858, Vermerk 8.6.60; Heigl to Kirchhoff, 8.6.60; Niederschrift zu Sitzung am 29.3.60; Niederschrift, 21.3.61; 12872, Stock to Guthsmuths, 1.12.60.
65. BHA, MWi, 12816. Trischler, *Luft- und Raumfahrtforschung in Deutschland 1900–1970,* 446f.
66. BHA, MWi, 12835, Niederschrift 25–26.4.60; 12823, Heigl to Stelle, 25.9.61.
67. BHA, MWi, 12823, Strauß to Baeumker, 30.7.62, and Baeumker to Heigl, 4.2.61 and 23.8.62; 12827, Sitzung, 6.7.61; 12881, DVL Wirtschaftsplan für 1958/1959. BA, B136, 9956, Strauß to Adenauer, 25.1.58; Wiederaufbau der deutschen Luftfahrtforschung, 25.1.58.
68. Helmuth Trischler, *Luft- und Raumfahrtforschung in Deutschland,* 362–364; Johannes Weyer, *Akteurstrategien und strukturelle Eigendynamiken. Raumfahrt in Westdeutschland 1945–1965* (Göttingen: O. Schwarz, 1993), 121.
69. *WBH* 7, no. 5 (2.2.61). Lanzinner, *Zwischen Sternenbanner und Bundesadler,* 347.
70. Kelleher, *Politics of Nuclear Weapons,* 64ff.
71. Strauß, *Erinnerungen,* 310. Schmückle, *Ohne Pauken und Trompeten* (Stuttgart, 1982), 196.
72. Strauß, *Erinnerungen,* 313–316. Krieger, *Strauß: barocke Demokrat,* 40f.
73. Kelleher, *Politics of Nuclear Weapons,* 104ff, 149ff, 198f.
74. *Flugwelt* 7/1958, p. 482. Brandt, *Rüstung und Wirtschaft,* 291f.
75. Franz Josef Strauß, "Die europäische Luftverteidigung," *Wehrtechnische Monatshefte,* 3/1959, 101–103.
76. Brandt, *Rüstung und Wirtschaft,* 277, 294.
77. FRUS, 1958–1960, vol. VII, no. 186, Telegram, 23.1.59.
78. MILITÄR, BV3, 11783, Konzentration der Luftfahrtindustrie, 14.2.58; Niederschrift 23.5.58, 28.5.58, p. 3. Andres, *Luft- und Raumfahrtindustrie,* 231.
79. Schwarz, *Adenauer,* vol. 2, 394–401.
80. Brandt, *Rüstung und Wirtschaft,* 300.
81. Abelshauser in *Anfänge westdeutscher Sicherheitspolitik,* vol. 4, 156.
82. MILITÄR, BV 3, W II, 16235, Bericht, 21.5.63.
83. Deutscher Bundestag, Stenographische Berichte, 2.7.58, 2209D.
84. Schmückle, *Ohne Pauken und Trompeten,* 198–211. Andres, *Luft- und Raumfahrtindustrie,* 213ff.
85. *Parlamentarisch-Politischer Pressedienst,* 27.10.1958. Schlotter, *Rüstungspolitik in der BRD,* 118.
86. Andres, *Luft- und Raumfahrtindustrie 1945–1970,* 214f. Abelshauser in *Anfänge westdeutscher Sicherheitspolitik 1945–1956,* vol. 4, 168.
87. *Flugwelt,* 12/1958, p. 910.
88. Schmückle, *Ohne Pauken und Trompeten,* 196ff.
89. Kelleher, *Politics of Nuclear Weapons,* 103.
90. MILITÄR, BV3, 11783, Besprechungsprotokoll, 5.2.58. Mechtersheimer, *Rüstung und Politik,* 18–19. Peter Schlotter, *Rüstungspolitik in der BRD,* 117.
91. Schmückle, *Ohne Pauken und Trompeten,* 197–211. Wolfgang Hoffmann, "Akte eines Akten-Dramas," *Die Zeit,* 8.1076. Voss, *Den Kanzler im Visier,* 397ff.
92. Schlotter, *Rüstungspolitik in der BRD,* 19. Benecke, "Aufgabe für die deutsche Luftfahrtindustrie," *Flugwelt,* 11/1958, p. 830.
93. BA, B102 15564, H1, BMVdg, Vermerk, 21.7.58.
94. BHA, MWi, 13332, Aktenvermerk, 10.7.58; 13340, Schedl to Strauß, 6.10.58.
95. Johannson, *Vom Starfighter zum Phantom,* 25. Andres, *Luft- und Raumfahrtindustrie,* 209ff, 220 (at about this time a representative of the Defense Ministry said that Germany would eventually procure one thousand Starfighters). Schlotter, *Rüstungspolitik in der BRD,* 20.
96. BA, B102, 162166, Niederschrift, 23.2.61. Schlotter, *Rüstungspolitik in der BRD,* 108.
97. BA, B102, 76252, Niederschrift, 8.12.59. Schlotter, *Rüstungspolitik in der BRD,* 23, 108. Johannson, *Vom Starfighter zum Phantom,* 26.
98. BA, B102, 162166, Niederschrift, 23.2.61.
99. Ulrich Kirchner, *Bundesdeutschen Verkehrsflugzeugbaus: der lange Weg zum Airbus* (Frankfurt a.M., 1998), 44.
100. Johannson, *Vom Starfighter zum Phantom,* 28f, 53, 58ff. *Interavia* 4/1962, 486–491.

101. Andres, *Luft- und Raumfahrtindustrie,* 401ff. Trischler, *Luft- und Raumfahrtforschung in Deutschland,* 400.
102. Weyer, *Technische Visionen - politische Kompromisse,* 18f.
103. Andres, *Luft- und Raumfahrtindustrie,* 510.
104. MILITÄR, BV3, 16341, Rede, 17.5.61.
105. Trischler, *Luft und Raumfahrtforschung in Deutschland,* 402f.
106. BA, B106, 21399, Strauß to Schröder, 2.5.61; Mitteilung aus Kabinettsprotokoll, 5.61, 9.5.61; Schröder to Strauß, 6.5.61. Weyer, *Technische Visionen - politische Kompromisse,* 63.
107. MILITÄR, BV3, 16341, Rede, 17.5.61.
108. BA, B106, 17801, Strauß to Bundeskanzleramt, 25.1.62. Trischler, *Luft- und Raumfahrtforschung,* 408ff. Kirchner, *Bundesdeutschen Verkehrsflugzeugbaus,* 111–116. "Spiel hinter den Kulissen," *Flug-Informations-Dienst* 9, no. 3 (2.2.62).
109. IFZ, NL Mintzel, Bd. 21, Strauß Rede, 8.7.61; Bd. 22, Strauß Rede, 13.10.62.
110. BA, B102, 36136, Vermerk, 24.11.61. Kirchner, *Bundesdeutschen Verkehrsflugzeugbaus,* 112. Trischler, *Luft und Raumfahrtforschung in Deutschland,* 412.
111. BHA, MWi, 12893, Strauß to Quick, 17.3.60. IFZ, NL Mintzel, Bd. 21, Strauß Rede, 8.7.61.
112. Andres, *Luft- und Raumfahrtindustrie,* 408f. Weyer, *Technische Visionen, politische Kompromisse,* 18, 62.
113. BA, B106, 1219, Schröder to Maunz, 5.10.61; Schröder to Ehard, 5.10.61. Wolfgang Krieger, "Zur Geschichte von Technologiepolitik und Forschungsförderung in der BRD. Eine Problemskizze," *Vierteljahrshefte für Zeitgeschichte,* 35, no. 2 (1987): 258f. Trischler, *Luft- und Raumfahrtforschung in Deutschland,* 416f. Andres, *Luft- und Raumfahrtindustrie,* 411, 413, 419.
114. MILITÄR, BV3, 16341, Rede Strauß, 17.5.61. Andres, *Luft- und Raumfahrtindustrie,* 431. Weyer, *Technische Visionen, politische Kompromisse,* 63. Trischler, *Luft- und Raumfahrtforschung in Deutschland,* 401.
115. Andres, *Luft- und Raumfahrtindustrie,* 404. Kirchner, *Bundesdeutschen Verkehrsflugzeugbaus,* 74f.
116. BA, B102, 15485, Strauß to Bundesfinanzminister, 28.2.58; Vermerk, 28.7.58; Fischer to Bölkow, 30.4.59. Trischler, *Luft- und Raumfahrtforschung in Deutschland,* 375. Kyrill von Gersdorff, *Ludwig Bölkow und sein Werk—Ottobrunner Innovationen* (Koblenz, 1987), 289.
117. Andres, *Luft- und Raumfahrtindustrie,* 233.
118. BA, B102, 36318, Betr., 26.3.62; Vermerk, 14.2.61.
119. BA, B102, 36318, Sitzung, 10.3.60, 11.4.60. Andres, *Luft- und Raumfahrtindustrie,* 231ff. Theodor Benecke and Günther Schöner, *Wehrtechnik für die Verteidigung. Bundeswehr und Industrie - 25 Jahre Partner für den Frieden (1956–1981)* (Koblenz, 1984), 219.
120. BA, B102, 36318, Sitzung, 10.3.60, 11.4.60; Niederschrift, 18.12.61.
121. ACSP, NL Strauß, Büro PV, 5368, Sörensen to Strauß, 5.4.63; Sitzungsbericht, 27.11.62. Boenke, *Entstehung und Entwicklung,* 42. Trischler and vom Bruch, *Forschung für den Markt,* 73f, 78. Rilling, *Kriegsforschung,* 51f.
122. Trischler and vom Bruch, *Forschung für den Markt,* 70f, 74–78. Deutinger, *High-Tech-Staat,* 190.
123. Deutinger, *High-Tech-Staat,* 189f.
124. ACSP, Rep. Landesgruppe, 3. Wahlperiode, 165, Schedl to Höcherl, 7.3.59. BHA, MWi, 22429, Flugplatz Oberschleißheim, 10.7.58; Ministerrat, 14.7.58. Benecke and Schöner, *Wehrtechnik für die Verteidigung,* 211, 217f.
125. BA, B102, 43525, Prass to Adenauer, 26.9.62; Strauß to Adenauer, 12.10.62; Adenauer to Erhard, 4.10.62.
126. Andres, *Luft- und Raumfahrtindustrie,* 313, 332ff.
127. ACSP, NL Strauß, Büro BMVg, I, Strauß to Berg, 7.2.59.
128. Schwarz, *Adenauer,* vol. 2, 677, 697, 724. Kelleher, *Politics of Nuclear Weapons,* 66. Strauß's empire also had regions of which little more is known even today than their existence. He had numerous "special accounts" (Sonderkontos), some dating back to at least the early 1950s. It is clear that the Economic Society of Bavaria (Volkswirtschaftliche Gesellschaft Bayern e.V., the

political arm of the LBI) and various firms paid money into various accounts that Strauß administered, some of them on a monthly basis, and that the accounts held great sums of money. Though it may be hypothesized that firms do not pay money to people who are not helping them, not enough is known about the transactions to draw any conclusions about their influence on our story. See, "Das Geld, Die Macht und FJS," *Der Spiegel* 50, nos. 30, 31 (22.7.96 and 29.7.96): 52–60 and 50–57.

129. *WBH* 8, no. 9, 11, 23, 26. Erich Kuby, *Im Fibag Wahn, oder, Sein Freund, der Herr Minister* (Reinbek bei Hamburg: Rowohlt, 1962). Thomas Dalberg, *Strauß, Porträt,* 177–186. Krieger, *Strauß: barocke Demokrat,* 48.

130. *WBH* 7 no. 21, 28.

131. "Onkel Aloys," *Der Spiegel* 16, no. 39 (26.9.62): 29–43. Notwithstanding their extreme one-sidedness see, Wolfgang Roth, et al., *Schwarzbuch: Franz Josef Strauß* (Cologne: Kiepenheuer & Witsch, 1972), 53–59; Bernt Engelmann, *Meine Freunde, die Millionäre: Ein Beitrag zur Soziologie der Wohlstandsgesellschaft nach eigenen Erlebnissen* (Darmstadt, 1966).

132. Strauß, *Erinnerungen,* 431.

133. ACDP, NL von Hassel, 012/1, Gespräche, 10.12.62. BWA, LBI, Präsidialsitzung, 14.12.62. "Hinter den Bonner Kulissen," *Tagesanzeiger,* 15.12.62 (regarding Strauß and Balke). Müller, *Geschichte der Kernenergie,* 159. Radkau, *Aufstieg und Krise,* 141.

CHAPTER 4

NEW TACTICS IN A TIME OF TRANSITION, 1963–1969

Changing Times

In 1963 there was a serious question whether the circumstances that the CSU had turned to its advantage were changing. For by 1963 many Germans were aware that their country was entering a period of transition—certainly many politicians and journalists had a powerful sense of it at the time, and historians have agreed with them. Though the changes went far beyond Germany, having their parallels in France, Italy, Britain, and the United States, they took different form in each country. In Germany, the event that marked the transition was Adenauer's long-awaited retirement, which came in the fall of 1963. Ludwig Erhard, Adenauer's successor, soon showed that he was unable to manage the conflicts between the parties in the governing coalition, and this contributed to a sense that the end of the Adenauer era did not so much lead into a definable new era in postwar Germany as an interregnum.

Another mark of the transition touched its deeper nature: the accelerating decline of the Catholic and socialist Weltanschauungen, and the diffusion and transformation of the liberal Weltanschauung. While the CDU, the CSU, and the Social Democrats accelerated their own respective liberalizations, each in its own way, the FDP accelerated its transition from a predominantly "Right-liberal" into an increasingly "Left-liberal" party. The Social-Democratic vote grew steadily and people spoke of a "comrade trend" (traditionally, members of the Social Democratic Party addressed each other as "comrade"). The CDU lost much of its hold over Catholic voters and people wondered whether Christian Democracy, having per-

Notes for this section begin on page 164.

formed its historic task of integrating Catholics and Protestants into one political party, reconciling the market economy and social responsibility, and reintegrating Germany into the West, had made itself obsolete. The larger trends of postwar Europe seemed to be turning against Christian Democracy, toward secularism, de-Marxified Social Democracy, stronger central governments, and a build-down of tension with the Soviet Union. Another mark was the public's demand for politicians with a more flexible and moderate public image, and an appetite for youth, dynamism, and modernity. Many in the CDU wanted Adenauer to retire because they thought the crusty old man had lost his appeal—by the 1965 federal election he would have been eighty-nine years old. By the mid 1960s the imperative to be "modern" had become politically irresistible. Franz Josef Strauß responded to it, as we shall see, and it was reflected in the unexpected success of Alfons Goppel as Bavaria's new Minister-President and in the CSU's political campaigns, which presented a more modern and dynamic image of the party.

The time of transition was also marked by growing interest in technology, the growing salience of industrial modernization and technology development as a political issue, and a new confidence in the efficacy of state planning to promote industrial modernization. The 1950s had been characterized by a liberalism that saw modernization as a product of market competition; but the state planning hailed in the 1960s was less about socialism than Keynesianism, and focused on state support for science and technology development, including research, education, and subsidies for private industry, particularly in what were seen as "key" sectors of the economy. All this had implications for the CSU and the politics of industrial modernization, and the potential connections to Strauß's own politics are obvious.

Yet the 1960s was a time of transition and the economic liberalism that had carried everything before it in the 1950s by no means disappeared. From 1963 to 1966 its representative, Ludwig Erhard, held the chancellorship. Although the formation in Bonn of the Grand Coalition of the CDU/CSU and the Social Democratic Party in 1966 heralded a new willingness to involve the state with private industry, some Christian-Democratic politicians and many industrialists, particularly from smaller firms and smaller, more regional groupings like the LBI (less confident that they had the political pull to make state interventionism work for them), continued to prefer the liberalism of the 1950s.

Liberalism and Interventionism in Bavaria

Even within the CSU the political situation turned against Strauß, as aftershocks from the Spiegel Affair reverberated through the party. Strauß's rivals took the affair as an opportunity to renew power struggles within the party leadership, and this led to what was at the time referred to as a "CSU-crisis."[1]

It is instructive to consider how Strauß maintained his position. In January 1963 he had himself elected chairman of the State Group—since he had become Special Minister in 1953 it had been the State Group's practice to elect as its chairman the deputy next in line for a ministerial appointment—and concentrated on rebuilding the State Group's discipline, unity, autonomy, and will, reasserting its special status and reconfirming it as one of the bases of his own power.[2]

Yet Strauß's reelection to the CSU party chairmanship was in doubt for some time. In the months prior to the party conference in July, the party's conservative wing, led by the aristocratic federal deputy Baron von und zu Guttenberg and the Catholic press and clerics, subjected Strauß to harsh criticism. Guttenberg went so far as to tell the press that "the body of the CSU is healthy, but its head is sick." Strauß won reelection to the party chairmanship partly by refurbishing his image.[3] He took some time off, letting it be known that he was seeking the counsel of priests and considering his past mistakes. He traveled abroad, tourist class, and began the personal transformation that soon included taking flying lessons, studying economics and finance, impressing the British with a book, *The Grand Design*, on European integration, losing thirty pounds, cutting his hair more stylishly, reining in his violent rhetorical excesses, and even being polite to his opponents.[4] He also broke out of the corner of defense politics by speaking to German policy toward Europe, toward France, and toward East Germany. He positioned himself as the leading German friend of Gaullist France, which, though Strauß's Gaullism was more overtly anti-American than Adenauer's, allowed him to claim more or less plausibly to be the heir to the Adenauer tradition as against the Atlanticism of Erhard's government.[5]

In any case, the conservative revolt threatened more than it promised Bavaria's industrial modernization. The rebels had little interest in industrial modernization, and there is no reason to believe that, had they pushed Strauß aside, they would have accomplished anything for Bavarian industry. They attacked Strauß not from the center but from the Right, and can be characterized as conservative humanists, moralists concerned with foreign policy and German reunification, and hardly at all with interest-group politics. It said much about the nature of their challenge that Strauß met it not by becoming more conservative but, in a sense, by modernizing himself.

Yet if the CSU was shaken up, its governance of Bavaria went unchallenged in these years. In November 1962, at the height of the Spiegel Affair, it won its first absolute majority in the Bavarian parliament, and in 1966 it increased its majority slightly, and considerably so in 1970, when it won an unprecedented 56 percent of the popular vote. The CSU's success seems to have reflected the voters' contentment rather than its expectations, for Bavarian state politics were relatively quiet in these years. Under the Minister-Presidency of Alfons Goppel, and in accord with the spirit of the times, the CSU's "religious Right" accelerated its long retreat, the state government represented Bavarians' federalist aspirations vocally but without slipping into the antinational excesses that in the 1950s gave fuel to the other parties, and the Bavarian economy outstripped that of West Germany. Though the parties naturally had no trouble finding things about which to disagree, few of their contentions agitated the deeper waters of Bavarian public life, and voters' interest in state politics diminished markedly, as did the urgency of the other parties' resistance to the CSU.

Within Bavaria the politics of modernization was probably less politicized than elsewhere in Germany, largely because within the CSU government could be found effective advocates of both the liberal and the interventionist approaches.

This in turn was largely because Minister-President Alfons Goppel was unable to enforce his policy ideas on the ministers in his government, at least until the very end of the 1960s. Goppel was politically weak, having become Minister-President as a compromise candidate. Homely and uninteresting, almost unknown to the public when the CSU Managing Committee (*Landesvorstand*) selected him to succeed Hans Ehard in 1962, and having no band of loyal personal supporters in the party and few connections to Bavarian industry, Goppel could not use the Minister-Presidency to challenge Strauß. Far from it: though Goppel had been Seidel's and Ehard's Interior Minister, he had never held any significant leadership position in the CSU party organization. Nor did Goppel try to upset the reckonings that had put him in power. Strauß continued to control the CSU party organization and it represented his ideas. Goppel accepted these, for the most part, and chose to profile himself as a moderate but resolute federalist. One could even say that, in his political weakness, modesty, and federalism, Goppel's Minister-Presidency continued Ehard's more than it resumed Seidel's. Yet in the course of the 1960s Goppel acquired the image of an amiable uncle, an administratively competent father figure (*Landesvater*) concerned to protect the Bavarian tradition and alleviate the hardships of the rural Bavarian people. His image was neither populist, clericalist, nationalist, conservative, or liberal; in fact it was somewhat apolitical. This was made possible by the nonconfrontational spirit of Bavarian politics in the 1960s and by the contrast between Goppel and Strauß, who formed, as one CSU leader put it, a 'dream-team': "Strauß as a politician involved in global controversies, with obvious ability, knowledge and prestige, and Alfons Goppel as lovable, tolerant, competent, 'father of his people,' respected throughout Bavaria, were a perfect pair."[6]

Consequently, Culture Minister Ludwig Huber was able to chart his own course to a much greater degree than previous occupants of this controversial ministry. In harmony with the fashion for planning and state intervention in the economy, Huber actively pursued modernization in education, science, and research. At the same time Economic Minister Otto Schedl developed his liberal energy policy into a comprehensive strategy for Bavarian economic development.

We will deal first with the Economic Ministry under Otto Schedl, who represented the liberalism that had been fashionable in the 1950s. Schedl resisted the pressures to spend public money on science and in support of industry, believing that it would be money poorly spent. Though Schedl was no market dogmatist, he firmly believed that government's chief role in the economy was to create conditions favorable to free competition.

Regarding aerospace research, Schedl was reluctant to support it—and given the situation he was probably right. By 1963 Bavaria had won its struggle to become the home of the German aerospace industry and held onto half of the DVL, by far the most important aerospace research institute, so that, Bavaria having won the central points, the few remaining institutes had declined in importance. Other questions, such as the financing of the Central Collection of Aviation Documentation (Zentralstelle für Luftfahrtdokumentation) and the creation of further institutes in Bavaria related to existing Bavarian industries (as in satellite technology, which related to Bölkow and its successor corporations, or electronics, which related to Siemens), were of lesser importance. As a result, Schedl's Economic Ministry saw aerospace research as a good place to save money. We have already seen that, as part of a deal with North Rhine-Westphalia, in 1963 it allowed the German Research Institute for Glider Flight (Deutsche Forschungsanstalt für Segelflug) to be forced to merge into the DVL, in return for which Schedl cooperated with North Rhine-Westphalia to overcome financial difficulties in the building up of the DVL center in Oberpfaffenhofen, Bavaria. Now that Bavaria was nearly a "half-owner" of the DVL, it even supported North Rhine-Westphalia in its battle to remain the headquarters of the DVL: the aerospace research institutes still to be merged into the DVL wanted the headquarters moved from North Rhine-Westphalia to Bonn in the Rhineland-Palatinate, but North Rhine-Westphalia and Bavaria prevailed. In 1966 Schedl celebrated the completion of the DVL's Oberpfaffenhofen complex as the consolidation of aerospace research in Bavaria.[7] The Oberpfaffenhofen complex required that Bavaria make only an inconsequential increase to its contributions to aerospace research: whereas Bavarian contributions had been DM 950,000 in 1960/61 and 1962, from 1963 through 1968 they remained at DM 1,000,000. In the contest over aerospace research institutes, Bavaria emerged as the real winner, receiving an almost 50 percent share of the DVL, an outstanding return on a small investment.[8]

The Fraunhofer Foundation was a different case. Here Schedl's hands-off approach seems to have failed Bavaria. We have already seen how Schedl abandoned earlier plans to make Fraunhofer an engine of industrial modernization in Bavaria, plans that were perhaps ready to bear fruit. At this time Fraunhofer was very much open to Bavarian influence: though Strauß had had to resign from Fraunhofer's Senate as a consequence of his resignation from the Cabinet, in the mid and late 1960s Fraunhofer's Board of Directors and Senate included Siegfried Balke, Hugo Geiger (CSU state parliamentary deputy), Herbert Berg (General Manager of Wacker-Chemie), Odilo Burkart (chairman of the board of directors of Maximilianshütte, Bavaria's only large steel mill); Emil Sörensen (a member of the board of directors of the Bavarian firm of MAN) chaired its Senate, while Hermann von Siemens served as Fraunhofer's President until early 1965. Yet in 1965 Bavaria hosted only three of fourteen foundation-owned Fraunhofer Institutes, while Baden-Württemberg hosted six.[9] Though in the mid 1960s the Fraunhofer Foundation was still funded primarily by the Federal Economic Ministry and the Defense Ministry, the trend in funding research institutes was to require cofunding from host states. Baden Württemberg had been willing, but Otto Schedl, admitting Fraunhofer's worthiness in principle, insisted that he did not have enough money for it in his budget.[10] Only direct political threats could move the Bavarian state government to increase its support for

Fraunhofer, as when Fraunhofer threatened to close the Technical Development Site (Technische Entwicklungsstelle, TES, where Felix Wankel developed his engines) in Lindau, Bavaria for lack of Bavarian state contributions. Even here, the CSU state government responded only after the Social Democrats began to make a political issue out of the closing.[11]

Schedl's chief concern remained energy prices, an issue that had not gone away with the arrival of oil pipelines in Ingolstadt. After 1962 the coal interests prevailed over the CSU in obtaining legislation to raise the cost of oil: the federal parliament passed legislation that extended the tax on heating oil to refinery gas (a by-product of the refining process), in order to discourage the Bavarians from using refinery gas to drive power plants; additional legislation required the oil firms to maintain sizable "minimum stocks," ostensibly to secure Germany's supply but in truth to raise costs and drive smaller dealers out of the market; further legislation required the oil firms to give legal notice long before the construction of pipelines and refineries.[12]

Not even with Strauß's help could the CSU muster votes to block the heating oil tax, the coal industry's most effective weapon against oil. In its 1963 legislative plans the CDU/CSU-FDP government conceded the continuation of the heating oil tax for five more years. Schedl led the opposition to this in the Federal Senate, where the states far from the coalfields and ports pitted themselves against the coastal and coal-producing states. It was finally decided that the heating oil tax should be phased out at the rate of 25 percent per year until it disappeared in 1968.[13] But when the Grand Coalition of Christian Democrats and Social Democrats took office in 1966, there was never any doubt but that it would come to the aid of coal by further extending the heating oil tax. Not only was the CSU's weight within that government reduced, but the Social Democrats had absolutely committed themselves to the extension, which the CDU also supported.

Yet Bavaria was checked but not set back. The harassing legislation and heating oil tax did not equalize the prices of coal and oil, and oil continued to increase its market share. In the late 1960s the oil companies built yet more pipelines and refineries in Bavaria, so that by 1968 oil flowed to Bavaria from Marseilles, Genoa, and Trieste. And though Bavarian industry encouraged Schedl not to capitulate to the heating oil tax, it was satisfied with Schedl's and the CSU's best efforts, understanding that it had never lain within the CSU's power to completely block a heating oil tax.[14]

At the same time, Schedl took the tactic that had brought oil to Bavaria and raised it to the level of the basic strategic principle of a politics of Bavarian economic development. His idea was that the best thing the Bavarian Economic Ministry could do for the Bavarian economy was to lower energy prices. The way to do this was by promoting free competition in as many energy sources as possible. Just as he had played Mattei's ENI against the international oil cartel, he proposed to play various energy sources against each other.[15]

Yet the time was past when liberalization could secure such big breakthroughs for the Bavarian economy. Efforts to improve free competition in natural gas and nuclear power had little effect.

In the case of natural gas, Schedl sought to repeat his trick of a decade earlier. After several years of hesitating, due to doubts about the cost-efficiency of gas, in the mid 1960s he made some very public efforts to arrange a supply of natural gas for Bavaria, whereby, he hoped, the market would put pressure on existing energy suppliers to lower prices. Schedl undertook a variety of actions: he promoted the construction of natural gas pipelines from northern Germany to northern Bavaria, which allowed northern Bavarian industry to purchase natural gas as cheaply as Ruhr industry. Then, looking for yet more favorable prices, he opened negotiations with the Netherlands, Algeria, and Libya. These ultimately failed, and in 1969 he opened negotiations with the Soviet Union, which received press attention similar to that which he got in the "red oil campaign." Later he allowed Ruhrgas, a northern German firm interested in dealing with the Soviets, to negotiate the details of a deal that delivered gas to Bavaria beginning in 1973.[16] The issues resembled those Schedl had faced with ENI, and allowed Schedl to cast himself once again as the aggressive representative of Bavarian interests, securing Bavaria's supply of cheap energy. Yet the results seem to have been less significant, as natural gas became a significant energy source for Bavaria only in the 1970s, due largely to the cost of building the network of pipelines beyond Bavaria's major urban centers.[17]

Atomic power was a similar case, though more symbolic than substantial. Prior to the mid 1960s, the Bavarian power companies had been uninterested in atomic power, since it could not be produced economically. Schedl did little to encourage them in this direction, believing that power companies used atomic power projects as an excuse to raise electricity prices, and that it was wiser to let other countries pay the costs of experimentation. But in 1966, when the oil companies raised their prices in Bavaria and thereby called into question his achievement in bringing the pipelines and refineries to Bavaria, Schedl came to see atomic power as a counterweight to the oil firms, which seems to have been the origin of his idea that Bavaria must develop as many energy sources as possible. And so he gave new impetus to two atomic power plants being built in Bavaria, at Gundremmingen and Niederaichbach.[18] The former was a successful but very small light-water reactor in the arrangements for which the Bavarian state government played little role. The latter was a heavy-water reactor, which, though financed by the federal government, was heavily promoted by the Bavarian Economic Ministry. If it had been a success, Siemens, the contractor, would have become the world's leading constructor of heavy-water reactors. But the experiment with heavy water proved a failure, not to say an economic catastrophe, and was not repeated.[19] As a result, in 1970 Bavaria received only 1.7 percent of its primary energy consumption, or 5 percent of its electrical power, from atomic power plants.[20]

But Schedl was not dogmatically liberal. Rather he was quite willing to see his ministry intervene in the economy when it would clearly benefit Bavaria and did not cost money. The merger of the Bavarian aircraft firms provides the outstanding example of this.

After the Starfighter contract ran out in 1964, the federal government determined to force the aircraft firms to merge before it awarded the next round of major government contracts. Such mergers could endanger the Bavarian aircraft industry if they led to Bavarian firms merging with northern German firms on unfavorable terms. Of course, by 1964 the merger issue already had a history. Since the mid 1950s the federal government had intended to force the firms to merge, so that the industry, which lived from government contracts, achieved reasonable economies of scale. As Defense Minister, Strauß had delayed the process, accepting the firms' idea that as a first stage they would not merge but form subsidiaries in which they cooperated in the production of individual aircraft, like Flugzeug-Union-Süd for the production of the Fouga Magister jet trainer. Then he allowed them to take a step backwards, forming semi-serious, much undercapitalized working pools (Arbeitsgemeinschaften) for joint work on the development of V/STOL aircraft (EWR), the Fiat G91 (Arge 91), and the F104 G (Arge 104 Süd).[21]

After Strauß's resignation, the government renewed its threat to withhold contracts. This had little effect through 1966. Even with Strauß out of the Defense Ministry, the aircraft firms knew well enough that the politicians could hardly allow them to go broke for lack of work. Yet the policy of encouraging mergers did endanger the Bavarian aircraft industry, partly because the very notion of mergers implied breaking down the Bavarian domination in high-technology airplanes; partly because Strauß's successor at the Defense Ministry was a northern German, Kai-Uwe von Hassel, who would presumably push for mergers that favored the northern German industry; and partly because the northern German firms were more cooperative. In 1964, two northern German firms, Focke-Wulf and Weser Flugzeugbau, merged to form United Aircraft Manufacturers (VFW, Vereinigte Flugtechnischewerke). The southern firms could not come to agreement; for one thing, they remained family firms, dominated by egotistical aircraft designer-owners (Willy Messerschmitt, Ludwig Bölkow, and Claudius Dornier), none of whom could bear to submit to another. When in late 1964 Heinkel abandoned the southern bloc for the northern, merging into VFW, the southern bloc became a purely Bavarian bloc—another dangerous development.[22] By 1966 all of the firms were desperate for work, and in the Grand Coalition formed that year the Defense Ministry and Economic Ministry fell into unfriendly hands: the former was given to Gerhard Schröder, a Protestant Christian Democrat from North Rhine-Westphalia and a political enemy of both Strauß and the CSU, and the latter to Karl Schiller, a Hamburg Social Democrat with no debts to pay in Bavaria.

For the first time since the early 1950s, the CSU state government rather than the Defense Ministry became the Bavarian aircraft industry's chief advocate. But the deck seemed to be heavily stacked against Bavaria. The federal government began to discuss a new fighter jet and contracts for its development and production were as vital as oxygen to the aircraft industry. The federal government announced that firms that did not merge would not get contracts, and that only one contract would be awarded. Schröder and Schiller shared the goal of forcing Bölkow and Messerschmitt to merge with VFW, in which merger, as they intended it, the northern firm would probably have dominated. Bölkow was set up as the first firm to be merged into VFW—bad news for Bavaria since VFW, being larger than Bölkow, had a reasonable claim to dominate Bölkow. Ludwig Bölkow was also part of the problem: he was ambitious, capital-hungry, and actively looking for partners in northern Germany and abroad, and his personal commitment to Bavaria was slight. Moreover, Bölkow seems to have considered that it would be better for the future of the aircraft industry to de-Bavarianize it, so that other states would have an interest in its support. Yet in 1967 negotiations between VFW and Bölkow failed, largely due to Bölkow's insistence that he be the chairman of the board of directors of the new firm and that Munich, the location of his firm, be its headquarters. VFW opened negotiations with the sole remaining northern firm, Hamburger Flugzeugbau (HFB), a small firm that it thought it would swallow, thereby putting itself in a yet stronger position when it came time to merge with the southern firms.[23]

The Bavarian state government tried to forestall the ill effects of a VFW-HFB merger by promoting a Bölkow-Messerschmitt merger. The latter seemed unlikely because Willy Messerschmitt refused to be subject to his former employee Ludwig Bölkow, who for his part was equally determined to lead any firm into which his own merged.[24] The Bavarian state government had tried to promote a Bölkow-Messerschmitt merger several years earlier by selling its Messerschmitt shares to a Bölkow subsidiary, and in 1965 considered offering a Messerschmitt-Bölkow merger substantial financing. Nothing came of these initiatives and in 1967 the state government tried again. Franz Sackmann, the CSU State Secretary in the Bavarian Economic Ministry (that is, number two in the ministry, after Schedl), offered to act as an honest broker between the two firms.[25] Sackmann, a longtime ally of Strauß from the CSU's liberal wing, spoke to the press of Bavaria's interests, "which would find a very lucrative expression in the form of guarantees and loans," so long as the merger negotiations were not characterized by "openly egotistical individual interests."[26]

But only the threats of the federal government could overcome the personal rivalries.[27] When the Messerschmitt-Bölkow negotiations dragged into 1968, the Defense Ministry warned the aircraft industry that there would be no next-generation fighter jet or Airbus until the southern firms merged; soon Schiller's Federal Economic Ministry added its own warning and Balke, who since his ministerial retirement in 1962 had become a spokesman for industrial interests, warned that the federal parliament could no longer tolerate "such a fragmented aircraft industry," and that the frustration of the parliamentary deputies could turn into anger that would endanger the existence of the industry. Even Strauß was reported to be disgusted with the firms.[28] At the same time the federal government hardened its preference for the industrial model most dangerous to the Bavarian aircraft industry: that of a single national firm.[29] Schiller threatened that if the firms refused he would either refuse to proceed with Airbus, or have the firms merged by legislation; he seems to have had in mind a "Law for the Adaptation and Recovery of the German Aircraft Industry," analogous to that which had reorganized the Ruhr coal industry. In April 1968 the federal parliament unanimously declared corporate mergers to be the condition of further contracts and the government declared 31 October 1968 to be the deadline: if there were no agreement by that date, lead responsibility in the next-generation fighter would be given to VFW. Messerschmitt and Bölkow sat down once more at the bargaining table. Once more the Bavarian state government took up mediation, and an agreement preliminary to a merger was finally signed on 6 June 1968.[30] The new firm was named Messerschmitt-Bölkow, and it was led by Ludwig Bölkow.

The CSU can take some credit, not so much that a merger took place, but that Messerschmitt and Bölkow merged. Given the intense mutual dislike of the firms' principals, it seems likely that, were it not for the CSU's effort on behalf of a merger favorable to Bavarian interests, one of the two would have merged with VFW. For the Bavarian government provided Messerschmitt-Bölkow with low-interest loans of up to DM 50,000,000 and, Bavaria taking ownership of 16.6 percent of Messerschmitt-Bölkow, promised Willy Messerschmitt to use its influence to restrain Ludwig Bölkow.[31]

Yet the contest was replayed in 1969. The political question of northern German versus Bavarian dominance of the German aircraft industry had not been resolved, and in another dance of potential mergers, the CSU again acted as midwife to a merger favorable to Bavarian interests. Schiller, considering that the CSU had worked with Messerschmitt and Bölkow to frustrate his project for a single national aircraft firm, promoted a merger of Messerschmitt-Bölkow and VFW into a single national firm involving Krupp GmbH. But Messerschmitt-Bölkow and VFW could not agree on valuation, and Krupp was determined to set the business policy of the single national firm. Neither Ludwig Bölkow nor Willy Messerschmitt would accept this; and as Ludwig Bölkow held 16.66 percent, Willy Messerschmitt 33.33 percent, and Bavaria 16.66 percent of Messerschmitt-Bölkow, they were able to prevent this merger.[32]

Again the firms maneuvered for position. This time Messerschmitt-Bölkow and VFW were competing to become the dominant German firm. The Messerschmitt-Bölkow merger had left two firms unmerged: the small family-owned Bavarian firm of Dornier, which utterly refused to even enter into negotiations, and Hamburg Aircraft Construction (HFB, Hamburger Flugzeugbau GmbH), owned by the Blohm family. Both VFW and Messerschmitt-Bölkow opened negotiations with HFB but Blohm took VFW more seriously. The VFW-HFB merger seemed to be the preference of the federal government, and it would certainly have given VFW the upper hand over Messerschmitt-Bölkow. But when the Bavarians heard that Blohm felt the VFW executives were treating him in a high-handed manner, Messerschmitt-Bölkow renewed its offers. Blohm flew to Munich, where Bölkow and Bavarian state representatives met them with a generous offer. Bölkow offered the Blohm family more than HFB was worth, convinced that if he could link his firm to Hamburg, it would be safe even under a

Social-Democratic government—Hamburg was the home of heavyweight Social Democrats like Herbert Wehner, Helmut Schmidt, Karl Schiller, and Hans Apel.[33] Again the CSU pushed the deal over the top: the Bavarian state government promised a credit for the financing of a series of twenty of Blohm's executive transport jets (the Hansa-Jet HFB 320, of which he had sold only twenty-three), a cause dear to Blohm's heart.

On 14 May 1969, Messerschmitt-Bölkow-Blohm was created. The CSU's role had again been necessary if not sufficient in making Messerschmitt-Bölkow-Blohm Germany's largest and dominant aircraft firm, overcoming the north-south divide in the German aircraft industry in a way that secured the future of the Bavarian aircraft industry.

Under Ludwig Huber, the Culture Ministry took an approach different from Schedl's, consciously and consistently taking up an active role in planning and directing state support for research and the construction of universities. Thus did Hanns Seidel's legacy finally pass from his own former ministry to one with a very different past, indeed from 1964 to 1970 Ludwig Huber's task was precisely "overcoming the past," *Vergangenheitsbewältigung*—a term customarily applied to the National Socialist past.

Huber had to overcome a different past. Not only industrialists, and northern and exile Germans in Bavaria but many, and probably even most, native Bavarians suspected that the modernization of Bavaria had been retarded by obscurantist clericalism in the Culture Ministry. Obscurantism and clericalism were popularly attributed not only to the nineteenth-century Patriot Party and the pre-1933 Bavarian People's Party, but also to the CSU. Alois Hundhammer, the leader of the CSU's conservative wing and first postwar Culture Minister, had staffed his rebuilt ministry with conservative Catholics, resisted Americanizing reforms, defended separate schools for Catholic and Protestant students and the continued existence of very small village schools, and given the general impression of being far more concerned with preserving and extending religious education and Bavarian state prerogatives in educational, cultural, and religious affairs than in improving the quality of education. And he proved extremely tight-fisted when it came to providing money for reconstructing schools and universities, much less scientific research.[34]

As a result the Bavarian Culture Ministry became the focus of a *Kulturkampf* more heated than any other in postwar Germany, which had prevented it from spending money to improve education and fund research. The *Kulturkampf* meant that Hundhammer's successors, even when they wanted to pursue such a policy, lacked the political power to win budget battles. For while the CSU's conservative wing, still quite strong in the Bavarian state government, used all its influence to prevent its prize falling into the hands of anyone not of its stamp, Protestants, liberals, and Social Democrats saw anyone the CSU was willing to put in this ministry as their enemy. In coalition negotiations in 1950 the Social Democrats drove Hundhammer from the Culture Ministry but allowed him to be succeeded by Josef Schwalber, his protégé and a man very much of his stamp, but a political weakling who regularly emerged empty-handed from budget battles. In 1954 the Coalition of Four tried to pacify religious tensions by giving the Culture Ministry to August Rucker, a nonpartisan Professor of Transport, whose success in securing a larger budget for education was limited by Bavaria's real budgetary problems and was, indeed, a success only relative to Schwalber's failure. In 1957 Hanns Seidel did the same thing, giving the ministry to Theodor Maunz, a nonpartisan professor of constitutional law, who was therefore not powerful within the CSU, and who therefore lost his budget battles. Bavarian industry had a real question whether the historically substandard Bavarian educational system could educate the sort of employees required by advanced sectors of the economy. Since the 1950s industry had been pushing the CSU to take action to improve the situation, particularly in technical education.[35]

And so through the early 1960s education proved the CSU's weakest issue, most voters being convinced that the other parties could do better. As Alfons Goppel admitted in 1963, on the issue of education, the CSU remained "hopelessly behind the game."[36]

A political crisis created the possibility of reform. Hildegard Hamm-Brücher, an FDP state parliamentary deputy who had for years aggressively criticized the CSU's conservative and Catholic education policies, uncovered Culture Minister Theodor Maunz's Nazi past (in the postwar era a leading scholar of German constitutional law, before 1945 Maunz had justified the Nazi destruction of the rule of law).[37] Maunz resigned, and Strauß and Goppel tapped Schedl for the succession to the ministerial seat that had acquired the nickname of the "electric chair." Schedl managed to wriggle out of it, with the assistance of Bavarian industrialists pleased with his performance as Economic Minister, and Goppel offered the position to Ludwig Huber, a young CSU politician closely associated with Alois Hundhammer and the CSU's conservative wing.

Just as "only Nixon could go to China," the *Kulturkampf* over the Culture Ministry had created a gridlock that only a CSU conservative could break.[38] Huber certainly looked like the right man: insiders knew he was too ambitious to succeed Goppel as Minister-President to follow Hundhammer's path; yet he had the support of Hundhammer's faction; moreover he chaired the CSU state parliamentary delegation, which guaranteed his budgetary requests would be supported. Once confirmed in the office, Huber created an ambitious program to spend money on school and university expansion, in particular expanding the university system, opening new universities in Regensburg in the early 1960s and in Augsburg at the end of the decade; other universities were planned, and later created, for Bayreuth, Passau, and Bamberg, thus giving each of Bavaria's subregions its own university.[39] Huber's strategy of spending money, talking progressive while avoiding discussion of confessional questions succeeded in avoiding political disaster for the better part of a decade, and moved the CSU forward on educational issues (though expectations were moving forward too, so that at the end of the 1960s the CSU still remained somewhat "behind the game" on the issue of education).[40]

Under Huber, the Bavarian Culture Ministry promoted research more energetically and effectively than it had in the 1950s. An important example of this was its handling of the trend to research specialization. Whereas in the 1950s most German universities, especially Bavarian universities, tried to participate in nearly every field of research, in the 1960s they recognized that they would have to accept research specialization. Rather than resist a division of labor with the other states in the name of Bavaria's "cultural sovereignty," Huber's ministry played the game, and played it very well. It acted quickly to secure some of the most industrially relevant research fields for Bavaria, such as biochemistry, molecular biology, solid-state physics, particle physics, plasma physics, atomic physics, aerospace technology, electrotechnology, and technical chemistry.[41]

It was of course no coincidence that many of these fields connected to Bavaria's aerospace industry and its electrotechnology industry (particularly Siemens, as in response to its request a technical faculty emphasizing electronics, control engineering, and process technology was created at the University of Erlangen).[42] The development of these fields often amounted to working out and expanding plans laid in the mid 1950s, often enough in the Munich suburb of Garching, which by the mid 1960s had become a world-class scientific center, boasting the Institute for Plasmaphysics and the Research Reactor of the Physics Department of the Technical University of Munich, a Radiochemical Institute, and an Institute for Low Temperature Research. Also planned for Garching were a Tandem Accelerator and Siemens' Reactor Research Station. The expansion of the Foundation for Radiology in Neuherberg, another suburb of Munich, and Siemens' Research Center in Erlangen, which Siemens constructed at a total cost of more than DM 100,000,000 and where it pursued research in reactor development, among many other things, also issued from earlier policies.[43]

Under Goppel and Huber, the Bavarian state government and the Culture Ministry continued to cultivate the Max Planck Foundation.[44] Huber, a senator of the Max Planck Foundation as was his predecessor Maunz, promoted the expansion of the network of Max Planck Institutes in Bavaria, particularly in atomic science and energy, such as the laboratory for atomic controls and security (part of the Max Planck Institute for Measurements Technology), the Max Planck Institute for Radiochemistry, and the Institute for Plasmaphysics, as well as in biochemistry, biology, and in medical research near Erlangen and Nuremberg, where many firms specialized in medical equipment and pharmaceuticals.[45] In 1966 Goppel offered the Max Planck Foundation office space in the royal palace in Munich. Butenandt, the foundation's president, accepted, and the Max Planck Foundation received an unlimited right of use to its offices in the palace, while the Bavarian state government arranged a loan to expand the offices. In 1968 Munich became the foundation's official headquarters.[46]

In some ways relations with the Max Planck Foundation had run a course similar to those with the DVL (Deutsche Versuchsanstalt für Luftfahrt, or German Aviation Research Institute). In the early 1950s both the DVL and the Max

Planck Foundation were suspicious of Bavaria's stinginess and evident desire to host institutes without supporting them. Later, under the influence of a CSU liberal (Seidel in the case of the DVL, Meinzolt in the case of the Max Planck Foundation), relations between the state government and the research foundation improved, particularly when Bavaria made up for its lack of money by offering the research foundation an attractive site (the FFO in the case of the DVL, the former royal palace in the case of the Max Planck Foundation). Both moves succeeded, and by the end of the 1960s both the DVL and the Max Planck Foundation called Bavaria home.

But Bavaria did not always get off cheaply. In the course of the 1960s the Institute for Plasmaphysics (IPP) became the jewel in Bavaria's scientific crown, one of the world's leading centers for the study of plasma physics. But it was extremely expensive. And since its creation in the late 1950s, the Bavarian state government had quarreled with the federal government and the Max Planck Foundation over its financing.[47] The Max Planck Foundation was funded jointly by the federal government, on the one side, and by the states collectively, on the other, a method of financing that favored states—like Bavaria—that hosted expensive institutes. Bavaria lost the quarrel when the federal government created the category of "Big Research" (Großforschung) as a device to separate the most expensive Max Planck Institutes from the Max Planck Foundation: the MPF supported many institutes, but a handful of them were fantastically more expensive than the others—mostly those institutes, such as the IPP, which used a single, very large device to conduct atomic research, and employed large numbers of people. The federal government and the MPF decided to separate the super-expensive institutes from the Max Planck Foundation so as to renegotiate their funding, forcing the host states, individually, to pick up more of their tab. The Bavarian government resisted to no avail, but in October 1968 the decision was made and Bavaria was then forced to pay a much larger bill for its two and a half "Big Research" institutes (that is, the IPP, the Foundation for Radiology, or Gesellschaft für Strahlenforschung, and the Oberpfaffenhofen half of the DVL).[48]

Such was the honest price of success: at two and a half institutes, Bavaria hosted more "Big Research" than any other German state.

The National Scene

Things were different in Bonn, where the resignation of Strauß and Balke left the CSU on the defensive. It was true that the CSU was on a new defensive, quite unlike that which it had been on prior to the mid 1950s, when it struggled to prevent its position within the West German party system from being undermined or even destroyed by the CDU. Now it defended a recently won position of influence all out of proportion to its nominal size—and the benefits Bavaria had reaped from that position.

Strauß had to make hard choices after the Spiegel Affair.[49] He had two basic options. First, he could accept his exclusion from the Cabinet and his reduced prestige, and, showing himself much more moderate, reasonable, and chastened, extend his hand to some of his erstwhile rivals, try to divide them from his committed opponents, and angle for readmittance to the Cabinet. Such an approach had definite drawbacks: it did not correspond to his basic belief that in politics things are most worth having when they are taken rather than given, nor to his combative personality; nor did it exploit his rhetorical, not to say demagogic, abilities; nor did "appeasement" make the best use of his leadership of a disciplined bloc of over fifty CSU deputies. It gave him no guarantees but left his fate in the hands of others, most of whom would never trust him. The chief advantage of "appeasement" was speculative: unless Strauß could change the FDP's mind about him before it firmed up its identity as the "anti-Strauß" party, its opposition would make it very difficult for him to attain the highest offices. Second, he could do the very opposite. He could lead a Christian Democratic opposition to Erhard's government, working to weaken and humiliate that government and his rivals in the CDU. If successful, this could result in his being brought into Erhard's government as the price of his cooperation, or, on the other hand, it could lead to the fall of the government and Erhard's replacement by a CDU/CSU-Social Democratic coalition. He could manage either case as the situation unfolded, fighting his way back into Erhard's government if he thought it had a future, or extending an olive branch to the Social Democrats if he thought it didn't. This approach was certainly more suited to his personality, political talents, and position as head of the State Group. Though it had the drawback of giving fuel to his rivals and enemies in the CDU and FDP, they had plenty of fuel as it was, and many of them were irreconcilable. And so it seems to this writer to have been the wisest choice. Certainly it is the path Strauß chose.

As we shall see, in working out the second option, Strauß created for himself a new-old image, addressed a set of new-old issues in new-old ways, all to the benefit of his "interest solidarity" in new-old ways. That is, though everything was made new, or at least given a new significance in the political situation of the 1960s and in Strauß's expansion of his field of vision and activity, nothing was radically new. Strauß built on his past, working out the implications of positions he had long promoted, though sometimes in surprising directions. And, as ever, his new-old politics promoted Bavaria's industrial modernization.

Relations between the CDU and CSU were marked by conflict after the Spiegel Affair, due partly to the CSU's challenge to the CDU. After Erhard became chancellor in the fall of 1963, Strauß, whom Erhard and the proper, conservative, Protestant northern Germans with whom he surrounded himself did not like and did not include in the new government, led the State Group in guerrilla warfare against Erhard's government. He harshly criticized the CDU and FDP, and their foreign, defense, and economic policies. All this is well known.[50]

But it is not widely appreciated that the worsening was due also to a CDU challenge to the CSU. This began with Strauß's forced resignation and the accompanying removal of Balke in December 1962. The CDU did not fully compensate the CSU for these losses. From 1963 to 1966 the most important ministry held by the CSU was the Interior Ministry, and by this measure, the CSU, which from 1949 to 1957 had held the Finance Ministry and from 1956 to 1962 the Defense Ministry, had been demoted. When in the fall of 1963 Erhard succeeded Adenauer and re-formed the government, he acceded to FDP demands to continue Strauß's exclusion from the Cabinet, gave more weight to the FDP and, within the CDU, to Strauß's rivals Schröder and von Hassel, northern German Protestants close to the national-liberal tradition, and he did the same after the federal election of 1965. None of this gave Strauß or the CSU reason to be mightily pleased.[51] The result was that, while the proportion of Christian Democratic deputies who belonged to the CSU had not varied from 1961 to 1965, the CSU continually lost influence within the government. In the 1961 federal election the CSU received 9.6 percent of the national vote, and it received 9.6 percent again in 1965. But in 1961 this won the CSU four ministries: Defense, Interior, Atomic Affairs, and Post; in 1965, five ministries, Justice, Agriculture, Post, Affairs of the Federal Senate, and Treasury (no key ministries at all, only minor and patronage ministries—in Germany Treasury is a minor ministry). This aspect, the CDU challenge to the CSU, is given less attention than it deserves, not only because of Strauß's aggressive image, but because the image of the well-behaved CDU and the unruly CSU inheres in their big-sister/little-sister relationship: the CDU never attacked the CSU but tried to embrace it, while the CSU struggled to escape the embrace. "Harmony in the Union camp" was a euphemism for CDU domination of the CSU. Or as a CDU leader said, "the more our friend Strauß, whom I highly esteem, is rejected in the rest of Germany, the more his fortunes rise in Bavaria but the CSU cannot expect that its victory, purchased, as it were, with our defeat, should increase the Bavarian representation. This is only a friendly hint."[52]

The CDU challenge to the CSU extended to all of the important elements of Bavaria's industrial modernization. The CSU encountered growing resistance to Bavaria's success, as many in the CDU felt that the CSU had gotten far more than its fair share of the spoils of government.[53] With the CSU's demotion after the Spiegel Affair, CDU leaders were disposed to challenge many of the elements of the established way of doing things that had favored Bavarian industry. This included Bavarian success in breaking its dependence on coal by bringing oil pipelines to Ingolstadt, which the CDU sought to undo by perpetuating the tax on heating oil. It further included resistance to Bavaria's success in building up its relationship with the Max Planck Foundation, so that tax money from other states supported Max Planck research institutes that were disproportionally located in Bavaria.

Most of all it meant aerospace and defense contracting, where the argument that the others should have their turn was more than plausible to the northern German ears of Strauß's successor in the Defense Ministry, Kai-Uwe von Hassel. Von Hassel and Erhard, moreover, hoped to save money on the defense budget, and had little commitment to the Bavarian defense industry: they were unlikely to build unnecessary military airplanes just to keep the Bavarian aircraft industry occupied.

They even had ideas of moving the aircraft industry northwards. Hence the Bavarian defense industry's intense dislike of Erhard, von Hassel, and von Hassel's successor, Gerhard Schröder, and its continued reliance on Strauß and the CSU.

We must make an important period division. Late 1966 saw a change of government that resulted in a substantial increase in Strauß's and the CSU's influence. Strauß prepared the change by reconciling with the Social Democrats, turning sharply on the FDP and subjecting Erhard to attacks that eroded his prestige. Strauß tried to convince the CSU to resign from Erhard's government in September 1966 when the latter refused to make Strauß minister. He was unsuccessful, but the episode did teach the CDU leaders another lesson about trifling with Strauß, a lesson that was fresh in their minds a few weeks later when the FDP did the very same thing Strauß had tried to do. After the FDP resigned from the government, Erhard's fate was sealed and Strauß became kingmaker. He threw his support to Kurt-Georg Kiesinger, the moderate, modest CDU Minister-President of Baden-Württemberg, and in November 1966 Kurt-Georg Kiesinger's "Grand Coalition" government of the CDU/CSU and Social Democrats took office.

The CSU's regained influence came largely through Strauß's tenure in the crucial Finance Ministry. Though the Foreign Ministry is usually considered the most important, it was probably surpassed by the Finance Ministry in these years, which saw the high tide of Keynesianism, the recession of 1966 to 1967, and little foreign-political activity.

Regained influence came also through Strauß's political position and performance. Strauß was no longer the outsider, denied even a ministry, but the leading Christian-Democratic figure after Kiesinger. In general, the Grand Coalition was a great success for Strauß. For though he had a difficult job as Finance Minister during postwar Germany's first recession, he managed to increase his popularity and worked well with Karl Schiller, the Social Democrats' wiry Economic Minister (the team acquired the affectionate nickname "Plisch und Plum," a reference to two dogs, one fat and one lean, in children's stories). Strauß's popularity and prestige rose as it appeared that his financial policies beat the recession. From late 1966 to late 1969, unemployment and inflation fell, the federal budget moved from deficit into surplus, and the economy from recession into boom. The public image of Strauß, the vulgar Bavarian, the man of scandals and the nuclear militarist faded before a new image of Strauß as dynamic, modern, open—even progressive, a futurist, a creative thinker who could not be explained in conventional categories. He seemed in tune with the social-democratic tide as he adopted Keynesian policies, supported government planning, strengthened the economic powers of the federal government over the states, and showed himself surprisingly flexible toward the Soviet bloc.[54]

Under both Erhard's and Kiesinger's governments the "interest solidarity" created by Strauß in the late 1950s stayed together, and remained under his leadership, usually lined up with the CSU against the CDU. One of the major issues that kept it together, and at the same time allowed Strauß to represent his political beliefs and promote the interests of Bavarian industry, was the question of state intervention in the economy versus liberalism.

The decline of liberalism allowed Strauß and the CSU to "outflank" the CDU on the general issue of political economy just as it had earlier done on more specific issues. The postwar German economic miracle had been credited to Ludwig Erhard and his liberal ideas, summed up in the phrase "social market economy." Liberalism, having carried all rival political-economic ideas before it through the early 1960s, ebbed with Erhard's chancellorship. Other ideas were coming into fashion throughout the Western world—government planning, Keynesian economic policy, managed growth, state support for key industries, and state interventionism in general. These ideas answered the need of the Grand Coalition for a political economy on which both Christian Democrats and Social Democrats could agree and that would profile them against the more liberal FDP. Strauß and the CSU threw their weight behind the new ideas. This was easy enough for the CSU to do: as the most Catholic party representing the most Catholic state in Germany, the CSU had never committed itself to the liberal ideas as deeply as had the CDU. Not surprisingly, the Christian Democrats' coalition with the Social Democrats threatened to create tensions with industry, which was one of Strauß's major constituencies, and which disliked the Grand Coalition and took fright at the prospect of a new, more "red" CDU/CSU and the concessions it might make to its coalition partner.[55] Yet, in fact, it bound industry more closely than ever to the CSU.

For in the version promoted by Strauß and the CSU, the new political economy meant even more government intervention in the economy *to the benefit of industry*.[56] Even before the Grand Coalition gave Strauß the Finance Ministry, he had made himself useful to industry by speaking to economic issues and becoming industry's chief patron in Bonn. After the Spiegel Affair, Strauß studied economics, so that, with the facility for rapidly learning a great deal about complex subjects that allowed him to astonish physicists as Minister of Atomic Affairs and generals as Defense Minister, in January 1964 he astonished the federal parliament with a long and expert speech on economic policy (wags dubbed this the "Put-Put speech," referring to Strauß's dexterous overuse of the American neologisms, Input and Output). German industry noted Strauß's willingness to undertake dirty work on its behalf, as when in early 1966 he visited Rhodesia and South Africa, promoting German industrial and banking interests in these countries while defending apartheid.[57] When in September 1966 Strauß pushed to return to Erhard's Cabinet, he had the full support of industry, especially of the BDI and Friedrich Flick.[58] And several months later, while Strauß prepared his claim to the Finance Ministry in a new government, *Industriekurier* let everyone know that, "It's quite certain that from Abs (Deutsche Bank) to Beitz (Krupp), in the big banks and in heavy industry, Strauß is the politician they count on."[59] They counted on him, for example, to lead the resistance to codetermination, that is, the Social-Democratic drive for legislation requiring employee representation on corporate boards. During the Grand Coalition and in accord with the spirit of the times, many Christian Democratic politicians joined the Social Democrats' call for codetermination—even the CSU party program of 1968 came out, although ambiguously, for codetermination. But when LBI chairman Rolf Rodenstock declared that this "had very much alienated industry," Strauß made himself the leading opponent of codetermination within the Christian-Democratic camp, declaring that economic growth, not codetermination, was the best social politics.[60]

One example of the CDU challenge to the CSU was the Defense Ministry, both in its plans in the new era and in the ministers who directed it. The new era was perhaps the deeper problem. As the Cold War entered a long period of thaw in 1963, the Erhard and Kiesinger governments inevitably sought to save money on the defense budget and required the Defense Ministers to deny follow-up contracts to the defense firms until the defense firms merged. The drive to raise German troop levels, which still had not reached Germany's NATO quota, made the former all the more imperative. This had ominous implications for the defense industry. As one of Strauß's successors admitted after his retirement: "they [the Americans] worked on us [to buy American materiel], and the French said, if you do that, if you buy American weapons, the European defense industry is finished ... and Strauß said that, and indeed he was right, absolutely right."[61]

As to the new Defense Ministers themselves, Kai-Uwe von Hassel, Strauß's successor from 1963 to 1966, came from northern Germany. He had been Minister-President (CDU) of Schleswig-Holstein, and would naturally favor the northern over the Bavarian defense industry, which would be legitimized by the flexible-response doctrine, more or less accepted by the German government, which meant that Germany would have to strengthen its capacity for conventional ground warfare. For that it would require the sort of weapons and equipment produced by the northern German defense industry rather than the aerospace and electronic products of the Bavarian.[62] But though such was the fear in Bavaria, we shall see that von Hassel proved amenable to Bavarian influence. In late 1966 Gerhard Schröder, the Atlanticist CDU deputy from North Rhine-Westphalia who had served as Adenauer's Interior Minister and Erhard's Foreign Minister, succeeded von Hassel, and he promised to be worse for the CSU. Schröder had the weight to stand up to Strauß and had little to gain from Bavaria or the CSU—it is not too much to say that Strauß and Schröder were enemies.

But von Hassel's and Schröder's tenures were shaped by an unexpected crisis. The Starfighters began to crash, and the resulting controversy weighed on von Hassel and Schröder—and drew in Strauß. From 1961 to 1963 nine Starfighters crashed, resulting in six deaths; then in 1964 alone nine crashes resulted in three deaths; and in 1965 twenty-six crashes resulted in fifteen deaths. Pilots grew reluctant to fly the Starfighter, which acquired the nicknames "widowmaker" and "flying coffin." Critics of the plane had never been lacking, but the crashes multiplied their number and gave them wide press coverage, including, in 1965, a feature article in the newsmagazine *Stern*.[63] In 1966 a parliamentary inquiry took place that led to finger-pointing between the air force and the military-industrial complex, resignations, and firings, and in succeeding years the planes' safety record waxed and waned. The list of criticisms made of the Starfighter was long: the Starfighter had never been the ideal plane for Germany's military needs, since interception was a hopeless task for a country the size of Michigan bordering the Warsaw Pact countries; moreover it was a "fair weather" interceptor, unsuited to the difficult weather conditions that prevailed over central Europe; its substantial redesign into a nuclear fighter-bomber had been equally ill-conceived, since America already had plenty of nuclear weapons aimed at the Soviet Union, and America's exclusive retention of the arming codes for the nuclear weapons held by Germany reduced the Starfighters to a German-financed adjunct to the American air force; its redesign had also been a technical failure, since the new plane was nearly a third heavier, many of its features did not work properly and it flew poorly; the purchase of unnecessary numbers of an unnecessary plane and its redesign into another unnecessary plane was a gamble that Germany would be able to secure some form of control, either alone or in conjunction with its allies, over nuclear weapons; and that gamble had failed, as in 1960 the Kennedy administration began to centralize control of nuclear weapons in Washington, and to frustrate any discussion of German participation in nuclear decision-making—later it even stopped delivery to Germany of components necessary to deliver the nuclear weapons that the Starfighter carried.[64] All of these criticisms had more than a little truth to them, and the desk where the buck stopped on them was Strauß's own. Yet the crashes were a somewhat different matter. They seemed to be due to a complex series of factors, certainly including the extraordinary demands the "unforgiving" Starfighter placed on pilots, but including pilot and mechanic errors, faulty workmanship in the German aerospace plants, and insufficient pilot training, most of which did not point back to Strauß.

Strauß, von Hassel, and Schröder were all criticized for much of this in the mid and late 1960s. But the latter two took most of the heat, and they and their ministries often reacted to it by pointing the finger at the defense industry. Strauß did otherwise. He treated his critics as opportunists who would weaken Germany's military posture, and unhesitatingly defended his Starfighter decision as necessary to Germany's defense and its industrial future.[65]

As a result these clouds over the Bavarian defense industry had a silver lining for the CSU. The pressure on the defense budget, flexible response, and the Starfighter crisis tended to consolidate the solidarity between the aerospace and defense industries and the CSU. While refusing new weapons development contracts and pointing fingers at the aerospace industry, von Hassel and Schröder and the CDU were unable to displace the CSU as their special patron. In fact the aerospace and defense industries became von Hassel's and Schröder's open enemy, calling regularly for their replacement. Particularly the aircraft industry had no use for Defense Ministers who were liberal in their economic philosophy, Atlanticist Francophobes in their foreign policy, and accepted both the flexible response doctrine and the Balance of Payments Offset Agreement. They desperately needed someone to represent them against the United States and to promote European defense-industrial cooperation, preferably with the French, who were pushing ahead determinedly with their political, military, and industrial challenges to America.[66] All this favored Strauß and his CSU lieutenants, such as Fritz Zimmermann, who, if they had never been the defense industry's servants, had always been its great allies.

Yet there were other examples of how Strauß and the CSU could still exercise their clout on behalf of their Bavarian clients. One of the best examples was the contract to produce the Leopard tank. Von Hassel had reason enough to award the contract for the Leopard—postwar Germany's first contract for the production of a battle tank and its biggest non-aircraft defense contract—to a non-Bavarian firm. For one thing, Germany's tanks had always been built in the Rhineland and northern Germany, near the steel industry, and these regions had qualified firms to nominate for the contract. For another, many people in the Defense Ministry and in government circles did not want the Leopard contract to be awarded to a Bavarian firm, arguing that Bavaria had already gotten far more than its fair share of defense work.[67] Before his resignation as Defense Minister, Strauß had earmarked the Leopard contract for the Quandt-Group: the industrialist Herbert Quandt was close to Strauß and planned to construct the Leopard in Augsburg, Bavaria. After Strauß's resignation, Quandt announced his intention to set up his assembly line for the Leopard in Hamburg, in order to rescue one of his idle plants in that city; perhaps he thought this would appeal to the new minister, who had been Minister-President of Hamburg's neighbor, Schleswig-Holstein. But other government circles opposed the creation in Hamburg of new defense-industrial capacities that the government would then come under pressure to keep busy with more contracts. The decision to award the contract to Quandt had not yet been made final when Friedrich Flick began to press for the Leopard contract. Flick was Germany's wealthiest industrialist, whose empire, rebuilt after he served a prison term for using slave labor during World War II, included several Bavarian provinces, among them the firm of Krauss-Maffei, which built locomotives and heavy machinery and looked to the Leopard contract to help it make the transition to defense work.[68]

In order to keep the contract in Bavaria, Strauß threw his weight behind Flick. He had continued to take a proprietary interest in his former ministry, contacted von Hassel and, though it is not known what Strauß said, it is reported that he "really stood up for" Krauss-Maffei. In July 1963 von Hassel, who freely admitted that he had "no desire for trouble with Strauß," awarded the contract to Krauss-Maffei.[69] The Leopards were delivered to the German army in the mid 1960s; by 1972 Krauss-Maffei had delivered over two thousand to the German army alone, and sold more to Germany's allies, including Italy, the Netherlands, Belgium, and Norway, who chose it over British, French, and American alternatives. And the Bavarian Krauss-Maffei did indeed make the transition to defense work, graduating from the Leopard to produce the Leopard II and other military vehicles, such as mobile armored antiaircraft guns and the chassis for bridge-laying vehicles.[70]

The Western Alliance

On the complex plane of relations with the Western allies, calculating how to make the most of Germany's peculiar strengths and vulnerabilities, Strauß operated with great skill. Here the key issues with implications for Bavarian industry concerned the argument between German "Atlanticists" and "Gaullists," the question of how Germany should react to the evolution of American strategic doctrine from "massive retaliation" toward "flexible response," and the question of the Balance of Payments Offset Agreement.

In 1964 the Christian Democratic parties began to argue bitterly whether Germany should follow an "Atlanticist" or a "Gaullist" foreign and defense policy. The French President Charles de Gaulle had demanded Germany choose between the two allies, and Adenauer had chosen France, so far as was possible for Germany. As soon as Erhard's government took office it set about revising that choice, which provoked an argument that divided the Christian-Democratic parties into two camps. "Atlanticist," or pro-American (and to a lesser degree, pro-British), deputies came for the most part from Protestant northern Germany. "Gaullist," or pro-French deputies, typically came from Catholic southern and western Germany, very often from the CSU. Chancellor Erhard, Foreign Minister Schröder, and Defense Minister von Hassel led the Atlanticists, arguing that only American nuclear forces could deter Soviet attack and that America's vision of a global free-trade regime would benefit no country so much as Germany. They thought de Gaulle a nationalist seeking to dominate Germany, the French offer to defend Germany from the Soviet Union ludicrous, and the French vision of a trade wall around Europe inimical to German interests.

Strauß was the leader of the German Gaullists. In mid 1964 he began to subject the Atlanticist attempt to reorient Germany away from France and toward the United States to sharp criticism. Strauß's German "Gaullism" was adapted to global changes, to the thaw in the Cold War that followed the Cuban missile crisis, to the movement of the two superpowers toward each other and away from their allies, and to the weakening of the sharply bipolar global power structure of the 1950s. It took sharp account of Germany's peculiar strengths and vulnerabilities. In Strauß's view, the Germany of 1964 was not so desperately needy as it had been in the 1950s; Germany was increasingly needed by others, and it was in the German interest to adapt its policies to this new political situation. Admitting that Germany depended, ultimately, on the American security umbrella, Strauß argued that in 1964 this "ultimately" was less immediate and put less pressure on German policy than it did prior to the erection of the Berlin Wall in 1961. Now that Gaullist France built up its nuclear "*force de frappe*" Germany had an alternative defense umbrella. Even though the French umbrella was not as reliable as the American, and even though it was doubtful that the *force de frappe* could really deter the Soviet Union, it created a new situation. Germany could flirt with the French and, by doing so, exert pressure on the United States. For Strauß was much less nervous about being abandoned by the United States than most Christian-Democratic politicians. He understood that after the Berlin crises the U.S. was fully invested in its alliance with Germany, and that, having gone to the brink of war over Berlin, it could hardly walk away from Germany now; that it had massively built up its conventional and nuclear forces and had little desire to reduce them; and that the U.S., in a sense, *wanted* to be the country chiefly responsible to defend Europe, if only in order to control NATO defense policy.

Strauß's Gaullism emphasized military defense. He insisted that the American nuclear umbrella, indispensable as it was at the time, did not give Europe lasting security because it was not credible over the long term that the Americans would put their own territory at risk to defend Europe. The new element in Strauß's Gaullism, not present in his pre-1963 rhetoric, was his vision of a European nuclear deterrent, which he hoped would come about through closer Franco-German relations. In 1966 Strauß's Gaullist manifesto, *The Grand Design: A European Solution to German Reunification,* proposed pooling the French and British nuclear armory into a European Nuclear Force, so that, interdependently with the French and British, the Germans would have their thumb on the nuclear button. European nuclear interdependence, Strauß urged, would solve many problems: Europe would be more secure (it *was* credible that Europeans would use nuclear weapons in the defense of Europe); America would be relieved of the burden of defending Europe; even the Soviets would feel more secure, since American troops could leave Europe; and this would prepare the way for the solution of bigger problems, such as the division of Germany and Europe. The Atlanticist-Gaullist quarrel was indeed about "high politics."

Yet Strauß's Gaullism had definite material implications. It meant a brighter future for the Bavarian defense and aerospace industries. For these industries, whose refounding in the late 1950s at a high technological level had been made possible by Strauß's cooperation with American firms, were now being stunted by Germany's close relations with America. To Strauß's way of thinking, the American government exploited Germany's dependence on it to force the German government to buy billions of dollars of American weapons; and the American defense firms, making everything the Germans needed only too well and too cheaply, moreover refused to work together with the German firms on anything like an equal basis. It was impossible for the German defense industry to survive unless Germany reduced its military dependence on America, which it could securely do only if it took up closer relations with France. If Germany accepted de Gaulle's offer of a "special relationship," a partnership extending to defense and defense-industrial cooperation, Germany could produce fighters, bombers, rockets, and control electronics—and so far as these things were produced in Germany they would be produced largely in Bavaria, by Bölkow and Messerschmitt and Siemens.

The material implications were neither central nor accidental to Strauß's Gaullism. Few doubted that Strauß deeply believed in his Gaullism. His new "Francophilia" was grounded in ideas about national defense, prestige, and position that he had been proclaiming for over a decade; few doubted, at the same time, that it was powerfully driven by his desire to get back into government—his Gaullism signaled to the Social Democrats that he was open to new ideas on foreign and defense policy and that they should therefore accept him as possible coalition partner. Yet at the same time Strauß's correspondence with Bavarian industrialists shows that their interests were on his mind too.[71]

Yet Strauß was wrong, at least in the short term. Neither de Gaulle nor the British would consider sharing control of their nuclear forces with Germany. In another example of the dynamic that had occurred so often in the previous fifteen years, the CDU had to make the real choice and could not afford to choose France, but Strauß was free to do so and in so doing to set themselves up as the most energetic protectors of the Bavarian aerospace and defense industry. And some of the material implications of Strauß's Gaullism were soon realized, as we will see.

German politicians also divided over the evolution of American strategic doctrine from the "massive retaliation" of the Eisenhower era toward the Kennedy-Johnson era doctrine of "flexible response." "Massive retaliation" held that NATO would meet a Soviet attack on Western Europe with an all-out American nuclear strike on the Soviet Union. Kennedy's and Johnson's advisors considered that, as the Soviet Union developed the capacity to launch a devastating retaliatory strike on the United States, this threat had lost credibility, and that it therefore tempted the Soviets to launch a conventional attack on Western Europe. Kennedy's and Johnson's advisors theorized that a strategy of "flexible response," a policy to meet a Soviet conventional attack with NATO conventional forces, and to use theater nuclear weapons only if these failed to halt the attack and after a warning, would be more credible and therefore of greater deterrent effect. This meant, however, that NATO's conventional forces, which had been allowed to remain much smaller than those of the Warsaw Pact, as "massive retaliation" had rendered them almost superfluous, would have to be built up. Especially Germany's conventional forces, which Strauß had neglected as he concentrated on building up his high-tech air force, would have to be built up.

Strauß and other German politicians resisted the American attempt to move NATO toward "flexible response." Ultimately, again, the Germans could not prevent the Americans, who controlled the nuclear weapons carried by the German air force, from instituting the new policy. But from their new position of strength within the alliance, they could doggedly resist it, flirting with the French and putting pressure on the Americans to modify their policy or to be more forthcoming on other alliance issues. Strauß argued that "massive retaliation" was still credible, that "flexible response" invited the Soviet leaders to try their luck (they could launch a conventional attack, halt when they received warning that NATO was about to use nuclear weapons, and keep the territory they had occupied!), and that the Americans wanted to use "flexible response" to move toward an alliance division of labor according to which America would provide the nuclear forces, and the European nations the ground forces, for the defense of Europe. Even the most Atlanticist of German politicians bridled at such a demotion.[72] Moreover, "massive retaliation" fit better with the budgetary concerns of both Erhard's and Kiesinger's governments, since "massive retaliation" nuclear forces were cheaper than "flexible response" conventional forces, especially for Germany, which had to cover the cost of both its own conventional forces and the balance of payments losses that America accrued through the forces it stationed in Germany (see below).

Beyond this, Strauß had personal reasons to oppose "flexible response." Before anyone else in Germany, he had descried the gathering wave of "massive retaliation" and ridden it into the Defense Ministry. His promotion of a small, highly modern, and nuclearized German armed forces, which had won him the Defense Ministry and the support of the defense industry, had been nothing but a translation of "massive retaliation" into German circumstances. And so he mightily resisted flexible response in 1961 and 1962, when it was less a policy than the direction of thought in Washington. But the Johnson administration pressed "flexible response" even harder than had Kennedy, demanding the expansion of the German army, and that Germany's new Starfighters carry only conventional weapons, in which case the enormously expensive planes, which had been purchased and redesigned for use as instruments of "massive retaliation," would lose their raison d'être.[73]

As with Gaullism, the question of "massive retaliation" versus "flexible response" had industrial implications, and it was not by accident that the doctrine Strauß stood for favored Bavaria. "Massive retaliation," with its emphasis on the air force, had built the Bavarian aerospace industry. "Flexible response" meant de-emphasizing the air force in favor of the army, de-emphasizing state-of-the-art fighter-bombers and rocketry and hence the Bavarian aircraft industry in favor of troop transporters, which would be produced by the northern German aircraft industry. A true believer in the policies he advocated, Strauß was well aware of his interest in protecting the Bavarian defense and aerospace industries, as we will see. And as in the case of Gaullism, governing responsibility forced the CDU to leave its industrial flank unprotected from CSU attacks: the CDU was not in a position to make too many problems for the Americans over "flexible response," but Strauß and the CSU did not hesitate to position themselves as the protectors of the Bavarian aerospace and defense industry. And though they could not determine alliance strategy, we will see that they did defend the industries that corresponded to their preferred force structure.

The Balance of Payments Offset Agreement was yet another source of division. In 1960 the American government requested Germany to pay monetary compensation for the huge balance of payments losses involved in maintaining hundreds of thousands of American troops in Germany. But Strauß convinced the Americans to settle for an agreement to purchase American materiel. The Balance of Payments Offset Agreement, signed in 1961, favored the Germans in the sense that the Germans had planned to make enormous purchases of American materiel anyway—these were the peak years of licensed production of the Starfighter; it favored the Americans in the sense that it connected Germany to American defense systems and a high dollar value was agreed upon—Strauß agreed to "Buy American" in 1961/1962 to the tune of $1.45 billion. Shortly before the Spiegel Affair, Strauß renewed the agreement under identical terms for 1963/1964. But as Starfighter production petered out, the Germans had no real need to make large purchases of American materiel and sought to be excused from the agreement. The American government insisted it be fulfilled. The agreement was duly renewed and in 1965 and 1966 the German government fell behind in its obligations, Erhard and his ministers thinking that the Americans would allow them to beg off the agreement; by June 1966 the Germans were almost $1.5 to 2 billion under the agreed amount. But when the Germans pleaded their inability to make up the deficit, the Americans announced plans to reduce American troop levels in Germany to a level proportionate with Germany's actual payments. The American ambassador created terrible scenes with Erhard, and, with his back against the wall, Erhard requested a tax increase to meet the American demands.[74] The FDP refused to approve the tax increase, and this became one of the proximate causes of Erhard's fall.

Strauß led the opposition to fulfilling the Balance of Payments offset agreement (which he had originally made), harshly criticizing attempts to meet the American demands.[75] Again, Germany's strength in this quarrel with America was the existence of a French option, and American dependence on the German state that had once been completely dependent on it. Strauß and the enemies of the Balance of Payments Offset Agreement played on this but were not motivated by it. A big part of Strauß's motivation was plainly the German aircraft industry, of which the Balance of Payments Offset Agreement was the deadly enemy, since the sums required could hardly be met without buying American military aircraft, which would destroy the nascent German aircraft industry. Moreover, the years 1964–1969 saw that industry in crisis for lack of work. As Strauß saw it, almost certainly correctly, the only long-term solution to this lack of work was for Germany to break free of its obligation to buy American aircraft and to build them in cooperation with other European countries.

In the late 1960s, Strauß and the opponents of the Balance of Payments Offset Agreement won a victory—a partial victory, but enough to keep the German aircraft industry alive. After Erhard fell, the Grand Coalition remained reluctant to meet the American demands. As Finance Minister, Strauß was a big part of this reluctance, and his concurrence was necessary when the German government finally agreed to make good America's balance of payments losses through a combination of materiel purchases and complex monetary transactions and manipulations—much better for the Bavarian defense industry than by materiel purchases alone. But Strauß continued to criticize the idea of a Balance of Payments Offset Agreement, and the fourth agreement (for the period 1 July 1967 to 30 June 1968) was yet better for the German aircraft industry, allowing the German government to purchase U.S. government bonds. Subsequent agreements continued this development, so vital to the German—and Bavarian—defense industry.[76]

The controversies over Gaullism, "flexible response," and the Balance of Payments Offset Agreement were about general policy orientations. The immediate question facing the aerospace and defense industry was which military aircraft Germany would purchase and manufacture, and the choices were already on the table in Bonn in 1967. Finance Minister Strauß and the State Group were well positioned to influence decisions in Bavaria's favor.

Even under the terms of the renegotiated Balance of Payments Agreement Germany remained under pressure to buy American materiel, not least in order to perform its reconnaissance mission under "flexible response," by now NATO's official doctrine. Germany needed these new aircraft quickly, more quickly than reconnaissance aircraft could be designed and built by German firms. Discussion in Bonn focused immediately on the reconnaissance version of McDonnell-Douglas's F-4 Phantom (reconnaissance version, RF-4). This airplane was to the 1960s what the Starfighter had been to the 1950s: the ne plus ultra of American aviation technology. But while McDonnell-Douglas refused to permit German firms to construct its planes on license, Lockheed, which had on offer a new reconnaissance Starfighter at half the price of the Phantom, was more than willing to do so. The German aircraft industry spoke with one voice in favor of the new Starfighter, but in June 1968 Defense Minister Schröder decided in favor of the Phantom.[77]

The CSU nearly overthrew Schröder's decision in the parliamentary Defense Committee. The Defense Committee had acquired a de facto veto power over major arms purchases, and Strauß lieutenant Fritz Zimmermann, who had succeeded to its chairmanship in 1965, claimed that a Phantom purchase would endanger the understanding that Germany's next jet fighter be of German design and construction. The CSU deputies on the Defense Committee emphatically rejected the Phantom; outnumbered, they managed to delay a vote on the issue until the fall of 1968, when, though all three CSU deputies voted against the Phantom, the Defense Committee narrowly voted to accept it.[78]

Yet the squeaky wheel got its grease. In compensation for the Phantom purchase, on the same day the Defense Committee accepted the Phantom, it voted to approve the purchase of other aircraft to be produced on license in Germany: an additional 50 Starfighters (Lockheed F-104G), 135 transport helicopters (Sikorsky CH-53 A), and 25 tactical trainers (various firms). The lion's share of this work went to the Bavarian firms of Messerschmitt-Bölkow, Dornier, and MAN-Turbo (the successor firm to BMW Triebwerkbau and MAN Turbomotoren). The German government further agreed that before the Phantom purchase was finalized, it would demand that the Americans reserve DM 500 million in Phantom subcontracts and other contracts from the American government for German firms. When the U.S. Department of Defense balked at this, leaving the German firms to the hazards of competitive bidding, the German government undertook to subsidize their bids to the tune of nearly 50 percent; the firms demanded more, so that they could underbid American firms and still make their accustomed German profits; and this demand, too, the German government met. The lion's share of the German Phantom work also went to Messerschmitt-Bölkow—over DM 100 million.[79] In all of this the aircraft industry was unblinkingly supported by Strauß, Fritz Zimmermann, and the CSU.

Yet the real successor aircraft to the Starfighter was not the Phantom but the MRCA Tornado. This jet fighter-bomber was produced in the 1970s by cooperating German, British, and Italian firms.

From its founding, the Western alliance had struggled with the question of a division of labor in defense-industrial work. It was a struggle for many reasons: each ally sought to secure its own industry, and to do so by securing Germany as a customer; each ally was determined to secure for itself, in any cooperation with another country, the most advanced work; and both America and France (at least after de Gaulle returned to power in 1958) were determined to avoid substantive cooperation in any defense items necessary to their national security. America and France again provide the instructive contrasts. America could afford to maintain its own industry, since its own enormous purchases were enough to sustain its defense industry, and it viewed cooperation as a means to retard the development of its allies' defense industries. America therefore sought agreements to standardize NATO equipment, since standardization could only mean its allies' purchase of America's advanced weapons, which were superior to anything its allies could produce, or it sought a "Defense Common Market," since, again, the smaller continental firms would not be able to stand up in competition against the American giants (the European countries frustrated both standardization and the Defense Common Market). France also had a "go-it-alone" attitude, seeking to avoid dependence on its allies for any weapons necessary for national defense, though this policy was difficult for France to sustain, both technically and financially. Technical and financial considerations pointed the French toward defense industrial cooperation, though the purpose of their policy, independence, pointed the other way. Germany, of course, was the dream client for both France and the United States: as the front-line state against the Warsaw Pact, Germany's defense needs were considerable; Germany had the financial means to be a big customer; and, since Germany had a small and backward defense industry, favorable deals could be made with it. So it seemed in the 1950s.

Germany entered the search for defense-industrial patrons and partners with peculiar strengths, chiefly the ability to choose. Even its very weakness was a strength—its industry was so small and backward that almost any cooperative arrangement must be a benefit to it. In the 1950s Strauß had chosen to cooperate chiefly with the United States. It is true that, even then, he had pursued cooperative projects with France, but the really big and important cooperative projects had been with the United States—above all, the license production of the Starfighter. But in the mid 1960s things changed. Having cooperated with the United States to rebuild the German aircraft industry at a surprisingly high technical level, close to that of the French and British industries, Strauß understood that it was in German interest to turn away from America and cooperate with France or Britain. With either of these countries Germany could cooperate in a nearly equal partnership, pooling resources and gaining know-how to produce military aircraft to be purchased by both countries.

Yet at the beginning of the discussion of a Starfighter-successor the only thing that was clear was that the contract for the Starfighter's successor would be the biggest and most important defense contract since that for the Starfighter itself. Just as Strauß had chosen the Starfighter in order to rebuild the German aircraft industry, the CSU promoted and fought for a Starfighter successor that would raise the German aircraft industry to the standard of the British and French industries. Already in the mid 1960s, the German government accepted that the German aircraft industry would no longer be reduced to producing aircraft designed by others, though it was equally determined that the industry was not yet prepared to design and produce a world-class fighter. The Starfighter successor would be produced and designed by German firms working in cooperation with another country's firms.[80]

The crucial question was, which country? The United States was not dismissed in Bonn. Its aerospace industry was the most advanced in the world. In the mid 1960s the German government began to subsidize what became known as the AVS project, in which Messerschmitt and Bölkow cooperated with Republic Aviation in designing a supersonic fighter that combined the Germans' new V/STOL technology with American variable geometry technology (hence the name, advanced V/STOL, or AVS). But each country treated cooperation as an intelligence operation, trying to pick up the other's know-how while protecting its own, while neither country's air force had much interest in procuring AVS aircraft.

Here was an unusual instance of Strauß wanting one thing and the Bavarian aircraft industry the opposite. Strauß and, therefore, Fritz Zimmermann insisted that the German industry cooperate with other European countries.[81] Strauß emphasized the "European political significance" of the Starfighter-successor, steering Germany toward participation in the Franco-British projects (AFVG and Jaguar). As we have seen, in these years Strauß's entire foreign policy conception pointed away from American and toward European cooperation. Moreover, after 1966 the CDU and CSU leaders resented the role played by the Americans and the Balance of Payments Offset Agreement in the overthrow of Erhard's government. This weakened the CDU Atlanticists and strengthened those who looked for European partners—above all, Strauß. In March 1967 Strauß actually demanded that Germany's technological cooperation with the United States be reduced, and, with Strauß as Finance Minister, the AVS project had little future. The governments cancelled the project in 1968. Yet the Bavarian aircraft industry feared being treated like a country cousin by the French and British, and wanted to cooperate with America in the AVS, or at least to maintain an American option until admitted on acceptable terms to a Franco-British project.[82]

As to France, Strauß's Gaullism indicated cooperation with the French. But the French government was unwilling to cooperate with the Germans in the highly prestigious sensitive area of advance fighter aircraft, at least on terms the Germans could accept.

That left the British. They were eager to cooperate with the Germans, but an Anglo-German project presented its own problems. For one thing, while the Germans required an air superiority fighter that could also perform close air support, the British wanted a long-range fighter-bomber, and the two roles were well-nigh impossible to reconcile in one design. For another, the British believed that their more advanced aircraft industry gave them the right to dominate a common project.[83]

But in 1968 and 1969 the German government decided to cooperate with the British on an aircraft to perform multiple roles—a Multi-Role Combat Aircraft, or MRCA, given the moniker Tornado. For, though both countries recognized the danger that the countries' divergent needs might result in an expensive plane that did neither task well, subtle pressures drove the Germans to conform to the British design preferences: the German aircraft industry strongly preferred the same kind of plane the British wanted (since a fighter-bomber was a more advanced aircraft and had a higher price tag), and many in the German government agreed, especially those, such as Strauß, who sought to preserve a nuclear strike role for Germany within the Western alliance.[84]

And the British claim to leadership was negotiable. At the urging of Ludwig Bölkow, Finance Minister Strauß pressed Germany's claims. Speaking to the Federation of the German Aircraft Industry, he said that "the German aircraft industry absolutely possesses the required management skills which are required to take lead responsibility for this project," and, agreeing with Bölkow, called British leadership, "inopportune." And indeed the German government, by deciding to purchase far more Tornados than the British—here again we may suspect that Finance Minister Strauß had a role—trumped the British claim and secured the lead responsibility for the German aircraft industry. But the decision of Schröder's Defense Ministry to include the northern German group in the development of the new fighter disappointed the Bavarians, for it blurred the old division of labor according to which the southern industry produced fighters and the northern transporters.[85]

The CSU promoted the MRCA unreservedly, publicly, within the government and parliament. If many of the Parliamentary Defense Committee's members oriented themselves to industrial interests, none did so more than the CSU members, and no one member more than its chairman, Fritz Zimmermann, who positioned himself as second only to Strauß as an advocate of the Bavarian aerospace and defense industries.[86]

Bavaria received the lion's share of the spoils. Messerschmitt-Bölkow-Blohm, BAe (on the British side), and Airitalia (an Italian firm) created Panavia to produce the MRCA, which is to say that VFW was reduced to accepting subcontracts from MBB, and Panavia chose Munich to be the firm's headquarters.[87] It was similar with the plane's jet engines: the Bavarian firm of MAN Turbo joined with Daimler-Benz to found MTU, which produced the engines in cooperation with Rolls-Royce and Fiat.[88]

The MRCA appeared on German runways in 1980, but, though most of its design and production controversies lie beyond the time limits of this study, we can say shortly that the German, British, and Italian governments acquiesced in the production of a second-rate aircraft, heavy and awkward, that performed none of its roles well, at the same time the American aerospace industry was making another leap forward in the development of the F-14, F-15, and F-16 series, so that the MRCA was almost obsolete by the time it entered service. But it was extremely expensive to produce, its cost increasing astronomically as production was repeatedly delayed to load ever more features onto the plane, with the purpose not so much of improving the plane but of providing work for the aircraft industry (the British joked grimly that, "MRCA = Military Requirements Come Afterwards"), until Helmut Schmidt apostrophized it as the "biggest arms contract since the birth of Christ."[89] Hence the MRCA benefited the German air force less than it did the Bavarian aerospace industry.

The American Challenge and Airbus

No issue showcased Strauß's abilities so much as technological competitiveness. Around and beneath the large issue of technological competitiveness he manipulated a dozen or more smaller issues and concerns in such a way that they combined to benefit Bavaria, the CSU, German and especially Bavarian industry, himself, various streams of public and elite opinion including nationalism, anti-communism, and anti-Americanism, and even interests, such as European integration, not part of the "interest solidarity" we wrote of earlier. His mastery of the political issue of technological competitiveness, in the 1960s apostrophized with the phrases "technological gap" and "American challenge," sprang from the same sources as his facility with military-strategic thought: his great intelligence and his deeply ingrained tendency to think in global terms, to see political, economic, military, social, and cultural questions in the light of universal history—the rise and fall of civilizations. This had been evident in his choice of a topic for a doctoral dissertation—"the idea of world empire" in the work of a minor Roman historian—and it remained his fundamental, "organizing" theme until his death in the late 1980s.[90] But it was in the late 1960s that this basic Straußian concern most closely corresponded with the issues dominating German public life.

The fashion for state research and development policies took off in the Western European countries in 1964, when an OECD report warned of a "technological gap" opening between the United States and the Western European countries. The report documented that the European countries spent one-third what the Americans did on research and development and that far fewer Europeans attended university.[91] Publicists and politicians began an earnest debate of measures to close the gap. While some genuinely feared that Europe was falling hopelessly behind America, others used the debate to promote other agendas, such as government planning and state intervention in the economy (especially among Social Democrats), government money for projects favored by industry (Christian Democrats and the FDP), and the need for a federal ministry to take the place of the state culture ministries and direct a national policy in education, research and development (the FDP, nationalists, and industrialists).

The German debate climaxed in 1968 with the publication of *The American Challenge,* a book on the political economy of European-American relations. A dry enough topic, no doubt, but the book sold ten million copies around the world.[92] Jean-Jacques Servan-Schreiber, the author and moderately left-liberal publisher of the French newsmagazine *L'Express,* recommended that the only effective way to prevent the complete domination of the European economy by American business was to undertake a discriminating Americanization. According to Servan-Schreiber, Europe had to admit that American dominance proceeded only from European inferiority, to change its mentality, and to educate more young people in technical fields, marketing, and management. The road forward led through European political integration, for, in order to finance significant research and development, firms would have to operate over areas larger than

European nation-states. Servan-Schreiber argued that America had not acquired its edge through liberalized markets but their opposite, and that therefore the political entities that assisted them had likewise to be bigger than the European countries. Specifically, it had been government money, much of it defense-related, that had allowed American aerospace, electronics, and nuclear-industrial firms to undertake the research that made them superior.[93] Therefore, the argument went, European firms needed government contracts to become competitive.

As a political issue in Germany, the technological gap and the American challenge seemed to favor the FDP and the Social Democrats. The FDP easily made hay out of the issue, for it had long argued that educational and scientific policy be centralized in a federal ministry. It represented the special interests of industry, profiled itself against the stuffy humanism of the Christian Democrats, and associated itself with the national interest and "the future." Likewise the Social Democrats, which found the answer in more government spending on education—an issue on which Social Democracy had the voters' trust. The CDU, on the other hand, found itself in a difficult position, for it had created the postwar German state and had quite a job admitting that radical change was necessary without implying that it had done something wrong. As for the CSU, the party and its chairman had different connections to this debate. For all of the obvious reasons, the CSU in general was on the defensive: voters considered it the most conservative party in Germany and associated it with obscurantism and clericalism; for almost two decades it had boasted that it protected state prerogatives in education, science, and research against the constitutional encroachments of federal programs.

But Strauß had a different profile than the CSU. On famously poor terms with his party's leading clericalists, for over ten years he had promoted technology, research and development, and the strengthening of Europe's scientific capabilities.[94] He eagerly took up the debate, since closing the technological gap required, as he argued it, policies that happened to serve German and Bavarian industry. He took it up all the more easily insofar as Servan-Schreiber's arguments corresponded to his own on many points. As was apparent in Strauß's foreword to the German edition of *American Challenge* and Servan-Schreiber's foreword to Strauß's *Challenge and Response: A Program for Europe* (a reworked version of *The Grand Design*), both men saw history as a competition between civilizations, considered that America represented a new type of civilization, and believed that the new struggle for civilizational dominance would be won by those who had the most effective foreign and industrial policies. Both also appealed to resentment of American power. Strauß's foreword to Servan-Schreiber's book was wholly positive: full of world-historical reflections, calls to greatness, remarks on Toynbee's civilizational challenges and responses, fate, new civilizations, planetary epochs, and military metaphors, Strauß emphasized supersonic air travel, space flight, atomic energy, electronics and computers, the emigration of scientists to America, and "big research." He considered that Servan-Schreiber's book was "a cry of warning against a mentality that tends to assign the Europeans the role of the Greeks, the despised 'Graeculi,' vis-à-vis the Roman Empire." "For Jean-

Jacques Servan Schreiber the challenge to Europe is no longer the Soviet Union but the USA. If after 1945 the European peoples outside the Russian occupied areas had to defend themselves against being drawn into the area of Soviet power, which was only possible with the help of the USA, then today they fight—actually they don't fight—against the threat of growing domination of the USA."[95] On the material level, Servan-Schreiber's recommendations implied nothing so clearly as European cooperation in aerospace and defense, which Strauß believed the Bavarian industry needed in order to survive against the American.

Strauß acted as industry's chief mouthpiece in the debate. His call for state support for the development of new technologies, particularly in aerospace, and his promotion of conferences on science policy that brought politicians and scientists together, obviously corresponded to industry's interests.[96] Beyond the specific issue of state support for research and development, Strauß addressed the related issues of measures to limit American direct investment (particularly in high-technology fields such as computers), and to stiffen Germany's back against American corporate domination and technological superiority. When investments became an issue, as they were in 1966, with Bölkow's encouragement, Strauß put himself in the forefront of those insisting that foreign parent firms not be allowed to raid the fruits of German scientific research.[97] He awakened the general public's interest in the debate by appealing masterfully to industrial self-interest, concern for Germany's future, and national pride, not to say nationalism, and this made him a central figure in the national debate.[98] For postwar Germany's technological failures had not distressed the average voter in the least, and the only way to create political support for a substantial and therefore costly effort in technology development was to cultivate public resentment of American power. Strauß specialized in creating and playing on such resentments.

All of this rather directly promoted Bavaria's industrial modernization, for state support for high-technology and growth industries meant, more than anything, championing Bavarian electronics, aerospace, and defense firms. In the 1960s, the Defense Ministry accounted for roughly 30 percent of federal expenditure for science. One continually heard the argument that "defense technology is extreme technology, cutting-edge technology, and therefore pacesetting technology."[99]

And it promoted Bavarian interests indirectly as well, through the ways Strauß's positions on nationalism, anticommunism, European integration, anti-Americanism, and intervention in the economy, and the need to close the "technological gap" and meet the "American challenge" tended to reinforce each other. Here we will indicate only the main lines of this mutual reinforcement. For example, the politics of technological development fit Strauß's political need to reinvent himself as a more progressive figure. We have already seen how whatever promoted Strauß's advancement tended to promote Bavaria's economic interests. On another level, the politics of technological development built up the CSU's political strength, since substantial industrial contributions were to be won on this issue from leaders of the export, growth, and defense industries that benefited from the policies the CSU promoted in the Adenauer, Erhard, and Kiesinger governments. The list of those who contributed to the CSU at election time reads like a Who's Who of German industry: Friedrich Flick, Herbert Quandt, Ludwig Bölkow, Willy Messerschmitt, the Siemens family, Karl Diehl, Fritz Berg, Hermann Abs, Gerd Tacke, the leaders of the chemical industry, particularly, it seems, Karl Winnacker and Rolf Sammet of Hoechst, elements within the steel-processing industries of the Rhine and Ruhr areas; and along with these industries came their banks and the publisher Axel Springer.[100] Further, the politics of technological development complemented Strauß's "Gaullism" and the vision of Europe he outlined in *The Grand Design:* a unified Europe as an equal partner of the United States would mean more European military spending, especially within Europe, and most especially within Bavaria. Regarding anticommunism, nationalism and anti-Americanism, all of these things lent their weight to the drive to close the technological gap, functioning as a stimulus and justification for the presence of the defense industries in Bavaria, just as the presence of the defense industries functioned as both a reward and (to a lesser extent) a stimulus for anticommunism and nationalism; so it was that Strauß and the CSU worked to maintain the Cold War atmosphere that justified the expenses.[101] Likewise, Strauß's and the CSU's statism supported government assistance to research and development, as well as to the growth- and future industries that were concentrating themselves in Bavaria. Regarding foreign and defense policy, Strauß's brand of *Der Primat der Außenpolitik* ("the primacy of foreign policy") sought to recover for Germany a position of equality with France and Britain, militarily, of course, but even more so politically, industrially, and commercially, so that his foreign and defense policy were symbiotic to his economic policies.[102] Naturally, this led into support to close the technological gap, and could only have been applauded by German industrialists—and not only defense industrialists—who believed that they suffered from their government's timidity in representing the national interest.

One project more than any other came to symbolize the attempt to close the technological gap and answer the American challenge: Airbus. The idea for a European consortium to produce a commercial jetliner did not originate with Strauß or the CSU but dated back to the early 1960s, when various European countries were discussing cooperation in civilian aircraft production. Two airplanes came out of these discussions, the Concorde and the Airbus.[103] The Germans stayed out of Concorde because they believed that the French and British had invited them in chiefly to help pay for the project; one sign of this had been that the latter invited Germany to join the project only after it was under way. With Airbus, on the other hand, the Germans had participated in the initial discussions. By the mid 1960s the French, German, and British governments were on board, attracted above all by the prospect of sharing the cost of supporting their respective aircraft industries with other governments. For everyone knew that subsidies would be required, at least for a transitional period, and that they would not be small. But it seemed a necessary investment to break the aircraft firms' near-total dependence on the military market—to escape the system Strauß had helped to create, in which political pressures forced the governments to award defense contracts, not according to the need for military aircraft, but according to the firms' need for work.

Technically, it was not a great feat for a large European country to build a commercial jetliner. The difficulty lay rather in earning a profit doing it, and, what was necessary to take on the overwhelming market dominance of the American firms of Boeing and McDonnell-Douglas, in creating and sustaining the national will necessary to see the project through an uncertain number of years in which the governments of the participant countries would have to absorb losses of many billions of dollars. That was the real "American challenge" in civilian aircraft. Everyone understood that Airbus was likely to lose money for the better part of a decade, perhaps, some thought, for more than a decade. Its industrial and political backers worked to make Airbus into an issue of national honor and a test of the European idea and determination to overcome the technological gap, so that failure, throwing in the towel, would be too crushing for the governments to contemplate.

The political background in Germany was marked by the Grand Coalition's bipartisan consensus. The consensus covered a range of connected issues, including Keynesian economic policy and the desirability that the government take some action to integrate Europe against American corporate domination and to close the technological gap by spending money to promote high-technology corporate projects. Despite the consensus, in Germany Airbus moved forward slowly for several years, due largely to the reluctance of the aircraft firms to merge, which was why, when the German Cabinet voted in March 1966 to support Airbus financially, it refused to make concrete promises of when and how much money would be made available. Likewise, though the federal parliament strongly supported Airbus, it voted to make its support dependent on prior mergers in the industry.[104] After Messerschmitt and Bölkow merged in 1968, and although market and organizational prospects darkened considerably in that year, the government declared itself ready for large financial subsidies to Airbus. In May 1969 France and Germany signed an agreement to construct a prototype Airbus.[105]

The CSU played a supporting role through 1969, but one that steadily grew. When he was Defense Minister, Strauß had led the political effort to fund civil aircraft production, but at that time it had been a matter of executive jets rather than commercial jetliners and the amount of money made available was small. During the Erhard and Kiesinger governments, the CSU supported the move toward Airbus, which in the late 1960s came under the ministerial jurisdiction of Karl Schiller's Economic Ministry. As Finance Minister, Strauß's role was to examine new expenses critically, and he is said to have been skeptical of the Airbus project, at least at first, apparently wanting to see airlines committed to purchasing the Airbus before he committed to supporting it financially. But the German government had to make its decision whether to commit to the project in 1969, before any airlines would commit to purchase the Airbus, and Strauß committed the financing. He expanded his role in 1969, when, despite Kiesinger's efforts to keep them involved, the British, who were to produce the Airbus's wings, backed out of the project. Strauß pushed the German government to subsidize a British firm to build the Airbus's wings in order to keep the project alive.[106]

Since the real challenge was to create and sustain national will, Strauß was made to order for a leading role in the project. Not only did he have in his pocket the political party that controlled the state where half of the German aircraft industry was located, and a long record of supporting aerospace, but he had made the argument frequently and powerfully that to stay out of aerospace was to be technologically backward; that short-term profits did not count so much as gaining technical know-how; and that government should support the development of technologies the "spin-off" effects of which would benefit the entire economy. Airbus would benefit from his understanding of the close connection between a nation's aircraft industry and its ego, and from his ability to play cleverly on national feeling and anti-American resentments. Moreover, he knew how to throw his political weight around, and was a "go" man, one who would look for reasons to push Airbus forward rather than try to minimize losses. The French connection was also there: for six years Strauß had been the leader of the German "Gaullists" and advocated cooperation with France in order to achieve independence from the Americans. Strauß even knew how to fly, having acquired a pilot's license in 1968. The CSU party paper, *Bayernkurier* (Bavaria Courier), did not exaggerate when on 2 May 1970 it editorialized: "Franz Josef Strauß is no Johnny-Come-Lately to This Field."[107]

But for one thing: the CSU was now out of power in Bonn. Federal elections in the fall of 1969 led to the formation of a Social-Democratic-FDP coalition. The CDU and CSU had, as in every previous election, outpolled the Social Democrats, but in course of the 1960s the Social Democrats and FDP had moved steadily toward each other on many issues. This created the danger that the new government engineer the transfer of the German aircraft industry, or at least that part of it involved in Airbus, to Social-Democratic states. The Social Democrats could, after all, have no interest in breaking the budget for the German aircraft industry so long as it remained concentrated in CSU-controlled Bavaria.

Yet the Social Democrats, who quite dominated the new government, agreed to make Strauß chairman of the board of directors of Airbus Germany (Deutsche Airbus GmbH). Obviously, the position would normally have gone to someone connected to the governing parties, but the Social Democrats had less interest in the project than we might expect. Social Democrats tended to see it as a form of what we would now call "corporate welfare" for firms whose employees, skilled labor and engineers, do not necessarily vote Social Democratic, especially when they were Bavarian. Moreover, Karl Schiller, whose Federal Economic Ministry had responsibility for the project, had never taken much interest in it. Leading Social Democrats anticipated that Airbus would impose financial burdens so great that the project would require Christian Democratic support. This was where Strauß came in. Sepp Hort, a CSU party member who was close to Strauß and at the same time a longtime employee of Bölkow, for whom he managed relations with the CSU, suggested to the Messerschmitt-Bölkow-Blohm board that Strauß lead Airbus Germany. Unable to convince the board members of the political wisdom of this, Hort took it upon himself to suggest Strauß to Hans

Hermsdorf, a Social Democrat and State Secretary in the Finance Ministry, who took the suggestion to Herbert Wehner. Wehner may have been the most powerful figure in the Social Democratic Party—as well the only figure in that party who possessed rhetorical and strategic talents equal to Strauß's, and whose Communist past had been a frequent target of Strauß's sharpest verbal arrows. Wehner needed little convincing. "Herbert never would have thought you could have such a good idea," Hort remembered Hermsdorf reporting back. Hort considered that Wehner intended to ease the task of government by creating an institution where cooperation would be the order of the day between the Social Democratic Party and Strauß, who was sure to lead a formidable opposition to the new government. Probably, too, Wehner was influenced by the location of the German aircraft industry—for its other stronghold, along with Bavaria, was Wehner's own home state of Hamburg. After Strauß agreed not to make partisan political capital out of the position, the government accepted him.[108]

A second promotion followed. After Strauß took his position as chairman of the board of directors of Airbus Germany in March of 1970 it remained for Airbus Germany to form, in cooperation with the French, the international firm of Airbus Industrie. It was agreed that the French industrialists would name Airbus Industrie's CEO, and the German industrialists the chairman of the board of directors. This time it was German industry that chose Strauß.[109]

Bavaria benefited enormously from all of this. MBB held 60 percent of Airbus Germany and southern Germany became a center of European commercial aircraft production. In Strauß, Bavaria had its insurance policy, for, though Airbus was created at a time when the Social Democrats were in power, the center of aircraft manufacturing in Germany was not moved to northern Germany.

Here we see what should by now be a familiar pattern. Once again, the CSU secured Bavarian interests against parties and nations much larger and more powerful than itself. Once again, Franz Josef Strauß championed Bavarian industrial interests. And once again, Bavarian industrial interests were not his priority. Airbus was less the result of the CSU's active work on behalf of Bavarian interests than it was the "natural" result of work the CSU had done a decade or more earlier.

Bavaria and the Big World

Even in the mid and late 1960s, when every party in western Europe took up the politics of industrial modernization, the CSU did not operate in this field according to any comprehensive plan. It adopted no general strategy, and its most successful leaders imposed no overall approach on the party or on Bavaria. Rather the politics of industrial modernization remained what they had always been for the CSU, individual politicians responding to events and developing approaches suitable to their personalities, ideas, and circumstances, arranging their positions in ways calculated to benefit and attract political and industrial constituents. The individual politicians transmitted modernizing impulses to the field for which they set or at least approved policy directions, each according to his own ambitions and ideas. This was the key to both the CSU's successes and failures. If Ludwig Huber could claim to have been successful, this was probably less because he worked in sync with the spirit of the times than because his policies suited the circumstances of the cases before him. If Otto Schedl used the authority he had won for himself on energy-political questions to promote a liberal policy of structural modernization that must rate as one of the most self-conscious modernization strategies developed by any of the politicians that promoted Bavaria's industrial modernization, it was not notably successful after 1963.[110] But Strauß continued to play the leading role, though not the same leading role he had played before the Spiegel Affair.

In the low politics of the years 1963 to 1969, that is to say, in the ministerial decisions as to what firms got what government contracts, Strauß and the State Group rarely got to make the decisions. Though the aerospace and defense contracts continued to be awarded, to a considerable extent, to Bavarian firms, it might seem to someone studying this era in isolation from the preceding that events had quite by accident, or quite luckily, worked out well for Bavaria. But we have seen that in previous years Strauß and the CSU State Group had arranged things so that they would do so, chiefly by concentrating the German aerospace and defense industries in Bavaria. In these years it was in high politics that the CSU played its role. The debates over political economy, Gaullism, flexible response, the Balance of Payments Offset Agreement and the technological gap determined whether there would be any research and defense contracts worth speaking of for Bavarian industry to win. These debates naturally moved far above the Bavarian industries, in the realm of high politics where hardly anyone in the CSU other than Strauß could exercise influence. But Strauß influenced these debates considerably.

Between 1963 and 1969 Bavaria became part of the big world. This happened as the CSU, but above all the State Group and Strauß, promoted policies that profiled the CSU on issues much bigger than narrow Bavarian interests and the traditional Bavarian concerns for federalism and agriculture, yet that promoted Bavaria's interest in industrial modernization. It is certainly true that after at least the early 1960s, Bavaria's interests became less important to an understanding of Strauß's politics. Although he never lost sight of them, he occupied himself with bigger questions, especially so far as he could manipulate them to promote his own drive for the German chancellorship. Yet exactly this marks Bavaria's arrival. A special concern with narrow, provincial, or backward Bavarian economic interests was no longer necessary. Bavaria having been hitched onto the modernization engine by the CSU in the late 1950s and early 1960s, it no longer mattered why the CSU pulled the wagon, so long as the train moved. It did not even make much difference whether the CSU pulled the wagon, for, with Messerschmitt and Bölkow and Airbus, and Siemens and Krauss-Maffei, the oil refineries, the Max Planck and Fraunhofer Foundations, the IPP and the DVL, Werner Heisenberg and Adolf Butenandt in Bavaria, almost any general program that promoted Germany's industrial modernization favored Bavaria. The CSU's role was to ensure that Bavaria was not unhooked from the wagon. And it proved that, under Strauß's leadership, this was within its power.

It also turned out that the big world was not a threatening place for the CSU and Bavaria, as least not so threatening as might have been expected. The larger trends of postwar Europe, toward more state intervention in the economy, secularism, centralized government, détente, and the reassertion of national feeling, did not hurt the CSU. Nor was Christian Democracy living on borrowed time. Outside of Bavaria, the CDU adapted to survive, continuing to integrate Catholics and Protestants in one party, but as its policy of integrating the working and middle classes faltered and its project of integrating Germany into Europe and the Western military alliance was taken up by the Social Democrats and the FDP, the CDU adapted to become a very moderate northern European conservative party. The CSU, on the other hand, still had work to do. And it did it, continuing, under Strauß's leadership, to integrate the Protestant and national-liberal traditions with the Bavarian Catholic and Christian-Democratic traditions. In the late 1960s it reversed the "Comrade Trend" and continued to increase its own vote throughout the 1960s and beyond, until in the 1974 Bavarian parliamentary election it received a phenomenal 62 percent of votes cast—more than twice the percentage of the Social Democrats.

But we end our story in 1969, since this year closed the era of uninterrupted Christian-Democratic government in Germany. By 1969 the FDP had completed its evolution into a left-liberal party, and, though the CDU/CSU received 46 percent of the vote in the federal election of that year, the FDP threw its 6 percent in with the Social Democrats' 43 percent, and it was enough to form a government. Most of the political dynamics and relationships that conditioned the politics of modernization we have described ended with the Christian-Democratic government in Bonn. Little changed in Bavaria in 1969. The CSU continued to govern Bavaria, in fact from 1962 up to this writing it has held an absolute majority in every Bavarian parliament. Though Otto Schedl retired from politics in 1969, Goppel and Huber soldiered on in Munich until 1978, when Strauß took over the Minister-Presidency of Bavaria, using it as a springboard from which to launch his 1980 candidacy for the chancellorship. For through the 1970s Strauß remained the first or second leading Christian-Democratic politician in Germany, and was the CDU/CSU's candidate for chancellor in 1980. But he lost, as he was indeed bound to: the FDP's enmity toward Strauß, forged in the Spiegel Affair and by Augstein, would have certainly prevented it from ever joining a Strauß government. Two years later the FDP abandoned the Social Democrats to form a government under the leadership of Helmut Kohl, Strauß's Christian-Democratic rival of the 1970s, and Kohl's coalition held power for a remarkable sixteen years. Strauß had by that time withdrawn from the national scene, trying to content himself with the Minister-Presidency of Bavaria, and died of a massive heart attack while hunting in 1988.

And Bavaria's industrial modernization continued apace. Bavaria had become part of the big world, even a privileged part of the big world, connected to developments in the world economy, moving and changing with it, no longer lagging behind or relatively isolated from that economy; and privileged because in the crucial postwar years a handful of CSU leaders found ways in which a small regional party could influence great national and international developments.

Notes

1. ACSP, Rep. Landesgruppe, 4. Wahlperiode, 69. Ulrich Wirz, *Karl Theodor Freiherr von und zu Guttenberg und das Zustandekommen der Großen Koalition* (Grub am Forst, 1997).
2. ACSP, Protokolle der Landesgruppe, 22.1.63. Treml, *Geschichte des modernen Bayern,* 441.
3. ACSP, Protokolle der Landesgruppe, 11.2.63. Dalberg, *Strauß: Porträt,* 222ff.
4. Anthony Sampson, *Anatomy of Europe: A guide to the workings, institutions and character of contemporary Western Europe* (New York, 1968), 22ff.
5. Wolfgang Krieger, "Franz Josef Strauß und die zweite Epoche in der Geschichte der CSU" in *Geschichte einer Volkspartei,* 176.
6. Franz Heubl interview in *Geschichte einer Volkspartei,* 557.
7. BHA, MWi, 12842, Betreff, 28.4.64; NL Schedl, I, Ministerreden, 1, Band 1–14, Ordner 26, Ansprache, 7.6.66. Trischler, *Luft und Raumfahrtforschung in Deutschland,* 446–450, 489.
8. BHA, MWi, 12902, 12842. Deutinger, *High-Tech-Staat,* 175, n. 773. Trischler, *Luft- und Raumfahrtforschung in Deutschland,* 511f.
9. BHA, NL Schedl, I, 1, Ordner 8. BHA, MK, Repertorien Band—Vorläufiges, VI/ 1088; MWi, Janssen to MK, 25.5.65. LT-Protokolle, 13.3.63. LT-Protokolle, 13.3.63. Rilling, *Kriegsforschung,* 53. Ludwig Bußmann, ed., *Die Wirtschaft des Landes Nordrhein-Westfalen* (Cologne, 1988), 108. Pohl, *Das Bayernwerk,* 375, 385f. Kock, *Der bayerische Landtag,* 149.
10. BHA, MK, Repertorien Band—Vorläufiges, VI/ 1088, Aktennotiz, 25.11.66. MAXIMILIANEUM, Finanzausschuß, 5. Wahlperiode, Bd. 5, 12.2.65; 6. Wahlperiode, Bd. 2, 21.2.68.
11. BHA, MK, Repertorien Band—Vorläufiges, VI/ 1088, Motoreninstitut Lindau, 2.6.65; Schedl to Goppel, 14.7.65. Deutinger, *High-Tech-Staat,* 190.
12. Abelshauser, *Ruhrkohlenbergbau,* 108.
13. BHA, MWi, 27190, Schedl to Strauß, 21.3.67; Strauß to Schedl, 12.4.67; 271911, Schedl to Schiller, 4.1.67. ACSP, Protokolle der Landesgruppe, 7.1.63, 14.1.63, 20.9.63. BHA, NL Schedl, I, 1. Amtliche Tätigkeit, Ordner no. 8. *CSU-Correspondenz,* 1964, no. 27 (7.12.64).
14. BHA, StK, 114379, Grundsätze, 2.12.66; Stellungnahme, 5.4.66. BHA, MWi, 27190, Noris to Schedl, 4.66. BHA, NL Schedl, I, 1, Ordner nos. 8, 10; I, 2, Band 80, 14.4.65; Band 81, 12.10.67; Band 81, 29.7.69; II, 2, nos. 52, 55, esp. Südpetrol to Innenministerium, 21.09.65; III, 52, no. 2. Bößenecker, *Bayern, Bosse und Bilanzen,* 39f. Pohl, *Das Bayernwerk,* 377.
15. BHA, NL Schedl, III, Bearb. Kart., no. 61, Rede no. 13; NL Schedl, I, Ministerreden, 1, Band 1–14, Ordner no. 27, Ansprache, 5.5.67; Ordner no. 29, Ansprache, 16.5.68; Ordner no. 30, Rede, 23.7.69, and Vortrag, 28.10.69. "Energie ins Land gelockt," *Der Spiegel* 19, no. 31 (28.7.65), 31ff.
16. BHA, NL Schedl, I, 2, Band 66, Schedl to Woltschkow, 5.7.67; Band 80, 30.12.65, 15.6.65, 15.7.69; Band 81, 12.2.70, 14.8.67. Bößenecker, *Bayern, Bosse und Bilanzen,* 47. Hans Baumann, *Männer und Mächte an Rhein und Ruhr. Von Banken, Bossen und Genossen* (Munich, 1973), 268. Bußmann, *Die Wirtschaft des Landes Nordrhein-Westfalen,* 109ff.
17. BHA, NL Schedl, I, Ministerreden 1, Ordner no. 30, Rede, 18.12.69; Ordner no. 31, Vortrag, 16.4.1970; Ministerreden 2, Band 51, no. 653, 13.5.71; NL Schedl, III, Bearb. Kart. no. 61, no. 13, "Aktuelle Probleme der bayerischen Struktur- und Energiepolitik," 1970. Stephan Deutinger, "Eine 'Lebensfrage für die bayerische Industrie'. Energiepolitik und regionale Energieversorgung 1945 bis 1980," in Die *Erschließung des Landes 1949–1973,* vol. 1 of *Bayern im Bund,* eds. Thomas Schlemmer and Hans Woller (Munich, 2001), 73f.
18. Bößenecker, *Bayern, Bosse und Bilanzen,* 43. Hermann Bößenecker, "In Bayern geht es auch ohne Hausmacht," *Die Welt,* 1966. Deutinger, "Eine 'Lebensfrage für die bayerische Industrie'" in, *Bayern im Bund,* vol. 1, 73f.
19. BA, B138, 2255, Weyand to Bundesfinanzministerium, 9.2.68. Henninger, "Kernforschung und Kerntechnik in Bayern," 46. Pohl, *Das Bayernwerk,* 381f. Bößenecker, *Bayern, Bosse und Bilanzen,* 46. Wolfgang Krieger, "Zur Geschichte von Technologiepolitik und Forschungsförderung in der Bundesrepublik Deutschland. Eine Problemskizze," *Vierteljahrshefte für Zeitgeschichte* 35, no. 2 (1987): 265 ("erfolglose Vorhaben"). Oskar Hatz, "Blick hinter die Kulissen,"

PNP, 6.7.68. Johannes Bähr, "Die 'amerikanische Herausforderung': Anfänge der Technologiepolitik in der Bundesrepublik Deutschland, *Archiv für Sozialgeschichte* 35 (1995), 96.
20. Stephan Deutinger, "Eine 'Lebensfrage für die bayerische Industrie'" in *Bayern im Bund,* vol. 1, 81. Manfred Treml, *Geschichte des modernen Bayern,* 448.
21. Kirchner, *Bundesdeutschen Verkehrsflugzeugbaus,* 97ff.
22. Andres, *Luft- und Raumfahrtindustrie,* 457ff, 462f. Schlotter, *Rüstungspolitik in der BRD,* 87f.
23. BA, B102, 43514, Notiz, 28.9.62; Vermerk, Troll, 2.12.63; Ergebnisprotokoll der Sitzung 28.11.63. Andres, *Luft- und Raumfahrtindustrie,* 459ff, 468. Kirchner, *Bundesdeutschen Verkehrsflugzeugbaus,* 202f. Mechtersheimer, *Rüstung und Politik,* 139.
24. BHA, MWi, 25926, Bayerische Flugzeugindustrie, 10.3.64.
25. MAXIMILIANEUM, Finanzausschuß, 6. Wahlperiode, Bd. 2, 21.2.68.
26. Schlotter, *Rüstungspolitik in der BRD,* 88f. Andres, *Luft- und Raumfahrtindustrie,* 465, 470f. Kirchner, *Bundesdeutschen Verkehrsflugzeugbaus,* 204f.
27. ACSP, Rep. Landesgruppe, 5. Wahlperiode, no. 208, no. 319.
28. Andres, *Luft- und Raumfahrtindustrie,* 471ff.
29. BHA, NL Schedl, I, Ministerreden 2, Band 62, Srbik to Schedl, 28.6.68; Srbik to Schedl, undated; Srbik to Schedl, 20.2.68. Andres, *Luft- und Raumfahrtindustrie,* 473. Schlotter, *Rüstungspolitik in der BRD,* 92.
30. Franz Sackmann interviewed by author, 12.8.99 in Roding. Kirchner, *Bundesdeutschen Verkehrsflugzeugbaus,* 205ff. Johannson, *Vom Starfighter zum Phantom,* 109. Andres, *Luft- und Raumfahrtindustrie,* 474ff. Schlotter, *Rüstungspolitik in der Bundesrepublik Deutschland,* 92f.
31. Franz Sackmann interviewed by author, 12.8.99 in Roding. Andres, *Luft- und Raumfahrtindustrie,* 476. Johannson, *Vom Starfighter zum Phantom,* 110. Schlotter, *Rüstungspolitik in der BRD,* 94.
32. Schlotter, *Rüstungspolitik in der BRD,* 94.
33. Sepp Hort interviewed by author, 7.6.00 in Munich. "Neue Konzentration in der deutschen Luftfahrtindustrie mit der neugegründeten Messerschmitt-Bölkow-Blohm, GmbH," *Wehr und Wirtschaft* 13, no. 5 (May 1969): 234. Kirchner, *Bundesdeutschen Verkehrsflugzeugbaus,* 225f. Schlotter, *Rüstungspolitik in der BRD,* 94f. Andres, *Die Luft- und Raumfahrtindustrie,* 480.
34. Oliver Braun, "Das politische Weltbild Alois Hundhammers (1900–1974)" (M.A. thesis, University of Regensburg, 2000), 77ff, 145ff. Johannes von Elmenau interviewed by Karl-Ulrich Gelberg, 23.10.91 in Munich, copy of transcript in possession of author.
35. BWA, LBI, Jahresbericht 1966.
36. ACSP, Protokolle der Landesgruppe, 20.9.63.
37. "Traumhafte Schau," *Der Spiegel* 17, no. 23 (5.6.63): 42–46. "Guter treuer Menschenstoff," *Der Spiegel* 18, no. 30 (22.7.64): 32f.
38. "Ist der neue Kultusminister in Bayern ein starker Mann?" *MM,* 7.10.64. "Kulturpolitik im Brennpunkt, Ludwig Hubers 100 Tage," *Main-Post,* 31.12.64. "Genug der Reden—nun die Reform," *Die Zeit,* 10.5.68.
39. BHA, MK, 66164.
40. "Mit so einem Minister ist kein Streit zu machen," *Quick,* 31.7.68. "Huber auf dem Elektro-Stuhl," *Welt am Sonntag,* 7.7.68.
41. ACSP, Rep. Landesgruppe, 5. Wahlperiode, Sitzungsniederschrift, 20.09.67; no. 326, Hort to Strauß, 15.3.66. ACSP, NL Strauß, Büro BMFinanz (1966–1969), Aktenzeichen, 8/261, Hort to Strauß, 14.7.67. MILITÄR, BW 1/ 181185, 22283, Hassel to Huber, undated. BHA, MK, 66165, 68691. *CSU-Correspondenz,* 1964, no. 11 (3.11.64): 5. *CSU-Correspondenz,* 1965, no. 36 (15.1.65): 2. Heinz Höfl, "CSU fordert eine Wehrsteuer," *SZ,* 14.11.66; Fred Schmid, *Der Militär-Industrie-Komplex* (Frankfurt a.M.: Verlag Marxistische Blätter, 1972), 170–176. Rilling, *Kriegsforschung,* 61–68.
42. Winfried Müller, Ingo Schröder, and Markus Mösslang, "'Vor uns liegt ein Bildungszeitalter.' Umbau und Expansion - das bayerische Bildungssystem 1950 bis 1975," in *Bayern im Bund,* vol. 1, 340 (control engineering and process technology = Regelungs-, Anlagen- and Verfahrenstechnik).
43. Henninger, "Kernforschung und Kerntechnik in Bayern," 45.

44. BHA, MK, 65988, Niederschrift, 27/28.6.63.
45. BHA, MK, 66165, 1.6.67. *CSU-Correspondenz*, 1966, no. 74 (13.7.66): 8. BHA, MK, 68691, an Sekretariat der Kultusministerkonferenz, 22.6.66. BHA, MK, 65988, 65989, Niederschrift, 10.5.63, 18.12.64.
46. Deutinger, *High-Tech-Staat*, 48.
47. BA, B138, 5859, Vermerk: IPP, Garching, 1.9.69.
48. BHA, MK, 65991, Plenarsitzungen, 14/15.6.66, 22/23.9.66, 3.11.66. BA, B138, 5862, Vermerk, 23.5.66; 5863, Vermerk, 22.6.66. Deutinger, *High-Tech-Staat*, 149ff, 217. Boenke, *Entstehung und Entwicklung*, 229ff, 241.
49. NL Strauß, Büro BMVg, VI, 373, Balke to Strauß, 28.12.62.
50. ACSP, Protokollen der Landesvorstand, 21.9.65, 23.10.65.
51. Strauß, *Erinnerungen*, 426.
52. See, e.g., ACSP, Protokollen der Landesvorstand, 9.4.65. *Adenauer: "Stetigkeit in der Politik". Die Protokolle des CDU-Bundesvorstands 1961–1965*, ed. Günter Buchstab (Düsseldorf: Droste, 1998), 767f (27.11.64).
53. ACSP, Protokolle der Landesgruppe, 20.9.63. BHA, BBbB, Dienststelle Bonn, Abgaben 1972–1978, 6, no. 33, Rutschke to Schedl, 17.10.63.
54. Wolfgang Krieger, "Franz Josef Strauß und die zweite Epoche in der Geschichte der CSU," in *Geschichte einer Volkspartei*, 179. Krieger, *Strauß: barocke Demokrat*, 61–64.
55. *WBH*, 5.1.66, p. 2 (industry reportedly reducing its financial contributions to the Christian-Democratic parties).
56. Conrad Taler, "Die Wiederkehr des Franz Josef Strauß," *Blätter für deutsche und internationale Politik* 12, no. 6 (June 1967), 587.
57. Josef Oertgen, "Apartheid-Propagandist Strauß," *Blätter für deutsche und internationale Politik* 11, no. 5 (May 1966), 360–362. Josef Oertgen, "Rhodesien und sein 'Handelspartner,'" *Blätter für deutsche und internationale Politik* 11, no. 9 (September 1966), 759–761.
58. Conrad Taler, "Die Wiederkehr des Franz Josef Strauß," *Blätter für deutsche und internationale Politik* 12, no. 6 (June 1967), 581.
59. Schmid, *Der Militär-Industrie-Komplex*, 167, citing *Industriekurier*, 10.11.66.
60. "Das Geld, die Macht und FJS," *Der Spiegel* 50, no. 30 (22.7.96): 59. Detlef Bischoff, *Franz Josef Strauß, die CSU und die Außenpolitik: Konzeption und Realität am Beispiel der Großen Koalition* (Meisenheim am Glan, 1973), 121.
61. MILITÄR, Ministerbüro Kai-Uwe von Hassel, BW 1/181172, Hopf to Berg, 20.8.63. ACDP, NL Hassel, I–157, 003/3, Hassel interview, p. 22.
62. MILITÄR, Ministerbüro Kai-Uwe von Hassel, BW 1/181172, 20789–20789/3, Gespräche BMVg mit Wirtschaft, 1964–1966.
63. Karl Wienand, "Die ganz große Verschwendung," *Stern* 24, no. 1 (1965).
64. "Ein gewisses Flattern," *Der Spiegel*, no. 5, 1966, p. 28, 33. Jim Upton, *Lockheed F-104 Starfighter* (North Branch, Minnesota, 2003), 77f.
65. Johannson, *Vom Starfighter zum Phantom*, 60–64.
66. MILITÄR, BW 1/ 181186, 22857, Stellungnahme zu dem Aufsatz 'Illustrierten-Demokratie oder echte Wehrdebatten.'" *Wehr und Wirtschaft* 9, no. 5 (May 1965): 239–246. See also, "Die deutsche Luft- und Raumfahrtindustrie 1968," *Wehr und Wirtschaft* 12, no. 4 (April 1968): 152. Mechtersheimer, *Rüstung und Politik*, 163.
67. MILITÄR, Ministerialbüro Kai-Uwe von Hassel, BW 1/ 181176, 21234/3, Fischer to Hassel, 19.4.63.
68. Sampson, *Anatomy of Europe*, 99. Schmid, *Der Militär-Industrie-Komplex*, 165.
69. Franz Sackmann interviewed by author, 12.8.99 in Roding ("machte sich stark"). ACDP, NL Hassel, I–157, 003/3, Interview with Hassel über die Zeit als Verteidigungsminister, p. 53f, 65 ("Ärger mit Strauß paßte mir gar nicht"). MÜNSTA, C III Firmen, Krauss-Maffei, no. 41, firm book, "Krauss-Maffei." BA, B136, no. 3104. Bößenecker, *Bayern, Bosse und Bilanzen*, 194.

70. Günter Papenbrock, "Krauss-Maffei baut den ersten deutschen Nachkriegs-panzer," *Wehr und Wirtschaft* 10, no. 4 (April 1966): 254–256. MÜNSTA, C III Firmen, Krauss-Maffei, no. 41, firm book, "Krauss-Maffei." "Holland bestellt 400 Leopard-Panzer," *Die Welt,* 25.10.68. "Nationale Rüstung ist notwendig,... und Rüstungsexport sinkt die Kosten, Ein Vorstoß von Dr. Zimmermann (CSU)," *Industriekurier,* 17.12.68. Bößenecker, *Bayern, Bosse und Bilanzen,* 195.
71. ACSP, NL Strauß, Büro PV, Korrespondenzakten, 5407.
72. Strauß, *Erinnerungen,* 332, 367, 409–410. Johannson, *Vom Starfighter zum Phantom,* 88, 96f.
73. Dalberg, *Strauß, Porträt,* 197–199. Johannson, *Vom Starfighter zum Phantom,* 83–87.
74. Harald Rosenbach, "Der Preis der Freiheit. Die deutsch-amerikanischen Verhandlungen über den Devisenausgleich (1961–1967)," *Vierteljahrshefte für Zeitgeschichte* 46, no. 4 (October 1998): 713–716. Schlotter, *Rüstungspolitik in der BRD,* 128f. George McGhee, *At the Creation of a New Germany: from Adenauer to Brandt: an Ambassador's Account* (New Haven, Connecticut, 1989).
75. Strauß, *Erinnerungen,* 428. Dalberg, *Strauß: Porträt,* 234.
76. Schlotter, *Rüstungspolitik in der BRD,* 11, 130.
77. Johannson, *Vom Starfighter zum Phantom,* 104f. Schlotter, *Rüstungspolitik in der BRD,* 12ff, 38–41, 124–145. Mechtersheimer, *Rüstung und Politik in der Bundesrepublik,* 130ff.
78. "Bonn kauft neue 'Starfighter' statt der 'Phantom'," *SZ,* 7.2.68. "FDP lehnt Kauf der 'Phantom' ab," *SZ,* 15.5.68. "Phantom-Ankauf noch möglich," *FAZ,* 3.10.68. "Unrühmliche Entscheidung," *Bayernkurier,* 2.11.68. Andres, *Luft- und Raumfahrtindustrie,* 226. Mechtersheimer, *Rüstung und Politik in der Bundesrepublik,* 78, 186. Schlotter, *Rüstungspolitik in der BRD,* 40ff, 185. Johannson, *Vom Starfighter zum Phantom,* 110ff.
79. ACSP, Rep. Landesgruppe, 5. Wahlperiode, no. 339. Seidl, "Schwieriger Neuanfang," 373–382 (MAN-Turbo). Johannson, *Vom Starfighter zum Phantom,* 113. Schlotter, *Rüstungspolitik in der BRD,* 46. Andres, *Luft- und Raumfahrtindustrie,* 227 (MBB share).
80. Mechtersheimer, *Rüstung und Politik,* 153.
81. Mechtersheimer, *Rüstung und Politik,* 39–42.
82. ACSP, NL Strauß, Büro BMFinanz (1966–1969), Korrespondenz, Karton 3/ lfd. 94, Hort to Strauß, 31.5.67; Hort to Strauß, 22.7.66. Andres, *Luft- und Raumfahrtindustrie,* 249–256, 273. Mechtersheimer, *Rüstung und Politik,* 28–35.
83. "Die Luftwaffe kann ein politisches Flugzeug nicht brauchen," *FAZ,* 5.12.68. Andres, *Luft- und Raumfahrtindustrie,* 273f. Mechtersheimer, *Rüstung und Politik,* 37–38.
84. "Es wird zwei neue Kampfflugzeuge geben," *Die Welt,* 27.12.68. Johannson, *Vom Starfighter zum Phantom,* 107. Mechtersheimer, *Rüstung und Politik,* 32–35, 43–84, 68.
85. Andres, *Luft- und Raumfahrtindustrie,* 270ff.
86. Mechtersheimer, *Rüstung und Politik,* 177–183.
87. "Differenzen um das 'Neue Kampfflugzeug,'" *Die Welt,* 3.12.68. Andres, *Luft- und Raumfahrtindustrie,* 276–278.
88. Benecke and Schöner, *Wehrtechnik für die Verteidigung* (Koblenz, 1984), 188.
89. Mechtersheimer, *Rüstung und Politik,* 113, 163.
90. Krieger, *Strauß: barocke Demokrat,* 17.
91. C. Freeman and A. Young, "The Research and Development Effort in Western Europe, North America and the Soviet Union" (Paris, 1965). "The Technology Gap," *Time* 89, no. 2 (13.1.67). Karl Steinbuch, *Falsch programmiert; über das Versagen unserer Gesellschaft in der Gegenwart und vor der Zukunft und was eigentlich geschehen müßte* (Stuttgart, 1968). Johannes Bähr, "Die 'amerikanische Herausforderung,'" 115. Sampson, *Anatomy of Europe,* 159–162.
92. Jean-Jacques Servan-Schreiber, *Passions,* vol. 2, *Les fossoyeurs* (Fixot: Paris, 1993), 28. Alain Rustenholz and Sandrine Treiner, *La Saga Servan-Schreiber,* vol. 2, *Le temps des initiales* (Paris: Editions du Seuil, 1993), 395–401.
93. Jean-Jacques Servan-Schreiber, *The American Challenge* (New York, 1968), 25, 66–67, 81.
94. FRUS, 1964–1968, Volume XIII, Western Europe Region, no. 255, Memorandum of Conversation, 2.6.67. Mechtersheimer, *Rüstung und Politik,* 47.

95. ACSP, NL Strauß, Büro BMVg, VI, 814, Korrespondenz mit Servan-Schreiber, 1954. ACSP, NL Elsen, 9.3.6. Jean-Jacques Servan-Schreiber, *Die amerikanische Herausforderung*, with a foreword by Franz Josef Strauß (Hamburg, 1968). Franz Josef Strauß, *Herausforderung und Antwort: Ein Programm für Europa*, with a foreword by Jean-Jacques Servan-Schreiber (Stuttgart, 1968).
96. ACSP, Protokolle der Landesgruppe, 7.2.66, Vorbereitung der Wissenschaftsdebatte. ACSP, Druckschriften, 13/23, "Dokumentation, Rede Strauß im Bundestag," (1965), p. 28. ACSP, Karton, Generalsekretär, 1965–1974. Forschungskreis Wehr und Wirtschaft, "Grundfragen der deutschen Wehrpolitik: II, Das militärische Bild," *Wehr und Wirtschaft* 13, no. 2 (February 1969): 95. "Strauß spricht mit Wissenschaftlern," *FAZ*, 7.2.66. BDI-Memorandum über die gesamtindustrielle Bedeutung der Luft- und Raumfahrttechnik, Köln, April 1966. *CSU-Correspondenz*, 26.9.66. Sampson, *Anatomy of Europe*, 161f.
97. ACSP, NL Strauß, Büro PV, Korrespondenzakten, 5407, Bölkow to Strauß, 12.8.66; Strauß to Bölkow, 20.8.66; Bölkow to Strauß, 16.8.66; Strauß to Bölkow, 26.8.66; Korrespondenzakten, 5204, Röbke to Strauß, 8.8.66; Strauß to Röbke, 26.8.66; Korrespondenzakten, 5411, Habsburg to Strauß, 19.8.66; Hepp to Habsburg. IFZ, NL Mintzel, Bd. 23, "Die deutsche Aufgabe Bayerns," Rede des Landesvorsitzenden der CSU, Bundesminister a.D. Franz Josef Strauß, anl. der CSU-Landesversammlung am 9.10.66, p. 18. Bischoff, *Franz Josef Strauß, die CSU und die Außenpolitik*, 125. Sampson, *Anatomy of Europe*, 97, 172f.
98. ACSP, Druckschriften, 13/23, Rede Strauß im Bundestag (1965).
99. Friedrich Zimmermann, "Rüstungspolitik und Verteidigungswirtschaft," *Wehr und Wirtschaft* 13, no. 1 (January 1969): 20.
100. ACSP, NL Strauß, Büro BMVg, III. 373, Balke to Strauß, 28.12.62. Klaus Voigdt, "Hinter Strauß ein Kreis. Interview mit dem ehemaligen Strauß-Berater Dr. Klaus Bloemer," *Vorwärts*, 23.10.69. Mintzel, *Die CSU: Anatomie einer konservativen Partei*, 370f, 376.
101. Albert von Buylaere, "Zwanzig Jahre nach Bastogne ist Europas Antwort: "Nuts!," *Wehr und Wirtschaft* 11, no. 6 (June 1967): 22–24. Schmid, *Der Militär-Industrie-Komplex*, 157–167.
102. Alf Mintzel, "Franz Josef Strauß," in, *Persönlichkeit und Politik in der Bundesrepublik Deutschland*, vol. 1, *Politische Porträts*, eds. Walter L. Bernecker and Volker Dotterweich (Göttingen, 1982), 203. Bischoff, *Franz Josef Strauß, die CSU und die Außenpolitik*, 117.
103. Kirchner, *Bundesdeutschen Verkehrsflugzeugbaus*, 87ff, 126ff.
104. Kirchner, *Bundesdeutschen Verkehrsflugzeugbaus*, 160–178. Jay L. Lorenzen, "A Statist Approach to High Technology Policy: The Case of Aerospace" (Ph.D. diss., University of Denver, 1990), 321f.
105. Andres, *Luft- und Raumfahrtindustrie*, 367–370. Lorenzen, "Statist Approach to High Technology Policy," 315. Ira C. Magaziner and Mark Patinkin, *The Silent War: Inside the Global Business Battles Shaping America's Future* (New York, 1989), 242f.
106. Andres, *Luft- und Raumfahrtindustrie*, 340f, 359. Ludwig Bölkow, "Verdienste um die europäische Luftfahrtindustrie, in, Friedrich Zimmermann, ed., *Anspruch und Leistung. Widmungen für Franz Josef Strauß* (Stuttgart: Seewald, 1980), 255. Ludwig Bölkow, *Der Zukunft verpflichtet: Erinnerungen*, 2nd ed. (Munich, 1994), 276f. Kirchner, *Bundesdeutschen Verkehrsflugzeugbaus*, 162, 231. Lorenzen, "Statist Approach to High Technology Policy," 316, 332.
107. Matthew Lynn, *Birds of Prey: The War Between Boeing and Airbus* (London, 1995), 41. Bölkow in Zimmermann, *Anspruch und Leistung*, 254. Schmid, *Der Militär-Industrie-Komplex*, 164.
108. Renate Höpfinger, Zeitzeugen-Interview mit Sepp Hort, in, *Franz Josef Strauß – Ludwig Bölkow - Sepp Hort*, vol. 2 of, *Bayerische Lebensbilder: Biographien – Erinnerungen – Zeugnisse*, Renate Höpfinger, ed. (Munich: Hanns-Seidel-Stiftung, 2004), 150–181. Bölkow, *Der Zukunft verpflichtet*, 283f. Bölkow in Zimmermann, *Anspruch und Leistung*, 256. Gersdorff, *Ludwig Bölkow*, 123. Kirchner, *Bundesdeutschen Verkehrsflugzeugbaus*, 230f, 270.
109. Andres, *Die Luft- und Raumfahrtindustrie*, 389.
110. BHA, NL Schedl, I, 1. Amtliche Tätigkeit, Zeitungsausschnitte, 1957–1970, Ordner nos. 9–12, 23–25.

CONCLUSION
BAVARIA, 1969

Circumstances and Their Masters

The CSU led what was probably the most remarkable regional renaissance in postwar Europe. But what does it say about its politics of industrial modernization that, until its achievement was realized, many CSU deputies were unaware that their party was up to something more than everyday pork-barrel politics? And that until the late 1950s it was driven more by personal ambitions and factional rivalries than a considered strategy? Interparty warfare and personal ambition hardly make a likely recipe for industrial modernization.

By now it should be clear that the CSU's politics of industrial modernization was not a formula susceptible of export. It depended utterly on Bavarian circumstances. These included the need of Bavarian industry for a party to represent it against the Ruhr industry and the CDU, the postwar presence on Bavarian soil of firms and research institutions with the potential for expansion, the desire of prominent scientists to enjoy Munich's charms, Bavarians' comparatively more anticommunist and hence pro-military attitudes, the combination of particularist passion and superior competence in many of Bavaria's upper-level civil servants, the weakness of the Social-Democratic and liberal political traditions in Bavaria, and, of course, two basic realities of the postwar party system, that the CSU securely dominated Bavarian politics and that the CDU could not form a national government without the support of the CSU, which enjoyed most of the benefits of governing but carried few of its burdens. Its success was equally dependent on what Alexis de Tocqueville called, "concatenations of secondary events." One thinks here of the mutual discovery of Franz Josef Strauß and the LBI at the very time Strauß was pressing for a trial of strength with the CDU and Bavarian industry was feeling itself dangerously vulnerable due to its lack of a powerful representative in Bonn. One thinks also of the triple congruence in the fall of 1956 of the "nuclearization" of American military strategy with Blank's

Notes for this section begin on page 176.

inability to adapt his own defense plans, and with Adenauer's need to shore up his position with German industry to prepare for the 1957 federal elections. Again, one thinks how Schedl's drive to introduce oil to Bavaria coincided with Mattei's struggle against the Seven Sisters.

Yet circumstances and concatenations of events did not produce a politics of industrial modernization. Politicians had to be able to see circumstances and events in the right way, to figure out how to master them. More than anyone else in postwar Germany, Strauß figured out how to arrange these things on the political chessboard in a way that benefited a remarkable list of entities: himself, the CSU, reefs of industries and branches of research, and, not least, Bavarian voters. Strauß was the game's grand master.

It was an interesting game, and must have had exciting moments for those who lived it, even if Servan-Schreiber's contention that we should read about the "fabulous struggle" for the conquest of technologies as breathlessly as we once read about great wars is not the experience of many readers of histories of the politics of modernization (present readers included).

At first Strauß and his CSU allies had nothing to lose. They allied themselves with Bavarian industrial interests: on the state level, Seidel took up industry's cause, while on the federal level Strauß showed Bavarian industrialists that he was willing and able to be useful to them, and gradually found opportunities to do the same for German industrialists outside of Bavaria. It was by learning to do the latter that he won the Ministry of Atomic Affairs and the Ministry of Defense, fulfilling his ambition to reshape the Western alliance in a way that promoted his personal ambitions and his determination that Germany return to the circle of European great powers. As the years went by, his efforts focused more on the "high politics" of the Western alliance and European integration, but he never neglected his Bavarian base, which he built up into the center of the German defense industry. Back in Munich, Seidel and his lieutenants learned from the Social Democrats' vision of a "second industrial revolution" to go from victory to victory. After Seidel's death, his epigones brought Bavaria along with them as they found their own formulas for advancing their careers, the party as a whole, and the industrial modernization of Bavaria. Some, like Hanns Seidel and Hans Meinzolt, supported research; Otto Schedl developed a liberal policy of stimulating competition to lower energy costs. Meanwhile, in Bonn, Strauß and his interest solidarity consolidated their achievements even while Strauß was out of office. In Munich the CSU was never out of office, but through the 1960s continued to build up Bavaria's scientific establishment.

Results

From 1949 to 1969 the Bavarian economy was *catching up* to the rest of West Germany. Here are some of the structural data. First, gross domestic product. From 1950 to about 1957 Bavaria's GDP grew more slowly, but from 1957 to 1970 and beyond more rapidly, than that of West Germany as a whole. In 1950, Bavaria's per capita GDP measured 85.3 percent of that of West Germany; by 1952 it had shrunk to 82.5 percent; in 1955 it had recovered only to 84.6 percent. After that it grew at a more rapid rate than that of West Germany, so that in 1960 it stood at 87.9 percent; in 1965 91.3 percent; and by 1970 92 percent. By 1980 Bavarian per capita GDP was 94.9 percent of that of West Germany. The numbers are even more impressive when one compares Bavarian growth rates to North Rhine-Westphalian: whereas in 1950 Bavaria's per capita GDP measured 72.3 percent of that of North Rhine-Westphalia, by 1970 it stood at 90 percent.[1]

Second, demographic figures. These tell the same story. In 1945 Bavaria was one of the least densely populated German states. This was not changed by the arrival in Bavaria of about two million German refugees; though other German states received refugees too, Bavaria received a disproportionately high number of them. From 1950 to 1960, Bavaria's population shrank relative to that of the rest of West Germany, increasing by only 3 percent while that of the latter increased by 11 percent. But from 1960 to 1970 Bavaria's population increased by 13 percent, that of West Germany by 11 percent.[2] In short, though Bavaria shrank in the 1950s, as people flowed west- and northward to prosperous states like North Rhine-Westphalia, it expanded in the 1960s, when the population flow reversed direction.

Third, occupational structure. These figures show Bavaria industrializing faster than West Germany as a whole. From 1950 to 1961 the percentage of the population working in agriculture fell by 9 percent in Bavaria, 8.6 percent in Germany, while the percentage of the population in industry and craft trades increased by 8.2 percent in Bavaria, by 6.1 percent in Germany. In the 1960s these changes accelerated. From 1961 to 1970, the number of Bavarians in agriculture declined by 8.4 percent, versus a West German decline of 6 percent, and the number of Bavarians in industry and craft trades increased by 2.9 percent, versus a West German increase of 0.6 percent. In 1950 those occupied in industry made up 7.2 percent of all Bavarians but 9.6 percent of all West Germans, but by 1971 the figures stood at 13 percent and 14 percent, respectively.[3]

But the transformation was more fundamental than is indicated by these figures. Bavaria had not remained the poorhouse of West Germany, but became a favorite location of the most modernizing industries. It became prosperous, and in an enviable way. It not only acquired the highly visible modern industries we have discussed in previous chapters, but enjoyed a well-balanced economy. Whereas in 1932 the Bavarian writer Oskar Maria Graf could observe, "Munich went to the dogs, so to speak, a long time ago; it is certainly the most provincial of all German cities," in the 1960s Munich acquired the nickname of "Germany's secret capital." Munich by no means became Germany's industrial, commercial, or financial center, yet it could not have acquired this nickname had it not become much more than a picturesque provincial backwater.[4] And not only the Munich metropolitan area, but also the Nuremberg and Augsburg areas, and even the smaller towns and countryside were doing well. Despite being made eccentric within the European trading area by the lowering of the Iron Curtain and the creation of the European Economic Community, Bavaria became increasingly important for industry and commerce. By 1969 modernity and Bavaria no longer seemed to exclude each other. It had become not only possible but suitable to speak of modernization with a Bavarian accent.

Even more telling than general growth figures, the CSU's politics of industrial modernization changed Bavaria's image—in the eyes of Bavarians and other Germans as well. The effects of this were far-reaching and incalculable.

Politics does much more to shape the way people think, the images in their minds, and the character they attribute to things, than most of us recognize. This is especially true of its outstanding personalities, their contests and rivalries. The old image of Bavaria had been formed in the struggle between Catholics and Protestants, especially by the *leyenda negra*, and in the conflicts between particularistic loyalties and nationalism, between socialism and antisocialism. Even today, anti-Bavarian sentiment continues to exist and is often connected to anti-Catholicism and anticonservatism. But though the older images have not gone away, from 1949 to 1969 the CSU superimposed on them a new layer of images, which transformed Bavaria's overall image in fundamental ways. And this necessarily affected every decision every industrialist and employee made about locating in Bavaria, or moving to Bavaria, or remaining in Bavaria. Whereas in 1949 the image German industrialists had of Bavaria would have been largely that of a charming, provincial place, conservative or even reactionary (in the European sense of those words—unfriendly to industry and capitalism), and where nothing much happened, by 1969 it was of a paradoxical place, traditional yet "happening," dominated since the war and for the foreseeable future by a pronouncedly industry-friendly party; moreover, one that not only invariably won in Bavaria but was a member of the coalition that governed Germany from 1949 through 1969, over which coalition it exercised considerable influence. They would think of a party that had repeatedly proved that it was able to take care of its own, and that by taking care of its own had changed Bavaria in some highly visible ways. For by 1969, when one thought of Bavaria, one thought of the CSU and Franz Josef Strauß, either explicitly or as an important aspect of one's image-complex of Bavaria.

Visibility was important. Not only was Strauß one of the most visible (and audible) politicians in Germany, but Bavaria forged ahead in the most visible industries, those most closely associated with the future and most closely covered by the news media. In the early and mid 1950s atomic power was treated as the horizon of the future. As its prospects faded, aerospace succeeded to its role. And news about atoms and aerospace was often enough news about Strauß, the CSU, and things going on in Bavaria. By the time the Starfighter was finished in 1964, the wave of interest in scientific research and development again focused attention on things that were happening in Bavaria. And the biggest economic story of the late 1950s and 1960s, the decline of coal and the heavy industry of the Ruhr and the rise of oil, often enough connected to a story of the CSU fighting, more or less successfully, for Bavarian interests. Due to the particular fields in which Bavaria forged ahead, in the late 1960s Bavarians and other Germans become aware of Bavaria as a place where remarkable things were happening—probably even more than they actually were.

One index of this was that the new, modern Bavaria became a journalistic cliché. Newspaper and magazine articles on the subject abounded and invariably one of their themes was the paradox of a conservative land modernizing yet remaining in some sense conservative. The changes in Bavaria were first remarked upon by *Der Spiegel*, which, though it invariably took an ironical tone when dealing with Bavaria and though it continued to pursue its publisher's vendetta against Strauß, nonetheless gave considerable credit to the CSU. Naturally, the business press took particular interest in what was going on in Bavaria, and *Der Arbeitgeber* (The Employer), the journal of the Federal Association of German Employer Federations (BDA, Bundesvereinigung der Deutschen Arbeitgeberverbände), devoted an entire issue to the theme "Bavaria: From Agricultural to Industrial State," as did *Der Volkswirt* (The Political Economist) to "Bavaria—An Industrial State," and some years later the French *Revue d'Allemagne* (Review of Germany). In the late 1960s and early 1970s books began to appear on the same theme, and we have already indicated that by the late 1960s Munich had acquired the significant nickname, "Germany's secret capital."[5]

A New CSU and a New Bavaria

All this points to something else. The CSU's politics of industrial modernization issued in something beyond new industries. It helped to create a new CSU and a new Bavaria.

By 1969 the CSU was no longer the party of conservative, rural, and Catholic Bavaria, but what Germans call a "people's party," appealing with considerable success to people of both Christian faiths, to all social classes, and to urban as well as rural voters, and representing all of the chief currents of political opinion other than Social Democracy. Nor was there any longer any question of the CDU absorbing the CSU: rather the latter exercised disproportionate influence over the CDU, and had proven its effectiveness far too well and identified itself far too closely with Bavaria, becoming the party even of Protestant nationalists in Franconia. Rather in the late 1960s Strauß raised the question whether the CSU should expand to become a national party. This never happened, though Strauß pushed very hard in this direction in the mid 1970s; but the very fact that he raised the question indicates how far the CSU had come in twenty years. The CSU had not only dropped its suspicion of democracy but had become demophile in attitude—as a party that receives over 50 percent of the vote in a variably four-to-five-party system can well afford to be. Representing the desire for modernization as well as Bavaria's baroque Catholic heritage, it had learned to treat the latter less as a legacy of religious faith than as cultural tradition and local folklore. And it had completely identified itself with Bavaria and with Bavarianness. As Alf Mintzel has pointed out, only the CSU could put up campaign posters with Bavarian symbols but without the party's name on them: "everyone knows which party is meant."[6]

By 1969, Bavaria was also no longer what it had been in 1949. The modernization of industry had led many other things to change. Most obviously, it lent Bavarian particularism a viability it otherwise would not have had. It broke the old association between particularism and backwardness. Within Germany, these two had long been felt to be almost two sides of the same coin. And no people would choose, over the long term, to remain backward. Conservative Catholic Bavarian parties had long been characterized by their propensity for a self-isolating, rigid, belligerent defense of particularism, and in the 1940s the CSU showed many signs that it would continue the tradition. But by 1969 it was clear that the CSU was about something else, a flexible defense of federalism, in the understanding, introduced to the party by no one so much as Strauß, that political and economic success was the best defense of federalism. Whereas in the past Bavarian politicians took positions and struck attitudes that practically invited others to force Bavaria to march in step, now the CSU's success invited others to emulate it.

Economic success also improved the character of Bavarian particularism, which further contributed to its viability. Feeling that under the government of the CSU Bavaria's identity was safe, Bavarian particularists became "nicer." They lost their angry, hard edge. In 1949 they cultivated chauvinism and particularistic resentments, and their tone was often accusing and sometimes hysterical, borne of their long experience of being on the losing side of history, of grievances over past defeats and despair of the future of their cause. Their rhetoric became somewhat less chauvinistic and more patriotic and their tone more reasonable after the Constitutional Convention in 1949, which more or less realized their federalist program (depending on how particularistic one was), but significant improvement came only as the 1950s and 1960s wore on. In these decades Bavarian voters saw what the CSU could do for Bavaria, but also, to the surprise of many of them, that the federalism of the Basic Law was only slightly undermined by federal legislation, and that in fact the other states quickly developed local loyalties. Even the Social Democrats found something to appreciate in federalism, as, out of power in Bonn from 1949 to 1969, they appreciated limits on Adenauer's power as well as their own ability to exercise meaningful power in the states they governed. By 1969, the angry hyper-federalists of the Bavaria Party seemed like antique figures; and almost all of the representatives of particularist-federalist opinion within the CSU, such as Minister-President Goppel, were less distrustful of the German state, more moderate, optimistic, reasonable, and pleasant. The particularist-federalist *Kulturkampf* had turned into a friendly debate. Similarly, though the climate of opinion in Bavaria had remained conservative, Bavarian conservatism had changed. It had become more self-assured, generous, popular, and progressive, as well as democratic, liberal, and tolerant.

And this brings us to something else Bavaria's industrial modernization made possible: a change in Bavarian consciousness. In 1969 Bavaria remained the most self-conscious and distinct German state. But the quality of its self-consciousness had changed. It was no longer defensive, but self-confident. Bavaria was no longer regarded as something of a joke, or if it remained the butt of many jokes, the jokes were more often tinged with envy than contempt. Now that the Bavarians' age-old desire to be German and stay Bavarian could be realized effortlessly, they found that other Germans wanted to become Bavarian—or, since this is said to be impossible, at least to savor Bavarianness. Non-Bavarian Germans coming to Bavaria who, generations ago, would have scorned to be mistaken for a Bavarian or to acquire the Bavarian accent and mentality were increasingly pleased to be mistaken for Bavarians, and happy that their children would be Bavarian. Manfred Baumgärtel, a CSU party manager who worked closely with Strauß, recalled that when, over the years, he visited Messerschmitt-Bölkow-Blohm plants he noticed that more and more engineers from northern Germany picked up a Bavarian accent. Things like this signified that important changes were taking place in people's attitudes: so long as non-Bavarian Germans saw Bavarianness as something desirable, mere politics posed little danger to Bavarian identity.[7]

The industrial modernization of Bavaria also made possible a change in Germany. Bavaria was no longer a remote "down there" where little happened to interest other Germans, and so Germany's center of gravity shifted southward. If through the early 1950s it seemed that West Germany would find its center of gravity in the lower Rhine and Ruhr, by 1969 that center of gravity had moved southward, up the Rhine, and eastward, closer to Bavaria, Baden-Württemberg, and Hesse. By the 1970s the northern German states were complaining that whereas Germany had long been marked by a "north to south gradient" ("Nord-Sud Gefälle," a slope from a northern height to a southern depth), now a "south to north gradient" was in the making.[8] This was nothing less than the reversal of a trend of centuries. From falling ever farther behind, through the nineteenth and first half of the twentieth centuries, southern Germany saw itself catching up to the rest of Germany. Thus a reversal in Bavarian history led to a reversal in German history.

In this way the industrial modernization of Bavaria also played its part in a reversal in European history. The centuries-old division of Europe into Protestant, enlightened, stable, prosperous, liberal, and later democratic northern Europe, and Catholic, backward, unstable, poor, and authoritarian southern Europe became obsolete between the end of World War II and the 1970s. Something like Bavaria's postwar economic boom had also happened in Austria and northern Italy, so that while the northern European countries saw their relative economic and industrial positions decline, while they lost empires and confidence, Bavaria and its southern neighbors became modern, stable, prosperous, liberal, and democratic. In many ways their situation was better than that of northern Europe, since, despite their religious secularization, the southern countries continued to enjoy the residual traditions, tastes, vital rhythms, and styles of their Catholic baroque religion-culture. Aware of their common lot as the despised southerners, they were also conscious of their common recovery. Though their common rise was not driven by common personalities, events, or strategies—never did they act together as anybody's "Greater Baroque Co-Prosperity Sphere" against northern

Europe—they all benefited from historical "long waves" and the basic conditions of the postwar world: the pressures exerted by the Soviet threat and American-led alliance over all of Western Europe; the ability of Christian Democracy and Social Democracy to cooperate in a way they had not prior to World War II to provide a hitherto unknown stability, legal order, and liberality; the expansion of trade; the relative decline of heavy industry, and the rise of the service sector and tourism. All of these things benefited southern Europe more than northern Europe, precisely because the southerners had not had them before. But perhaps the Bavarians, whose political leaders navigated the circumstances and "concatenations of events" best, drew the most benefit from them.

Notes

1. See, *Bayern in Zahlen,* which has appeared annually since 1947; see also, *Statistische Jahrbücher für den Freistaat Bayern* and *Statistische Jahrbücher der Bundesrepublik Deutschland.* The best discussion of the statistics and their meaning is in Erker, "Keine Sehnsucht." See also, H.H. Bergschmidt, "Das Wachstum der Bayerischen Wirtschaft seit 1950 im Vergleich zum Wirtschaftswachstum in der Bundesrepublik Deutschland" (Ph.D. dissertation, Munich, 1964). The figures given in the text were calculated by the author from figures in Erker, "Keine Sehnsucht," 485, citing, *Bayern in Zahlen* 22 (1968), Beilage, and "Das Bruttoinlandsprodukt in Bayern und im Bundesgebiet 1960–1982," in, *Bayern in Zahlen* 37 (1983): 156–162.
2. These figures were calculated by the author from figures in the *Statistisches Jahrbuch für die Bundesrepublik Deutschland 1971,* 27.
3. Erker, "Keine Sehnsucht," 492ff.
4. Oskar Maria Graf, *Notizbuch des Provinzschriftstellers 1932: Erlebnisse, Intimitäten, Meinungen* (Basel, 1932), 49f. Karl Bosl, "München, 'Deutschlands heimliche Hauptstadt.' Historische Bemerkungen zur Strukturanalyse des modernen Hauptstadt- und Großstadttypus in Deutschland," *Zeitschrift für bayerische Landesgeschichte* 30, no. 1 (1967): 298-313.
5. "Mir san mir," *Der Spiegel* 18, no. 1/2 (8.1.64): 30-42. "O'zapft is," *Der Spiegel* 18, no. 39 (23.9.64): 42-52. *Der Arbeitgeber* 22, no. 8 (24.4.70). *Der Volkswirt* (28.7.67)(supplement, "Bayern—ein Industrieland"). *Revue d' Allemagne* 19, no. 3 (1977). *Clipper Magazin* (October 1971), Beilage (publication of Pan-American airlines). Bößenecker, *Bayern, Bosse und Bilanzen.* Riehl-Heyse, *CSU, die Partei, die das schöne Bayern erfunden hat.* Bernd Rill, ed., *Bavaria Felix: Ein Land, das Heimat ist und Zukunft hat* (Percha am Starnberger See, 1986). Bosl, "München, 'Deutschlands heimliche Hauptstadt.'"
6. Alf Mintzel, "Bayern und die CSU. Regionale politische Traditionen und Aufstieg zur dominierenden Kraft," in *Geschichte einer Volkspartei,* 236.
7. Manfred Baumgärtel interviewed by author, 29.2.00 in Munich.
8. Rüdiger von Voss and Karl Friedrich, eds., *Das Süd-Nord-Gefälle: gemeinsame Strategien für neue Strukturen* (Stuttgart, 1986).

BIBLIOGRAPHY

Archival Sources

Archiv für Christlich-Demokratische Politik der Konrad-Adenauer-Stiftung, St. Augustin (ACDP)

Private papers

Nachlaß Siegfried Balke (NL Balke)

Nachlaß Kai-Uwe von Hassel (NL Hassel)

Archiv für Christlich-Soziale Politik der Hanns-Seidel-Stiftung, Munich (ACSP)

Party deposits

Bundestagswahl 1961 (BTW 1961)

Druckschriften (DS)

Flugblätter (FB)

Generalsekretär (GS)

Geschäftsführender Landesvorstand (GFLVor)

Landesausschuß (LAus)

Landesgruppe Repertorien (LGRep)

Landesgruppe Protokollen (LGProt)

Landesversammlungen (LVers)

Landesvorstandsprotokollen (LVor)

Landtagsfraktion (LtF)

Private papers
Nachlaß Franz Elsen (NL Elsen)
Nachlaß Karl Sigmund Mayr (NL Mayr)
Nachlaß Otto Seeling (NL Seeling)
Nachlaß Hanns Seidel (NL Seidel)
Nachlaß Franz Josef Strauß (NL Strauß)
Bayerisches Hauptstaatsarchiv, Munich (BAYHSTA)
Ministerial deposits
Bayerische Staatskanzlei (StK)
Bayerisches Staatsministerium für Finanz (MF)
Bayerisches Staatsministerium für Unterricht und Kultus (MK)
Bayerisches Staatsministerium für Wirtschaft und Verkehr (MWi)
Bevollmächtigter Bayerns beim Bund (BBbB)
Private papers
Nachlaß Werner Disko (NL Disko)
Nachlaß Hans Ehard (NL Ehard)
Nachlaß Johannes von Elmenau (NL Elmenau)
Nachlaß Otto Schedl (NL Schedl)

Bayerisches Wirtschaftsarchiv, Munich (BWA)
Bestände
Landesverband der Bayerischen Industrie (LBI)
Verein der Bayerischen Chemischen Industrie (VBCI)

Bundesarchiv, Koblenz (BA)
Ministerial deposits
Bundeskanzleramt (Bk)
Bundesministerium der Inneren (BI)
Bundesministerium für Wirtschaft (BMWi)
Bundesministerium für wissenschaftliche Forschung (BMwF)
Private papers
Nachlaß Karl Carstens (NL Carstens)
Nachlaß Karl Theodor Freiherr von und zu Guttenberg (NL Guttenberg)
Nachlaß Hermann Höcherl (NL Höcherl)
Nachlaß Hjalmar Schacht (NL Schacht)
Nachlaß Fritz Schäffer (NL Schäffer)

Institut für Zeitgeschichte, Munich (IFZ)
Repertorien
Fraunhofer Gesellschaft (FhG)
Private papers
Nachlaß Wilhelm Hoegner (NL Hoegner)
Nachlaß Alf Mintzel (NL Mintzel)

Maximilianeum, Munich (MAX)
Sitzungsberichte der Aussschüsse des Bayerischen Landtages
Ausschuß für Kulturpolitische Angelegenheiten (AKu)
Ausschuß für den Staatshaushalt (ASt)
Aussschuß für Wirtschaft und Verkehr (AWi)

Militärisches Archiv, Freiburg (MILITÄR)

Stadtarchiv München (SM)
Firmen (F)

Newspapers and Newsmagazines

Abendzeitung (Munich) (*AZ*), 1949–1971.

Bayernkurier, 1949–1971.

CSU-Correspondenz, 1949–1971.

Frankfurter Allgemeine Zeitung (*FAZ*), 1949–1971.

Frankfurter Rundschau, 1949–1971.

Mittelbayerische Zeitung, 1949–1971.

Münchner Merkur (*MM*), 1949–1971.

Neue Zürcher Zeitung (Deutschland edition) (*NZZ*), 1949–1971.

Passauer Neue Presse (*PNP*), 1949–1971.

Der Spiegel, 1949–1971.

Süddeutsche Zeitung (*SZ*), 1949–1971.

Vorwärts, 1949–1971.

Der Weiß-Blaue Hintergrund (*WBH*)

Die Welt, 1949–1971.

Die Zeit, 1949–1971.

Printed Primary Resources

Adenauer, Konrad. *Briefe 1945–1959.* Edited by Hans Peter Mensing. 5 vols. Berlin, 1983–2000.

Adenauer: "Es mußte alles neu gemacht werden." Die Protokolle des CDU-Bundesvorstandes 1950–1953. Edited by Günter Buchstab. Düsseldorf, 1986.

Adenauer: "Wir haben wirklich etwas geschaffen": die Protokolle des CDU-Bundesvorstands 1953–1957. Edited by Günter Buchstab. Düsseldorf, 1990.

Adenauer: "Stetigkeit in der Politik": die Protokolle des CDU Bundesvorstandes 1961–1965. Edited by Günter Buchstab. Düsseldorf, 1998.

Die Protokolle des Bayerischen Ministerrats 1945–1954. Edited by Karl-Ulrich Gelberg. Munich, 1995.

Foreign Relations of the United States.

Krone, Heinrich. *Tagebücher. Vol. 1, 1945–1961.* Edited by Hans-Otto Kleinmann. Düsseldorf, 1995.

Morsey, Rudolf and Hans-Peter Schwarz, eds. *Unter Vier Augen: Gespräche aus den Gründerjahren/ Konrad Adenauer; Theodor Heuss.* Berlin, 1997.

Verhandlungen des Bayerischen Landtags. Stenographische Berichte. Munich, 1946–1971.

Verhandlungen des Deutschen Bundestages und des Bundesrates. Munich, 1949–1971.

Books and Secondary Literature

40 Jahre Landesverband der Bayerischen Industrie e.V. (n.p., n.d.).

Abelshauser, Werner. *Der Ruhrkohlenbergbau seit 1945. Wiederaufbau, Krise, Anpassung.* Munich, 1984.

Abelshauser, Werner. "Korea, die Ruhr und Erhards Marktwirtschaft: Die Energiekrise von 1950/51." *Rheinische Vierteljahrsblätter* 45 (1981): 287–316.

Ammann, Jürgen. "Die Haltung der Christlich-Sozialen-Union in Bayern zur Frage der Wiederbewaffnung und Aufstellung der Bundeswehr, 1950–1956." Master's thesis, University of Augsburg, 1994.

Andres, Christopher Magnus. *Die bundesdeutsche Luft– und Raumfahrtindustrie 1945–1970. Ein Industriebereich im Spannungsfeld von Politik, Wirtschaft und Militär.* Frankfurt a.M., 1996.

Augstein, Rudolf, ed. *Überlebensgroß Herr Strauß. Ein Spiegelbild.* Reinbek bei Hamburg, 1980.

Baer, Fritz, ed. *Die Regierungen 1945–1962.* Vol. 9 of *Bayern im 19. und 20. Jahrhundert.* Part 3 of *Dokumente zur Geschichte von Staat und Gesellschaft in Bayern,* edited by Karl Bosl. Munich, 1976.

Bähr, Johannes. "Die 'Amerikanische Herausforderung.' Anfänge der Technologiepolitik in der Bundesrepublik Deutschland." *Archiv für Sozialgeschichte* 15 (1995): 115–130.

Balke, Siegfried. "Ein Vierteljahrhundert Organisationen der Chemiewirtschaft in Bayern," N.p., n.d.

Barbarino, Otto. *Ein Lebenslauf im 20. Jahrhundert.* 2nd ed. Munich, 1998.

Baumann, Hans. *Männer und Mächte an Rhein und Ruhr. Von Banken, Bossen und Genossen.* Munich, 1973.

Bazzoli, Luigi and Riccardo Renzi. *Il miracolo Mattei.* Milan, 1984.

Benecke, Theodor and Günther Schöner, eds. *Wehrtechnik für die Verteidigung: Bundeswehr und Industrie, 25 Jahre Partner für den Frieden (1956–1981).* Koblenz, 1984.

Bernecker, Walter L. and Volker Dotterweich, eds. *Persönlichkeit und Politik in der Bundesrepublik Deutschland: politische Porträts.* 2 vols. Göttingen, 1982.

Bickerich, Wolfram. *Franz Josef Strauß: Die Biographie.* Düsseldorf, 1996.

Bielfeldt, Carola and Peter Schlotter. *Die militärische Sicherheitspolitik der Bundesrepublik Deutschland: Einführung und Kritik.* Frankfurt a.M., 1980.

Bischoff, Detlef. *Franz Josef Strauß, die CSU und die Außenpolitik. Konzeption und Realität am Beispiel der Großen Koalition.* Meisenheim a. Glan, 1973.

Bölkow, Ludwig. *Der Zukunft verpflichtet: Erinnerungen.* 2nd expanded edition. Munich, 1994.

Boenke, Susan. *Entstehung und Entwicklung des Max-Planck-Instituts für Plasmaphysik, 1955–1971.* Frankfurt a.M., 1991.

Boesch, Frank. *Die Adenauer-CDU. Gründung, Aufstieg und Krise einer Erfolgspartei 1945–1969.* Stuttgart, 2001.

Bößenecker, Hermann. *Bayern, Bosse und Bilanzen: Hinter den Kulissen der weiß-blauen Wirtschaft.* Munich, 1972.

Bosl, Karl. "München 'Deutschlands heimliche Hauptstadt.' Historische Bemerkungen zur Strukturanalyse des modernen Hauptstadt- und Großstadttypus in Deutschland." *Zeitschrift für bayerische Landesgeschichte* 30 (1967): 298–313.

Brandt, Gerhard. *Rüstung und Wirtschaft in der Bundesrepublik.* Witten and Berlin, 1966.

Braun, Oliver. "Das politische Weltbild Alois Hundhammers 1900–1974." Master's thesis, Regensburg, 2002.

Braunthal, Gerard. *The Federation of German Industry in Politics.* Ithaca, N.Y., 1965.

Bührer, Werner. "Der BDI und die Außenpolitik der Bundesrepublik in den fünfziger Jahren." *Vierteljahrshefte für Zeitgeschichte* 40, no. 2 (1992): 241–261.

Bührer, Werner. "Geschichte des Bundesverbands der Deutschen Industrie" (forthcoming).

Bupp, Irvin C. and Jean-Claude Derian. *The Failed Promise of Nuclear Power: The Story of Light Water.* New York, 1981.

Bußmann, Ludwig, ed. *Die Wirtschaft des Landes Nordrhein-Westfalen.* North Rhine-Westphalia, n.d.

Deutinger, Stephan. *Vom Agrarland zum High-Tech-Staat. Zur Geschichte des Forschungsstandorts Bayern 1945–1980.* Munich, 2001.

Dexheimer, Wolfgang X. "Die CSU-Landesgruppe. Ihre organisatorische stellung in der CDU/CSU Fraktion." *Zeitschrift für Parlamentarische Fragen* 3 (1972): 307–313.

Eckert, Michael. "Die Anfänge der Atompolitik in der Bundesrepublik Deutschland." *Vierteljahrshefte für Zeitgeschichte* 37 (1989): 115–143.

Erker, Paul. "Keine Sehnsucht nach der Ruhr. Grundzüge der Industrialisierung in Bayern 1900–1970." *Geschichte und Gesellschaft. Zeitschrift für Historische Sozialwissenschaft* 17, no. 4 (1991): 480–511.

Freund, Hanns Egon. "Die Gründung des Landesverbandes der Bayerischen Industrie im Jahre 1949." In *40 Jahre Landesverband der Bayerischen Industrie, e. V.* (n.p., n.d.).

Gaddis, John Lewis. *Strategies of Containment: A Critical Appraisal of Postwar American National Security Policy.* New York, 1982.

Galli, Giorgio. *La sfida perduta: biografia politica di Enrico Mattei.* Milan, 1976.

Gelberg, Karl-Ulrich. *Hans Ehard: Die föderalistische Politik des bayerischen Ministerpräsidenten, 1946–1954.* Düsseldorf, 1992.

Gersdorff, Kyrill von, with the assistance of Winfried Brunner. *Ludwig Bölkow und sein Werk: Ottobrunner Innovationen.* Koblenz, 1987.

Graf, Oskar Maria. *Notizbuch des Provinzschriftstellers 1932: Erlebnisse, Intimitäten, Meinungen.* Leipzig, 1932.

Groß, Hans Ferdinand. *Hanns Seidel 1901–1961: Eine politische Biographie.* Munich, 1992.

Hanns-Seidel-Stiftung e.V., ed. *Geschichte einer Volkspartei. 50 Jahre CSU, 1945–1995.* Grünwald, 1995.

Hanns-Seidel-Stiftung e.V., ed. *Josef Müller—Der erste Vorsitzende der CSU. "Politik für eine neue Zeit."* Grünwald, 1998.

Hentschel, Volker. *Ludwig Erhard: ein Politikerleben.* Berlin, 1998.

Heuss, Theodor. *Theodor Heuss, Politiker und Publizist: Aufsätze und Reden.* Selected and commented on by Martin Vogt. Tübingen, 1984.

Hoegner, Wilhelm. *Der schwierige Außenseiter. Erinnerungen eines Abgeordneten, Emigranten und Ministerpräsidenten.* Munich, 1959.

Höpfinger, Renate, ed. *Josef Müller—der erste Vorsitzende der CSU.* Munich, 1998.

Hubensteiner, Benno. *Bayerische Geschichte: Staat und Volk, Kunst und Kultur.* 13th ed. Munich, 1992.

Huck, Burkhardt J. "The regional and occupational dependence on defense contracting in the Greater Munich Area." In *Defence Expenditure, Industrial Conversion and Local Employment,* edited by L. Paukert and P.J. Richards, 51–70. Geneva, 1991.

Johannson, Kurt. *Vom Starfighter zum Phantom.* Frankfurt a.M., 1969.

Kelleher, Catherine McArdle. *Germany and the Politics of Nuclear Weapons.* New York, 1975.

Kirchner, Ulrich. *Geschichte des bundesdeutschen Verkehrsflugzeugbaus: der lange Weg zum Airbus.* Frankfurt a.M., 1998.

Kock, Peter Jakob. *Der Bayerische Landtag: Eine Chronik.* Würzburg, 1996.

Koerfer, Daniel. *Kampf ums Kanzleramt: Erhard und Adenauer.* Stuttgart, 1987.

Köhler, Henning. *Adenauer: eine politische Biographie.* Frankfurt a.M., 1994.

Kreikamp, Hans-Dieter. "Die Entflechtung der I.G. Farbenindustrie A.G. und die Gründung der Nachfolgegesellschaften." *Vierteljahreshefte für Zeitgeschichte* 25, no. 2 (1977): 220–251.

Krieger, Wolfgang. *Franz Josef Strauß: der barocke Demokrat aus Bayern.* Göttingen & Zurich, 1995.

Kritzer, Peter. *Wilhelm Hoegner. Politische Biographie eines bayerischen Sozialdemokraten.* Munich, 1979.

Kuby, Erich. *Im Fibag-Wahn, oder, Sein Freund der Herr Minister.* Reinbek bei Hamburg, 1962.

Kuntz, Aline Marie. "Conservatives in Crisis: The Bavarian Christian Social Union and the Ideology of Antimodernism." Ph.D. diss., Cornell, 1987.

Lanzinner, Maximilian. *Zwischen Sternenbanner und Bundesadler: Bayern im Wiederaufbau 1945–1958.* Regensburg, 1996.

Lorenzen, Jay L. "A Statist Approach to High Technology Policy: The Case of Aerospace." Ph.D. diss., University of Denver, 1990.

Lynn, Matthew. *Birds of Prey: The War Between Boeing and Airbus.* London, 1995.

Magaziner, Ira C. and Mark Patinkin. *The Silent War: Inside the Global Business Battles Shaping America's Future.* New York, 1989.

Maugeri, Leonardo. *L'arma del petrolio. Questione petrolifera globale, guerra fredda e politica italiana nella vicenda di Enrico Mattei.* Florence, 1994.

McGhee, George. *At the Creation of a New Germany: from Adenauer to Brandt: an Ambassador's Account.* New Haven, CT, 1989.

Mechtersheimer, Alfred. *Rüstung und Politik in der Bundesrepublik: MRCA Tornado: Geschichte und Funktion des größten westeuropäischen Rüstungsprogramms.* Bad Honnef, 1977.

Militärgeschichtlichen Forschungsamt, ed. *Anfänge westdeutscher Sicherheitspolitik: 1945–1956.* 4 vols. Munich, 1982–1997.

Milosch, Mark. "Die Rolle von Franz Josef Strauß bei der Ansiedlung der Luftfahrtindustrie in Bayern," in *Franz Josef Strauß – Ludwig Bölkow – Sepp Hort,* vol. 2 of *Bayerische Lebensbilder: Biografien, Erinnerungen, Zeugnisse,* ed. Renate Höpfinger. Munich, 2004.

Mintzel, Alf. *Die CSU. Anatomie einer konservativen Partei 1945–1972.* Opladen, 1975.

————. *Geschichte der CSU: Ein Überblick.* Opladen, 1977.

————. *Die CSU-Hegemonie in Bayern: Strategie und Erfolg; Gewinner und Verlierer.* Passau, 1999.

Müller, Josef. *Bis zur letzten Konsequenz: Ein Leben für Frieden und Freiheit.* Munich, 1975.

Müller, Wolfgang D. *Geschichte der Kernenergie in der Bundesrepublik Deutschland.* Stuttgart, 1990.

Oertgen, Josef. "Apartheid-Propagandist Strauß." *Blätter für deutsche und internationale Politik* 11, no. 5 (May 1966): 360–362.

Oertgen, Josef. "Rhodesien und sein 'Handelspartner,'" *Blätter für deutsche und internationale Politik* 11, no. 9 (September 1966): 759–761.

Pietra, Italo. *Mattei, la pecora nera.* Milan, 1987.

Pohl, Manfred. *Das Bayernwerk: 1921 bis 1996.* Munich, 1996.

Prüß, Karsten. *Kernforschungspolitik in der Bundesrepublik Deutschland.* Frankfurt a.M., 1974.

Radkau, Joachim. *Aufstieg und Krise der deutschen Atomwirtschaft 1945–1975: verdrängte Alternativen in der Kerntechnik und der Ursprung der nuklearen Kontroverse.* Reinbek bei Hamburg, 1983.

Riehl-Heyse, Herbert. *CSU, die Partei, die das schöne Bayern erfunden hat.* Munich, 1979.

Rill, Bernd, ed. *Bavaria Felix: Ein Land, das Heimat ist und Zukunft hat.* Percha am Starnberger See, 1986.

Rilling, Rainer. *Kriegsforschung und Vernichtungswissenschaft in der BRD.* Cologne, 1970.

Rosenbach, Harald. "Der Preis der Freiheit. Die deutsch-amerikanischen Verhandlungen über den Devisenausgleich (1961–1967)." *Vierteljahrshefte für Zeitgeschichte* 46, no. 4 (1998): 709–746.

Roth, Wolfgang, Ingrid Matthäus, Dieter Lasse, Walter Haas, in cooperation with Bernt Engelmann. *Schwarzbuch: Franz Josef Strauß.* Cologne, 1972.

Rusinek, Bernd-A. "Das Porträt Leo Brandt (1908–1971)." *Geschichte im Westen 6,* no. 1 (1991): 74–90.

Rustenholz, Alain and Sandrine Treiner. *Le temps des initiales.* Vol. 2 of *La saga Servan-Schreiber.* Paris, 1999.

Sampson, Anthony. *Anatomy of Europe.* New York, 1968.

Sampson, Anthony. *The Seven Sisters: The Great Oil Companies and the World They Shaped.* New York, 1975.

Schlemmer, Thomas. *Aufbruch, Krise und Erneuerung. Die Christlich-Soziale Union 1945 bis 1955.* Munich, 1998.

Schlemmer, Thomas and Hans Woller, eds. *Bayern im Bund.* 7 vols. Munich, 2001–.

Schlotter, Peter. *Rüstungspolitik in der Bundesrepublik Deutschland: Die Beispiele Starfighter und Phantom.* Frankfurt a.M., 1975.

Schmid, Fred. *Der Militär-Industrie-Komplex.* Frankfurt a.M., 1972.

Schmückle, Gerd. *Ohne Pauken und Trompeten. Erinnerungen an Krieg und Frieden.* Stuttgart, 1982.

Schreyer, Klaus. *Bayern—ein Industriestaat. Die importierte Industrialisierung. Das wirtschaftliche Wachstum nach 1945 als Ordnungs- und Strukturproblem.* Munich, 1969.

Schwammberger, Adolf. "Otto Seeling." In volume 4 of *Fränkische Lebensbilder,* edited by Gerhard Pfeiffer, 243–257. Würzburg, 1971.

Schwarz, Hans-Peter. *Adenauer.* 2 vols. Munich, 1994.

Seidl, Jürgen. "Schwieriger Neuanfang—Wiederaufbau und Expansion der BMW AG unter besonderer Berücksichtigung der Unternehmensbeziehungen zum Staat (1945/48–1969)." Ph.D. diss., University of Regensburg, 2001.

Servan-Schreiber, Jean-Jacques. *The American Challenge.* New York, 1968.

Servan-Schreiber, Jean-Jacques. *Les fossoyeurs.* Vol. 2 of *Passions.* Paris, 1993.

Staudt, Florian. "Anfänge bayerischer Atompolitik in den 50er Jahren." Master's thesis, Munich, 1997.

Steinbuch, Karl. *Falsch programmiert; über das Versagen unserer Gesellschaft in der Gegenwart und vor der Zukunft und was eigentlich geschehhen müßte.* Stuttgart, 1968.

Stokes, Raymond G. *Divide and Prosper: The Heirs of I.G. Farben under Allied Authority, 1945–1951.* Berkeley, 1988.

Strauß, Franz Josef. "Ceausescus fünf Prinzipien der Souveränität. Gemeinsamkeiten bei den Gesprächen in Bukarest." *Epoche* 4, no. 3 (1980): 35–36.

Strauß, Franz Josef. *Die Erinnerungen.* Berlin, 1989.

Strauß, Franz Josef. *The Grand Design. A European Solution to German Reunification.* London, 1965.

Strauß, Franz Josef. *Challenge and Response: Program for Europe.* New York, 1970.

"The Technology Gap." *Time* 89, no. 2 (13.1.1967): 18–19.

Treml, Manfred, ed. *Geschichte des modernen Bayern: Königreich und Freistaat.* Munich, 1994.

Trischler, Helmuth. *Luft- und Raumfahrtforschung in Deutschland, 1900–1970: Politische Geschichte einer Wissenschaft.* Frankfurt a.M., 1992.

Trischler, Helmuth and Rüdiger vom Bruch. *Forschung für den Markt: Geschichte der Fraunhofer-Gesellschaft.* Munich, 1999.

Vierhaus, Rudolf and Bernhard vom Brocke, eds. *Forschung im Spannungsfeld von Politik und Gesellschaft: Geschichte und Struktur der Kaiser-Wilhelm-/Max-Planck-Gesellschaft: Aus Anlaß ihres 75jährigen Bestehens.* Stuttgart, 1990.

Voss, Friedrich. *Den Kanzler im Visier: zwanzig Jahre mit Franz Josef Strauß.* Mainz & Munich, 2000.

Voss, Ruediger von and Karl Friedrich, eds. *Das Süd-Nord-Gefälle: gemeinsame Strategien für neue Strukturen.* Stuttgart, 1986.

Votaw, Dow. *Il cane a sei zampe: Mattei e l'ENI—saggio sul potere.* Milan, 1965.

Weilemann, Peter. *Die Anfänge der Europäischen Atomgemeinschaft. Zur Gründungsgeschichte von EURATOM 1955–1957.* Baden-Baden, 1983.

Weitz, John. *Hitler's Banker: Hjalmar Horace Greeley Schacht.* Boston, 1997.

Weyer, Johannes, ed. *Technische Visionen, politische Kompromisse: Geschichte und Perspektiven der deutschen Raumfahrt.* Berlin, 1993.

Winnacker, Karl. *Nie den Mut verlieren: Erinnerungen an Schicksalsjahre der deutschen Chemie.* 2nd ed. Düsseldorf, 1974.

Wirz, Ulrich. *Karl Theodor von und zu Guttenberg und das Zustandekommen der Großen Koalition.* Grub am Forst, 1997.

Wolf, Konstanze. *CSU und Bayernpartei: Ein besonderes Konkurrenzverhältnis, 1948–1960.* Cologne, 1982.

Yergin, Daniel. *The Prize: The Epic Quest for Oil, Money, and Power.* New York, 1991.

Zimmermann, Friedrich, ed. *Anspruch und Leistung. Widmungen für Franz Josef Strauß.* Stuttgart 1980.

INDEX

C

D

G

H

I

T

U

V

W

Z